CHRIST IN TEN THOUSAND PLACES

Homilies toward a New Millennium

WALTER J. BURGHARDT, S.J.
Woodstock Theological Center

D0815816

PAULIST PRESS
New York / Mahwah, N.J.

also by Walter J. Burghardt, S.J.
published by Paulist Press

LET JUSTICE ROLL DOWN LIKE WATERS
LOVE IS A FLAME OF THE LORD
PREACHING: THE ART AND THE CRAFT
SPEAK THE WORD WITH BOLDNESS
STILL PROCLAIMING YOUR WONDERS

Cover design by Tim McKeen

Illustrations by Emil Antonucci

Library of Congress Cataloging-in-Publication Data

Burghardt, Walter J.
    Christ in ten thousand places : homilies toward a new millennium / Walter J. Burghardt.
        p.   cm.
    Includes bibliographical references and index.
    ISBN 0-8091-3905-7 (alk. paper)
    1. Catholic Church—Sermons. 2. Sermons, American. I. Title.
BX1756.B828C47   1999
252′.02—dc21   99–33816
                                                                                     CIP

Published by Paulist Press
997 Macarthur Boulevard
Mahwah, New Jersey 07430

www.paulistpress.com

Printed and bound in the
United States of America

TABLE OF CONTENTS

ORDINARY TIME

A FEAST & MEMORIALS

WEDDING HOMILIES

MEDLEY

PREFACE

Back in 1994, gifted preacher John Buchanan remarked perceptively to a group of fellow preachers gathered in Chicago by the editors of the journal *The Living Pulpit:*

> Part of what the preacher is about is knowing what the issues are, the questions being asked, which define a culture in a given time and place. The preacher must read and listen and see and participate in the world in which the congregation lives. We need to know what is being written by novelists, poets, journalists, essayists. Kathleen Norris in her wonderful bestseller *Dakota* says that Lemmon, South Dakota, is so small that the poets and preachers have to hang out together.

Read, listen, see, participate. Four verbs that declare with rare succinctness the experience that lies behind an effective sermon, behind all effective communication. In this way alone can a preacher get beyond abstractions, beyond generalizations, beyond pious pap for the multitude. In this way alone does a preacher touch *this* congregation, *this* culture or *these* cultures, the justice issues of *this* acre of God's world, where *these* men, women, and children hurt, where *they* find their joy, what *they* hope for. Yes, many injustices overleap a particular area, are far from parochial, and their extent should be impressed on a parish that is linked in ever-widening concentric circles to a diocese, to a church universal, to a world, a humanity that is our broader parish.

In the Woodstock Theological Center's project Preaching the Just Word—five-day retreat/workshops to improve the preaching of justice

1

issues—we experience across the United States, have experienced in Canada, Jamaica, and Australia, the truth of Buchanan's observation.[1]

In Kentucky I had to *read*. At my request, the Office of Catholic Charities of the Archdiocese of Louisville supplied me with data from Kentucky's "Kids Count." Only with such data could I presume to preach in Louisville's cathedral in 1996 under the title "Do I Hear the Children Crying?" Only because I discovered that in Kentucky one in four children was growing up below the poverty line; in every county in 1990 (the latest available year for accurate poverty data) children's poverty exceeded that of the general population; poverty rates were even higher for young families; in 1995 one third of all families with children whose parents were under 30 lived below the poverty level; for younger single-mother families the poverty rate was 70.7 percent; reports of child abuse and neglect increased almost twofold in ten years; more than one in four births was to an unmarried woman; and Jefferson County, where I was preaching, posted rates above the state average.

In Australia I had to *listen*. I was told that in a developed world that exalts the equality of the sexes the Australian macho is still a fixture. I was told that racism, if not rampant, continues to confront the Asian and the Aboriginal. Take an embarrassing incident on Qantas 461 from Sydney to Melbourne: A flight attendant asked a white lady if she wanted to move away from three Aboriginal artists with whom she was actually traveling. Not pretending to be an instant expert, I simply asked priests in my homily: Is this kind of discrimination exceptional or typical? And "why the discrimination in housing and employment among ethnic populations, unfair interest charges and wage structures? Is the spousal abuse that is slowly seeping into the headlines a sacrilege that arouses your rage? How have your people reacted to the gay and the lesbian? And why the increase in drug addiction, in teenage suicides?" In Jamaica it was instructive to see what it means in harsh living for 70 percent of the population to be out of the economy; for 40 Jamaican dollars to equal one American dollar; for parents in one largely Catholic community to have this only choice: Take drug money or see your children starve.

To preach effectively, I have learned to *see*. For all the advantages of a cab or the Metro, it is worth my while to walk some of Washington's ways. It dismays me to see acre after acre that was fired in 1968. It chills my heart to see children shoeless, emaciated; teenagers exchanging money for some white stuff; grown men and women rustling for food in garbage cans. It's instructive when, unlike the priest in Luke 10, I do not pass by "on the other side"

(Luke 10:31) but join Jesus' "little ones," the unnoticed, the unimportant, even glimpse an occasional note of hatred in sullen eyes. The difference? I have ceased to live in a rural seminary. I roam the United States uncovering the justice issues. I no longer need field glasses to see the hungry and the homeless, the jobless and the despairing, the abused and the AIDS-afflicted.

Participate? Here my PJW colleague Father Raymond Kemp is a more realistic guide. He was involved in two African-American parishes in the District of Columbia. He has lived among a people used to a struggle for survival: without food, education, work, wealth, luxuries. He has lived among the extended family, sometimes 13 to 16 in one house—a bonding of sisters and brothers, but often dysfunctional through crack and coke, deadly weapons, imprisonment. He has lived with their sense of healing. Not so much from doctors and priests; rather the expectation that *God* will bring healing. He has lived with a distressing nihilism, a pervasive feeling among so many that there is no future beyond this desperate moment, settling a score, proving yourself a man. And on the *Donahue* show, Father Kemp was asked by a teenager if he would officiate at her funeral!

On one level of participation I am uncommonly fortunate, can out-Kemp Kemp. Preaching on or to the elderly, I need no longer pretend. At 84, I can feel in my flesh what aging is like. Arthritic joints jab, oxygen reaches the heart more painfully, bones turn brittle, and sauerkraut makes for diarrhea.

It is my fond hope that this 12th collection of my homilies published by the Paulist Press will exemplify for preachers some types of the experience that stems from reading, listening, seeing, and participating.

In this context of diversified experience, I am delighted to borrow my title from a sonnet shaped by a unique master of rhythm, the Jesuit Gerard Manley Hopkins (1844–89). Untitled, the sonnet begins "As kingfishers catch fire" and closes as follows:

> ...Christ plays in ten thousand places,
> Lovely in limbs, and lovely in eyes not his
> To the Father through the features of men's faces.[2]

Walter J. Burghardt, S.J.
January 1, 1999

From Advent to Easter

1
BLESSED IS THE WOMAN
WHO HAS BELIEVED
Fourth Sunday of Advent (C)

- Micah 5:1–4
- Hebrews 10:5–10
- Luke 1:39–45

Some years ago, at a seminar on preaching, a lady theologian offered a gracious but telling critique of a homily of mine, "Advent with Mary." In the course of her critique she gave a sound reason why such a homily is best preached by a woman. Why? Because the Advent Mary is the pregnant Mary. And so, if experience is a factor in effective preaching, we would do well to listen to the daughters of Eve during these four pregnant weeks.

I agree, and I do listen. But, given the unfortunate factual situation—ordained but not pregnant—let this male presume to speak to you of our Lady, of Advent with Mary. I shall speak of her as Luke understands her, and with insights from gifted women.

Remember, we are still in Advent, still waiting with Mary for the most remarkable, most influential birth in human history. Three movements to my musings, three questions stimulated by today's Gospel: (1) How did Mary wait for Jesus that first Advent? (2) What did her kinswoman Elizabeth reveal to us that is so important about the pregnant Mary? (3) What might all this say to you and me about our own Advent, our waiting for Jesus?

I

First, how did Mary wait for Jesus that first Advent? Today's Gospel is revealing. Pregnant, she does not retire into isolation; she goes into the hill country of Judea to visit a relative, Elizabeth, wife of high priest Zechariah. Why? Angel Gabriel had told her that

Elizabeth was six months pregnant. So what? Well, Elizabeth was getting on in years, had been believed to be barren, had hidden her pregnancy for five months.

Now we the graying among Catholics have been told from childhood why Mary went visiting: She wanted to congratulate Elizabeth on her unexpected pregnancy, help the aging lady her last few months with child. I've preached that myself. My female critic sees it differently: Mary was seeking "support from another woman,"[1] from another pregnant woman. It makes sense. This young woman had never been pregnant; she was pregnant not by Joseph but by God's creative and active power;[2] she was to mother the "Son of God" (Lk 1:35).[3] She could hardly tell that story to any of her down-to-earth female friends in backwater Nazareth: "Gather round, ladies: I've just been made pregnant by the Holy Spirit!" Whom to tell but another woman some distance away, an older woman, a relative, "just before God" (Lk 1:6), beyond childbearing age, a woman also surprised by joy, surprised by God.

Mary pregnant with the All-Holy is not a confident, self-assured, triumphant queen of heaven. She is young, perhaps an adolescent, probably confused when Gabriel leaves her without a script for the future, not knowing quite what to do next, even how to tell Joseph.

II

Enough on why Mary went visiting. But that is hardly the whole story—Mary pregnant, Elizabeth pregnant, Mary seeking support from Elizabeth. Support she receives, but far beyond her imagining. As soon as Mary entered Elizabeth's home, "the child in [Elizabeth's] womb," John, the Baptizer to be, "leaped with delight" (Lk 1:41, 44). By a miracle of grace, the unborn child recognizes not his cousin but his Lord. "Filled with the Holy Spirit" (v. 41), Elizabeth recognizes not only her kinswoman but the mother of her Lord: "Why should this happen to me, that the mother of my Lord comes to me?" (v. 43).

But Elizabeth is not finished. "Blessed indeed," she cries, "blessed is the woman who has believed that what the Lord has promised her will see fulfilment" (v. 45). Here is our Lady at her most remarkable: She believed. She trusted that what God had promised her through an angel would be realized. But listen to what God had promised: "You are going to conceive in your womb and bear a son, and you will call him Jesus. He will be great and will be hailed as Son of the Most High,...and of his kingship there will be no end" (Lk 1:31–33).

Reflect on the utter trust in Mary's simple response to the angel, "Let it be with me as you say" (Lk 1:38). Gabriel had not left her with a "Here is your life" scenario. No details whatsoever. He never told her she would become a refugee with her infant to escape a king's anger. Never told her that, when her child grew up, some of his relatives would think him mad, that the people of Nazareth would try to cast him over a cliff. Never told her what aging Simeon foretold later, "This child is marked for the fall and the rise of many in Israel, to be a symbol that will be rejected—indeed, a sword shall pierce you too" (Lk 2:34–35). Never told her that some of his fellow Jews would charge Jesus with having a devil, that one of his closest friends would betray him with a kiss, that he would die shamefully on a cross between two thieves, but not to worry, for he would rise again shortly. Why, Gabriel never taught her a single thing about the Trinity, what it really meant to be unique Son of God; never a cram course in Christology, how one could be God and human in one and the same person.

God asked of Mary only this, "Trust me." And she did. Totally. That is why Luke sees in Mary a perfect disciple. Jesus would make that clear later on: "My mother and my brothers are those who hear the word of God and do it" (Lk 8:21). Mary listened and Mary did. Little wonder that in Christian tradition Mary has long been seen as the "woman of faith." Listen to St. Augustine: "Mary full of faith conceived Christ in her heart before she conceived him in her womb."[4] In fact, Augustine insists that it was precisely by her believing that Mary conceived Christ in her flesh. She believed, and in believing she conceived. "In other words, the human act whereby she conceived her Son was not an act of loving union with her husband but an act of loving faith in God."[5] What did she *do* to conceive Christ? Very simply, she made an act of faith. She said yes to God, without reservation: Whatever you want, dear Lord.

III

Why this accent on Mary believing? It raises my third question: What might all this say to you and me about our own Advent, our waiting for Christ? In a word, we too are asked to believe; Advent for us is preparation for a strong act of faith. But be careful! Not only an act of intellect—I accept with my mind what God has revealed to us: The infant in that stable is the unique Son of God, God in our flesh.

Important, of course; our Christian living, our Christian dying, depends on it. If that child is not God as truly as the Father is God, our worship here, our Eucharist, is dreadful deception, a horrible hoax. We might as well go home, get what comfort we can at eight o'clock from TV's "Touched by an Angel," give place of honor on Thursday to Santa Claus.

No, Christmas is the incredible creed you will shortly utter together: "We believe in one Lord Jesus Christ, God from God, one in Being with the Father, through [whom] all things were made, [who] for us and for our salvation came down from heaven, by the power of the Holy Spirit was born of the Virgin Mary and became" as human as you and I.

And still, for all its splendor, that affirmation is only a beginning of my faith; an important truth, but not the whole truth. With that response of my intellect must go a response of my whole person: an act of trust similar to our Lady's. I must trust, as Mary trusted, that "what the Lord has promised [me] will be fulfilled," will come to pass, will be realized.

Not easy. As with Mary, so with you and me. In Christ, God has not provided us with a scenario for our lives, what will happen to any one of us. God did not tell us what color would grace our faces, what manner of children would be born of us, whether we shall live in poverty or plenty, in love or rage, when we shall die and how. I cannot predict my tomorrow.

What, then, has God promised in that Child of Bethlehem? That the God who wore our flesh will never abandon us, will always be there for us, no matter how absent he seems, how far away, no matter how far we stray, how faithless we become. That even if we desert him, he will never wave good-bye to us. "The power of the Most High," God's holy Spirit, will always "cast a shadow over you" (Lk 1:35), the shadow that is a sign of God's presence.

The theology is clear enough; let me bring it down to earth. Two stories that unexpectedly came together. First true story: I heard it two decades ago in Nassau from a Bahamian priest, and in 1979 I used it in Georgetown's Dahlgren Chapel to end a homily on trust. A two-story house had caught fire. The family—father, mother, several children—were on their way out when the smallest boy became terrified, tore away from his mother, ran back upstairs. Suddenly he appeared at a smoke-filled window crying like crazy. His father, outside, shouted to him, "Jump, son, jump! I'll catch you." The boy cried, "But, daddy, I can't see you." "I know," his father called, "I know. But *I* can see *you.*"[6]

Second story: a letter to me dated last Sunday, from a lady in Chevy Chase who had just heard me speak at Blessed Sacrament parish. I quote word for word.

> When my sister Kathleen was diagnosed with cancer, we began walking each noontime for an hour, and you were a part of that ritual. We read and used as the fabric of that year's long journey [your homilies]. Some [of them] spoke eloquently [to us]. When she was at the very end and unconscious, my brother-in-law asked me if I could say something. We, my mother, my sisters Anne Miskovsky and Mary Stahlman had recited all our traditional prayers and still Kathy fought to stay with her young family. I remembered your fire homily and I said, "Jump, [Kathy]. He can see you." She died quietly.

Advent with Mary? When the chips are down, leap down from the theology. Like Mary, jump! It's a replay of Jesus on the cross: "Father, into your hands I entrust my spirit" (Lk 23:46), the whole of my living self.[7] And not only in a foxhole, not only at the very end; now, tomorrow, each night falling asleep. It's your advent, your coming to Christ; it's your response to his Christmas, to his coming to you. Whether you can see him is not all-important. He can see you; he does...always. Jump!

Holy Trinity Church
Washington, D.C.
December 21, 1997

2
FORGIVE, AND YOU WILL BE FORGIVEN
Second Week of Lent, Year 1, Monday

- Daniel 9:4b–10
- Luke 6:36–38

Not many years ago, in the Hashemite Kingdom of Jordan, in a tiny town named Mafraq, two Bedouin youths got into a fight, fell to the ground in their fury. One lad pulled out a knife, plunged it fatally into the other's flesh. In fear he fled for days across the desert, fled the slain boy's vengeful relatives, fled to find a Bedouin sanctuary, a "tent of refuge" designed by law for those who kill unintentionally or in the heat of anger. At last he reached what might be a refuge—the black-tented encampment of a nomad tribe. He flung himself at the feet of its leader, an aged sheik, begged him, "I have killed in the heat of anger; I implore your protection; I seek the refuge of your tent."

"If God wills," the old man responded, "I grant it to you, as long as you remain with us."

A few days later the avenging relatives tracked the fugitive to the refuge. They asked the sheik, "Have you seen this man? Is he here? For we will have him."

"He is here, but you will not have him."

"He has killed, and we the blood relatives of the slain will stone him by law."

"You will not."

"We demand him!"

"No. The boy has my protection. I have given my word, my promise of refuge."

"But you do not understand. He has killed your grandson!"

The ancient sheik was silent. No one dared to speak. Then, in visible pain, with tears searing his face, the old man stood up and spoke ever so slowly: "My only grandson—he is dead?"

"Yes, your only grandson is dead."

"Then," said the sheik, "then this boy will be my son. He is forgiven, and he will live with us as my own. Go now; it is finished."[1]

A powerful story, good friends. A story with a biblical background. A background in today's two readings: in Daniel and in Luke. Sin in Daniel, forgiveness in Luke. Let's look at Daniel, then at Luke, finally at ourselves.

I

First, sin in Daniel. A passionate prayer. It was not shaped by Daniel, but by an inspired scribe later on.[2] It is not the prayer of an individual; it is the prayer of a community. It does not ask for enlightenment, as the context would demand, enlightenment on why Jeremiah's prophecy of a restoration of Israel after 70 years has not been fulfilled; it is an admission of public guilt, and an impassioned petition for the restoration of God's privileged people.[3] With some changes in content and style, that prayer might well become our nation's prayer if this Lent is to become real. A suggestion from your homilist:

> Ah, Lord, great and awesome God, you are unfailingly faithful to the covenant your Son cut with us in his blood, steadfast in love for all those who love you and keep your commandments. We have sinned; we have done wrong; we have acted wickedly; we have rebelled; we have turned aside from your commandments and ordinances. We have not listened to our own prophets, to John Paul II and Martin Luther King, to Dorothy Day and Mother Teresa, who spoke in your name to our political leaders and to all the people of our land. We have not listened as you spoke to us of the millions of your infant images forcibly kept from the light of day; spoke to us of our children, one of every four growing up poor, living in some kind of hell, in the richest nation on earth; spoke to us of our elderly rummaging in garbage cans for the food we discard so casually; spoke to us of the AIDS-afflicted crying to us for compassion while so many of us see their affliction as your vengeance on their sin; spoke to us of the African Americans still second-class citizens in "the land of the free"; spoke to us of our Jewish sisters and brothers fearful that the Holocaust has not yet burned itself out; spoke to us of our judges empowering physicians to take the life that is yours alone to give and take.
>
> Righteousness is on your side, O Lord, but open shame falls on us, the inhabitants of the District of Columbia and all of

America, those who are near and those who are far away, because of the treachery they have committed against you. Open shame, O Lord, falls on us, our leaders, our elected officials, because we have sinned against you. To the Lord our God belong mercy and forgiveness, for we have rebelled against Him, and have not obeyed the voice of the Lord our God by following His laws, which He set before us by His servants our prophets.[4]

II

Second, forgiveness in Luke. I find it at once awesome and comforting in Luke how the father of the prodigal sees his wayward son from afar, is "filled with compassion," runs to meet him, and before the sinful son can say "I have sinned against heaven and before you," throws his arms around him and kisses him (Lk 15:20–21). Pre-eminently, that father is God—the God of whom the Psalmist sings,

> The Lord is merciful and gracious,
> slow to anger and abounding in steadfast love....
> He does not deal with us according to our sins,
> nor repay us according to our iniquities....
> As a father has compassion for his children,
> so the Lord has compassion for those who fear Him.
> For He knows how we were made;
> He remembers that we are dust.
>
> (Ps 103:8–14)

What is awesome and comforting is that our God, our Father, always takes the initiative in forgiveness; for without God's grace no one can cry to God "I'm sorry." The younger son, who squandered his inheritance in dissolute living, who devoured his father's property with prostitutes, could never have decided to say to his father, "I have sinned against heaven and before you" (Lk 15:18), if God had not touched his heart with divine tenderness.

But there is another side to forgiveness. You heard it from Luke's Jesus: "Forgive, and you will be forgiven" (Lk 6:37). I find it at once fascinating and frightening in Luke how Jesus links God's forgiveness with our own. If my sins are to be forgiven, it's simply not sufficient to say with sincerity "I'm sorry." Remember the slave in Matthew whose king forgave him the equivalent of 150,000 years' wages (Mt 18:23 ff.)? Remember the slave's refusal to have mercy on a fellow slave who owed him the equivalent of a hundred days' wages? Remember the king's anger? The unforgiving slave would be tortured until he paid the whole of his impossible debt. Remember Jesus' harsh application? "So my heavenly Father will also do to every one of you if you do not forgive your brother [or sister] from your heart" (v. 35).

III

This story leads to you and me, to our sinning and our forgiving. Our sinning. Yes, seminarians and priests though we are,[5] each of us can echo the strong sentence in the First Letter of John, "If we say that we have not sinned, we make [God] a liar, and His word is not in us" (1 Jn 1:10). Each of us can resonate to the anguish of Paul: "I delight in the law of God in my inmost self, but I see in my members another law at war with the law of my mind, making me captive to the law of sin that dwells in my members" (Rom 7:22–23). It is the endless tension in each Christian and in the Body of Christ: the Christian and the Church at once holy and sinful, linked to Christ in love and yet always in need of reform, in need of conversion, in need of forgiveness, in need of the Christ who says time and again, "Your sins are forgiven. Go and sin no more."

Still, I find it at once fascinating and frightening when Jesus tells me, "When you are offering your gift at the altar, if you remember that your brother [or sister] has something against you, leave your gift there before the altar and go, first be reconciled to your brother [or sister], and then come and offer your gift" (Mt 5:23–24). You know, I've never done that. Strange, isn't it, that I rarely if ever touch that command to the thrilling passage where Paul exclaims, "God has given us the ministry of reconciliation,...entrusting the ministry of reconciliation to us. So we are ambassadors for Christ, since Christ is making his appeal through us; we entreat you on behalf of Christ, be reconciled to God" (2 Cor 5:18–20).

I entreat others, "Be reconciled to God." What of my own reconciliation with those to whom God is making His appeal through me? A paradox, surely, this unreconciled reconciler. Luke's Jesus is uncompromising when his disciples ask him how to pray. "Whenever you pray, say: 'Father! ...Forgive us our sins, for we too forgive everyone who does wrong to us'" (Lk 11:4).[6] I still tremble when I voice that petition in our form, "Forgive us our trespasses, as we forgive those who trespass against us." I tremble because this bargain with

God scares me. God will be faithful, cannot be other than faithful. But I...I wonder.

Lent, good friends.... Lent is not primarily 40 days of giving up: an ice-cold Bud Lite, the sugar in your Starbuck,[7] the pizza that ups my poundage. Lent is an increasing involvement in the paschal mystery, in a dying/rising Christ. Its center is a cross, its focus a God-man whose very crucifixion is a cry for forgiveness—"Father, forgive them" (Lk 23:34a).[8] On my own crosses, my own calvaries, for whom shall I pray that prayer?

Theological College
Washington, D.C.
February 24, 1997

3
THE STRANGER: YESTERDAY AND TODAY
Third Sunday of Lent (A)

- Exodus 17:3–7
- Romans 5:1–2, 5–8
- John 4:5–42

A powerful Gospel, my friends.[1] A Gospel that should speak pointedly to each of us individually and to all of us as a Christian community. My homily has a strange title: "The Stranger: Yesterday and Today." Two stages: (1) Jesus and the stranger; (2) the stranger in our time.

I

First, Jesus and the stranger. To a Samaritan woman coming to draw water at a well in Samaria Jesus says, "Give me a drink" (Jn 4:7). It is difficult to exaggerate how unusual, how unexpected, how scandalous that request was. For one thing, this was foreign territory. Even more significantly, the people who populated that territory and the Jews with whom Jesus lived were bitter enemies; for the Samaritans refused to worship in Jerusalem. Recall the words of the woman to Jesus, "Our ancestors worshiped on this mountain [Gerizim], but you people claim that the place where God ought to be worshiped is in Jerusalem" (Jn 4:20). Recall her response to his request, "You are a Jew—how can you ask me, a Samaritan, for a drink?" And John adds, "Jews, remember, have nothing to do with Samaritans" (v. 9).

More than that, Jesus was speaking to a woman. Notice the reaction of the disciples when they returned from gathering supplies in town: "They were shocked that he was holding a conversation with a woman" (v. 27). More shocked that he was talking with a woman than because he was talking with a Samaritan.

The Jewish historian Josephus tells of attacks by Samaritans on pilgrims traveling to or from the temple of Jerusalem. And remember

17

one frightening Gospel scene. When Jesus "had set his face resolutely toward Jerusalem," toward his destiny, toward his death, he sent messengers ahead of him to make arrangements for his lodging. When they came to a village of the Samaritans, Luke tells us, "the villagers would not welcome him, seeing that his intention was to proceed to Jerusalem." It was then that James and John asked Jesus, "Lord, do you want us to call down fire from heaven to consume these people?" (Lk 9:51–54).

Not so Jesus. Not only did he rebuke James and John (v. 55). In his parable of the man who fell among robbers on the way down from Jerusalem to Jericho, Jesus proposed as an example of love of neighbor, proposed as neighbor to the half-dead Jew, not another Jew; a Samaritan, a man who lavished care on his enemy when a priest and a Levite both "passed by on the other side" (Lk 10:31–32). Recall, too, how Jesus cured ten lepers and the only leper who returned to fall at Jesus' feet and thank him was a Samaritan. Jesus' reaction is sobering: "Was no one found to return and give praise to God except this foreigner?" And Jesus said to him, "Get up and go your way; your faith has brought you salvation" (Lk 17:11–19).

A splendid Scripture scholar put it bluntly: "There was no deeper breach of human relations in the contemporary world than the feud of Jews and Samaritans, and the breadth and depth of Jesus' doctrine of love could demand no greater act of a Jew than to accept a Samaritan as a brother."[2]

II

The experience of Jesus with the stranger, with Samaritans who despised the Jews and were despised by them, what does this have to do with us? Rather than bog down in vague generalities, let me focus on one terribly real stranger in our time, a stranger who poses problems for many Americans right now, confronts our Christianity at a profound level. I mean the immigrant.

You see, during the 19th century and early in the 20th, Americans had little or no problem accepting immigrants from the Old World, had little difficulty making space rapidly for these newcomers, even rejoiced to welcome them to our shores. Little social conflict. Why? Three reasons. First, immigrants did not form a large percentage of American society—at its largest, in 1910, 14.7 percent. Second, immigrants supplied the labor that America's growing economy demanded. Third, the European immigrant stream was so varied—in culture, in religion, in nationality, in language—and distributed over so enormous a geographic region that it could not preserve its culture intact for more than a few generations, and could not effectively challenge America's way of doing things, could not, for example, dictate a new political order. Little wonder that back in 1903 we could read Emma Lazarus' famous inscription on the base of the Statue of Liberty:

> Give me your tired, your poor,
> Your huddled masses yearning to breathe free,
>   The wretched refuse of your teeming shore.
> Send these, the homeless, tempest-tost to me,
>   I lift my lamp beside the golden door!

Things have changed, and changed drastically. Europe has dried up as a source of immigration. The new sources are Latin America and Asia. For example, since 1970 some five million Mexicans have entered the United States to stay. It is now estimated that soon after the year 2050 non-Hispanic whites may form a minority of our population. Right now Hispanics compose 28 percent of the population of Texas, about 31 percent of the population of California.[3] And so, as I crisscross the country with my project Preaching the Just Word, I find controversy raging: Is the new migration doing harm to our economy? Is unskilled labor taking jobs from natives? And what will it do to our culture, our politics, our American way of life? And for Catholic Christians, we are already experiencing how hard it is to merge Hispanics and Anglo-Americans into a parish that is a single, well-knit, loving community.

A homily is not the place to solve complex problems. But a homily *is* the place for profound personal reflection. Allow me to suggest what I see as a Christlike attitude to today's special stranger—the immigrant. Christlike in the sense that it comes close to the way Jesus dealt with the Samaritan woman at Jacob's well. My own meditation made for a powerful, provocative, at times humorous reflection. Let me share it with you as I experienced it several days ago in the capital city of our nation.

First, I don't have to *like* today's immigrants, be they from Mexico or El Salvador, from Vietnam or the Philippines. Nothing in today's Gospel suggests that Jesus liked the lady, this stranger at the well. Still, in his eyes she was a person, a woman, human, as human as he was. Even more importantly, she had been shaped by God, shaped in the image and likeness of her Creator, gifted with intelligence and freedom, with a mind to know and a heart to love. And, for all her faults and fragility, she was still an image, a reflection, of God. Somewhat misshapen, like the rest of us, but still awfully precious in God's eyes, in Jesus' eyes. I ask myself: Is that the way *I* eye the immigrant, eye each immigrant?

Second, I don't have to *agree* with the immigrant, praise the legal immigrant's initiative, applaud the illegal alien's cleverness in crossing our border. I may even vote to limit the number of legal immigrants. What I may not do is simply turn my back on them, take out my frustrations on the children of the alien, refuse them medical care. Jesus held no brief for the Samaritan woman's life style, told her frankly that her adventures in marriage were a farce. Yet he never made this a pretext for disowning her, never gave her a cold shrug of the shoulder, never said, "Skip the drink, lady; your hands are unclean."

Third, it is the Christian's task, it is my privilege, to *reach out* to the stranger in trouble, the despised and the downtrodden, the bedeviled and the bewildered, the lonely and the unloved—the immigrant. Jesus took the initiative, the first step, with the Samaritan woman. He started the conversation; *he* asked *her* for water—even though his disciples would be shocked to find him talking to a woman in a public place. I too may not, on principle, wait for the stranger to make the first move. The age-old Christian virtue called "hospitality" is not primarily coffee and doughnuts after Mass; it is the warm hand of welcome to the stranger, to those who are different, to those who do not look, talk, smell as I do.

Fourth, I dare not forget that the *gift I bring* to the stranger is not simply bread or water, a peanut-butter-and-jelly sandwich or a Tequila Sunrise. Think back on Jesus. In return for her graciousness with a drink of cold water,[4] he held out to her a promise of "living water," the Holy Spirit to refresh and quicken her sluggish spirit.[5] The welcome I give to a stranger may well be the prelude to God's grace, God's way of using my very ordinary humanness to draw down light, strength, courage, and peace into a struggling human frame.

Not only for that individual in front of me; not only the Samaritan woman before Jesus. Because of that fascinating conversation, she turned from sinner to apostle. She rushed back to the people in her town, told them how impressively Jesus had spoken to her. "Could this possibly be the Messiah?" (Jn 4:29). The result? Crowds from the town came out to see this surprising visitor. At their urging he stayed with them two days. "No longer," they said to the woman, "no longer is our faith dependent on your story. For we have heard for ourselves, and we know that this is really the Savior of the world" (v. 42). So too for you and me. It's Presbyterian novelist and preacher Frederick Buechner's inspired insight: Humanity is like a gigantic spider web. Touch it anywhere and the whole thing trembles. For as we move about our world, a kind word here, an ugly act there, what we do for good or ill will touch this person, this person will touch another person, and so on and on, until who knows where the whole thing ends. No man, no woman, is an island.

A welcome to a stranger. The miracle in Samaria did not end there, at Jacob's well. The miracle continues, can only continue, through you and me. Only remember the response in today's responsorial psalm: "Today, if you hear God's voice, harden not your hearts." Today. Today's stranger.

Franciscan Renewal Center
Scottsdale, Arizona
March 2, 1997

4
PROPHET ACCEPTED, PROPHET REJECTED
Third Week of Lent, Year 2, Monday

- 2 Kings 5:1–15
- Luke 4:24–30

At first hearing, today's readings sound like two valid reasons for a preacher to invent a virus, stay at home, say a swift "private" Mass, and go to bed early. Fortunately, intense study and protracted prayer have brought rescue to a harried head, relief to a troubled heart. Let's see whether your version of Generation X agrees.

To clue you into my way of proceeding, I shall (1) suggest to you what sort of pyrotechnics Luke is producing in chapter 4, (2) spend some time on the lot of the prophet as Jesus saw it, and (3) focus on the significance of all this for your projected lives as prophets. More simply, (1) Luke, (2) Jesus, (3) you.

I

First, Luke. A bit of biblical discovery, quite important. At first reading, chapter 4 can puzzle us. Earlier in the chapter, Luke has Jesus outlining the program for his ministry: "The Spirit of the Lord is upon me, for [the Lord] has anointed me; He has sent me to preach good news to the poor, to proclaim release for prisoners and sight for the blind, to send the downtrodden away relieved, and to proclaim the Lord's year of favor" (Lk 4:18–19). His teaching, Jesus proclaims, is a fulfilment of Old Testament Scripture, specifically Isaiah 61.[1]

Jesus' fellow townspeople are impressed, delighted. When he proclaims, "Today this passage of Scripture has been fulfilled in your hearing," Luke tells us, "They all bore witness to him and were amazed that such gracious words came from his lips" (vv. 21–22).

The men and women of Nazareth love him; one of their own boys has made it big time.

Then, surprise. All of a sudden the situation changes for the worse. Jesus remarks, "Believe me, no prophet is accepted in his own homeland" (v. 24). And he exemplifies the proverb from two Old Testament prophets, Elijah and Elisha. The people in the synagogue grow furious; they take him "to the edge of the cliff on which the town was built, to throw him over it." But he slips through the crowd and goes on his way (vv. 28–30).

What has happened? Are Nazarenes so fickle that one moment they applaud, the next they kill? Not quite. Luke's chapter 4 is what scholars call a "conflation";[2] he has brought together two events, two stories, that happened at different times. Why? Call it Luke's theology. That theology has to do with Jesus as prophet. And that summons up my second point.

II

What is Luke emphasizing? Wherein lies the theology? Simply and profoundly this: Like all prophets, Jesus was accepted and Jesus was rejected. Accepted in his homeland, rejected in his homeland. It was predicted by old Simeon when the child Jesus was presented to the Lord in Jerusalem's temple. "Look," Simeon said to Mary, "this child is marked for the fall and the rise of many in Israel, to be a symbol that will be rejected" (Lk 2:34). Jesus himself predicted that, in consequence of his coming, peace within families would be destroyed. Sons will clash with their fathers, daughters with their mothers, daughters-in-law with their mothers-in-law. "One's foes will be members of one's own household" (Mt 10:35–36).

Earlier prophets had already experienced it. Jeremiah's first six years found him on a high; success came speedily; and such success, he reasoned, surely proved that God had called him. Then ensued a series of reversals; then commenced the second period of his ministry, the "long trek across the dreary plateau of failures." Time and again he disputed with God: "You are just, O Lord....Why does the way of the wicked prosper?" (Jer 12:1). And God's answer, when it came, was discouraging: Things will get worse before they get better. And Jeremiah would complain to his people, "For 23 years...I have spoken persistently to you, but you have not listened" (Jer 25:3).[3] Amos, too, could complain, "They hate the one who reproves in the gate, and they abhor the one who speaks the truth" (Amos 5:10).

Malachi experienced it. Malachi could not remain silent when he saw before him greedy priests who were offering in sacrifice animals that were blind or lame; had to protest when he saw Jewish men divorcing their wives and marrying attractive foreign girls; had to shout aloud against "those who oppress the hired workers in their wages, the widow and the orphan, those who thrust aside the alien" (Mal 3:5), abuse the stranger, the immigrant. For these and other violations of the covenant Malachi cried, "Have we not all one and the same Father? Has not the one God created us? Why, then, are we faithless to one another, violating the covenant of our ancestors?" (2:10).

Rabbi Abraham Joshua Heschel insisted that the prophets were a lonely lot. Lonely because they alienated simply everyone: not only the wicked but the pious, not only cynics but believers, not only princes but priests, not only false prophets but judges. What is surprising is not that the people turned a deaf ear to the prophets; what is surprising is that the people tolerated them. For "To the patriots, they seemed pernicious; to the pious multitude, blasphemous; to the men in authority, seditious."[4]

What Luke suggests in chapter 4 is Jesus' mission in miniature: acceptance and rejection, with the emphasis on rejection—rejection in his own homeland. A rejection that prophets before him had experienced time and again. Ultimately, Israel as a whole rejected him, and Jesus saw himself "as the cornerstone of a new Israel (Luke 20:17) and those who did respond to him entered it."[5]

III

Third, how does all this touch you? I mean as priests or priests-to-be. I suggest that it turns on one word, a word that designated a significant role of Jesus. The word? Prophet. Not predicting the future. A more primary sense: one who speaks in another's presence on behalf of someone. In Heschel's pithy sentence, "In the presence of God [the prophet] takes the part of the people. In the presence of the people he takes the part of God."[6]

What the prophet Jesus intimates, what the Hebrew prophets confirm, is that during your apostolate as priests/prophets two reactions are likely to greet you: acceptance *and* rejection. Even, or especially, or usually, in your homeland. In your parish. A disciple of Jesus, he himself insisted, cannot expect to be treated differently than his master. Partly your personality, who you are. Some adults will like you instinctively, others dislike you on sight. Some of the young will think you cool, others ugly. Some will find your mustache cute, others can't stand it on a priest. Some will not really accept you, or accept you halfheartedly, because you are male.

Even more important here is what you say, what you preach, your message. Retain the biblical word "Lord" for Jesus, "He" for God, "Father" for the First Person of the Trinity, and ears will close; you're not "with it." Change the words, and the chancery's mail sack will bulge. "No one," says an experienced lay friend of mine, "no one phones the rectory to tell you how well things are going."

Preach the option for the poor: The poor will cheer you, the not-so-poor may charge you with discrimination. Preach with the pope against capital punishment: The polls tell us 25 percent of your congregation may applaud, 75 percent will resent a heart that bleeds for the murderer rather than the victim. Plead for the AIDS-afflicted: You will be blessed by the afflicted, will antagonize those who see in AIDS God's own plague on the promiscuous. Preach justice for those on welfare: Some Catholics will join you, others will respond, "We'll give them justice, these wastrels who use up our hard-earned money." Preach against abortion: For all your fidelity to authentic teaching, prochoice Catholics will tune you out.

One concrete example will not leave me after almost two decades. It was the annual Mass on Argentina's national day at St. Matthew's Cathedral. The preacher was Capuchin Sean O'Malley, then head of the Spanish Secretariat of this archdiocese, now ordinary in Fall River, Massachusetts. His stole was a symbolic purple. Instead of the usual eulogy, he quoted statements by John Paul II and the bishops of Latin America about repression, torture, and disappearances; he began to focus on the people who had vanished under the Videla regime; he quoted Scripture on Herod's slaughter of the innocents. At that point the congregation, led by a high-ranking general, walked out. Some damned the homilist for "turning a religious event into a political one." Another said, "priests have no place in politics. He should have given a sermon on another subject, like the love of God."[7]

I am not suggesting that we bar the controversial from the pulpit. We cannot be content with glittering generalities: "No one can live on bread alone," "My peace I give to you," "Seek first the kingdom of God," "Love your neighbor as yourself," "Wives, be subject to your husbands." We must move the gospel to this age, to this people; but the meaning and demands of the gospel today are chock-full of complexity. On legitimately controverted social, political, or economic issues I dare not pontificate, speak in dogmatic fashion, as if I alone am the trumpet of the Lord. But if I dare not dogmatize, I must still raise the issues, lay them out, at times may even tell the faithful where I stand and why. Not to impose my convictions as gospel, but to quicken their Christian consciousness, to spur them to personal reflection.

And still, however prudent we may be, we cannot avoid being, like Jesus, symbols that are rejected. Many, perhaps most, of our people will say yes to what we proclaim as gospel, even approve our interpretation of an indistinct gospel. But in an age as educated, as sophisticated, as critical as ours, others will challenge what we call gospel, even if we can quote Rome till the cows come home. And when the gospel is not utterly clear, we preachers may inhabit a no man's land, treacherous territory where raising awareness, lifting consciousness, is misunderstood, is resented, is defied.

Even so, it is the prophet's privilege and burden: our privilege to speak for God to living men and women, our burden to face rejection. It is our role in the mission of Jesus. That role involves a cross, perhaps a daily cross. It may not be Jeremiah's 23 years of preaching without an ear that hears. Not likely tossed over the nearest cliff, not pinned to twin beams of wood between two convicts. But believe me—from years of travel across the country on my project Preaching the Just Word—it is the rare priest/prophet who does not cringe under criticism, does not suffer from ears that are deaf, from noses turned upward in opposition, from lips thinning in anger. But never forget the ultimate Christian paradox, the feast the Church celebrates explicitly each September 14: the *triumph* of the cross.

What shall we celebrate in and through our priesthood? Will it be only the "successes," the acceptances, the wisdom that emerges from our grace-filled intelligence? Will it be collection baskets as heavy as the nets of the apostles after Jesus' resurrection? Or will it be the foolishness of the cross, Christ crucified, the apparent "failures," the rejections? Celebrate indeed, for the only real failures take place when our love is absent. If we love, we can trust God to give the increase, as only God can.

Lent, you know, is a splendid period for celebrating what "the world" views as failure: no money, no power, no fame. Yes, rejection, the cross. Fifty-six years a priest, I love this ministry, the priest as prophet, my head and heart, lips and tongue outthrust to people for God, raised to God for people. Not primarily the applause, though I have never silenced it. More importantly, an awareness of weakness—how impotent I am of myself, for all my native gifts. Coming to sense how truly St. Paul spoke: "I will boast all the more gladly of my weaknesses, so that the power of Christ may dwell in me. Therefore I am content with weaknesses, insults, hardships, persecutions, and calamities for the sake of Christ; for whenever I am weak, then I am strong" (2 Cor 12:9–10).

Whenever I am weak, then I am strong. A question for Lent, beneath the cross: Do you believe that? Do you?

Theological College
Catholic University
Washington, D.C.
March 16, 1998

5
BORN BLIND, HOW DOES HE NOW SEE?
Fourth Sunday of Lent (A)

- 1 Samuel 16:1, 6–7, 10–13
- Ephesians 5:8–14
- John 9:1–41

A memorable Gospel. But there's a practical problem here. We can listen attentively, for it's a fascinating story—not only a striking miracle, but powerful dialogue. We can react admiringly, for this Jesus of ours shows himself stern to the powerful, compassionate to the little people. And all the while we can keep the story in the first century, in the Middle East, with a cast of characters mostly foreign to us. We can forget that the Jesus story has to become our story, that the pilgrimage of Jesus had for purpose to sketch our own human and Christian journey.

And so I suggest that we move the story to 1998. How? Ask three questions. (1) On a broad canvas, where do we find blindness today? (2) What, for Christians, is the light that can pierce the darkness? (3) What might all this say to us in the darkness we experience as a community and as individuals?

I

First, on a broad canvas, where do we find blindness today? I dare not speak for you. So, let me sketch my own vision: three areas where all too many men and women are blind, do not see as they should. The areas? Our world, our country, our church. Not everybody, not always; still, a frightening amount of blindness, across a frightening stretch of territory.

Our world. I see blindness in a world where human beings, children of one God, even Christians commanded to love as Jesus loved,

28

brutalize one another with hate in their hearts. Item: Northern Ireland. Blind because they do not see that, like Cain, they are killing their brothers and sisters. I see blindness in the Middle East, where peace is so elusive because hatred is etched into history. I see blindness in what was once Yugoslavia and in areas of Africa, where war knows no innocents, no mercy, where women are raped and children slaughtered. I see blindness in a world where 16 million refugees are forced by war or persecution to flee their native lands, where 25 million more are forced from their homes to walk to unfamiliar resting places. I see blindness in a world where over 250 million children have to work, many at risk from dangerous and exploitative labor.

Our country. I see blindness in a country where our black sisters and brothers still echo the cry of Yahweh to Pharaoh, "Let my people go"; where Americans claim to love their children and yet 1.5 million defenseless infants are aborted each year; where we constitute four percent of the world's population but consume 40 percent of its resources; where the younger you are the poorer you are; where we kill the killers to show that killing is wrong; where women still cry out against their powerlessness to shape their world in any but a masculine mold.

Our church. I see blindness in a church where only 30 percent of U.S. Catholics celebrate Eucharist at least twice a month; where all too often liturgy is lifeless, and Catholics leave us for more vibrant Protestant preaching; where Hispanics often feel unwelcome and African-Americans find little to entice them; where priesthood and religious life are no longer attractive; where churches and schools continue to close, and we are losing our young in heartbreaking numbers; where our internal, intramural dissensions hinder our mission, keep us from spreading the gospel outside our walls; where a large number still see abortion as a legitimate Christian choice; where rugged individualism and consumerism are just as rampant as in the rest of society.

One-sided? Of course. Is there another side? Yes indeed. But it doesn't cancel out the dark side; it's there, far more darkness than any homily can narrate. For that dark side, is there a remedy? The ultimate antidote lies in today's Gospel.

II

Hence my second point. Listen to Jesus once more: "We must work the works of Him who sent me while it is day. Night is coming when no one can work. As long as I am in the world, I am the light of the world" (Jn 9:4–5). Several observations here.

First, a lesson from Jesus. He tells us straight-out that in the man born blind we do not have just another miracle. The miracle is a sign. His disciples ask Jesus, "Rabbi, who committed the sin that caused him to be born blind, he or his parents?" Jesus' response? "Neither....[He was born blind] to let God's works be revealed in him" (vv. 2–3). The lesson taught by the story? The triumph of light over darkness. In curing the man born blind, Jesus acts out what he proclaimed earlier, "I am the light of the world. No follower of mine shall ever walk in darkness; no, he will possess the light of life" (Jn 8:12), that is, the light that gives life.

Lovely, but what does it mean? It is difficult to think of our Lord as light. It is easy enough to see him as a baby resting on straw; as a carpenter crafting a cabinet; as a healer cleansing a leper; as a teacher charming the temple; as a convict bleeding on a cross; even as risen from the grave and munching fish on a lake shore. But Jesus as light? How unreal can a three-point homilist get?

The fact is, this is reality. Priest Zechariah recognized it six months before the birth of Jesus. Filled with the Holy Spirit, he prophesied in awe: "In the merciful compassion of our God, the Dawn from on high will visit us, to shine on those who sit in darkness" (Lk 1:78–79). Aged Simeon saw it six weeks after the birth of Jesus. Guided by the Spirit, he took the child in his arms: "My eyes have seen your salvation...a light to give revelation to the Gentiles" (Lk 2:30–32).

But what does it mean? It means that redemption, God in our flesh, touches our minds: Our minds were darkened by sin, and God came to tear away the darkness. How? The Son of God was born not only to *do* something but to *say* something; he was born not only to die but to teach. "This is why I was born," he said to Pilate, "this is why I have come into the world: to bear witness to the truth" (Jn 18:37).

And the truth Jesus revealed is a brilliant light for our minds, for he told us secrets unsuspected about God and the image of God that is every man and woman. Told us of a God who sent an only Son to die in rare anguish for a race that had rebelled; of a food that would be his flesh, a drink that would be his blood; of a church that would be his body, prolong his presence till time is no more; of a new life that is God's life throbbing through our inmost being; of a life beyond this life, where, as the Mass for the Departed puts it, "life is not taken away, life is merely changed"—where our happiness is God "face to face," days without end, life rapturous and ecstatic, without pain, without tears.

All this Jesus told us, and a thousand truths more. This is the light that shattered the darkness one blessed midnight. But this light is not enough. Jesus did not thunder from a mountain, plead from a boat, and whisper from a cross so that his words might hover in the Judean air, or lie imprisoned in a Bible, or reach our minds like ancient history. Revelation calls for a response. If God speaks to us, it is so that we might speak to God. If Jesus proclaims, "Truly I say to you," it is our task to answer, "I believe, Lord; help my unbelief." If the first light is revelation, the corresponding light is faith.

And faith is indeed a light. With it I can affirm what a Huxley could only deny: that even an evolving universe needs a God. With it I can assert what an Aristotle could never suspect: that God is not only One but Three. With it I can see on a cross not injured innocence but God redeeming; in a small white wafer, not lifeless bread but the Bread of Life. With it I can see God in the water that bathes a baby's brow and in the oil that anoints an elderly woman's lips, in the hand of a priest upraised to forgive and in the words of self-giving a bride and groom murmur to each other. With it I can see in suffering a share in Jesus' passion, in death entrance into endless ecstasy. I can do so because in faith I use God's eyes to see, and so in the dark I can know breath-taking truths that only God has a right to see.

But it is not only in the area of faith, of God-given revelation, that Jesus can be light to us. His Holy Spirit, present deep within you and me, is a Spirit of wisdom. In an age-old hymn, "Come, Holy Ghost," we beg the Holy Spirit, "Enkindle light in our minds."[1] And rightly do we pray that prayer. For in the Sermon on the Mount, Jesus said to all who claim to follow him: "You are the light of the world....Let your light shine before men and women" (Mt 5:14–16). There is a wisdom not of this world, a wisdom the Spirit gives to those who in God's presence are like little children, a wisdom the Spirit gave to such as our Lady and the "good thief" on the cross, to Dorothy Day among the homeless and to parish priest St. John Vianney in his 12 hours in the confessional, to untold "ordinary" folk who believe with St. Paul that "God's foolishness is wiser than human wisdom" (1 Cor 1:25).

III

Finally, so what? What does this say to today's darkness, to you and me, as individuals and as a community? How can you be light in darkness? Basic to an answer is a process the Church asks of you at this stage in Lent. Where lies *your* darkness? How describe *your* Christian cataracts? I leave that scrutiny to you, while promising you a private investigation of my own blindness, where I do not see with the eyes of Christ. Here I would rather focus on one theme where your light is indispensable, where all of you can bring the light of Christ in varied ways to our church, to our country, perhaps even to our world.

Let me take you to the movies. Right now, six films up for Oscars have something extraordinary in common. The films? *Titanic, Deconstructing Harry, The Full Monty, Good Will Hunting, As Good as It Gets,* and *L.A. Confidential.* What do they have in common? All are statements. Statements of what? Statements of our social predicaments, darknesses of our time. And all employ images. What images? Images that suggest what I would call light: the renewal of the community.[2] Take just one of those films, *Titanic,* its social symbolism: "A technological wonder, the latest luxury commodity of industrial capitalism, [the Titanic] encodes in her decks and salons social hierarchies soon to be swept away in the maelstrom of the Great War...."[3] At the end, "White-gloved stewards open doors and the two young lovers enter the ship's elegant main salon. All around them are the characters of the film, but assembled as they never were in the real story—first-class passengers, immigrants from steerage, the ship's officers and musicians and waiters—all applauding Jack and Rose as they ascend the gilded staircase and embrace."[4] Even in the comedies on that list,

> The old flawed society...is transformed into a fundamentally new and reordered community. In this new community social relations are different; they are characterized by understanding, compassion, forgiveness. It is an image, not of the world we actually live in but of the one we want to live in, a community shaped by our profoundest hopes and desires.[5]

Such, good friends, are my expectations for you. Deepen this already remarkable community of yours. Not by agreeing on everything. How can you? You are not a community of clones. For all your similarities, you are so different one from another that this community is a miracle of grace. What makes you a community, literally one with one another? Not only the Creed you recite together; not only the hymns you sing as one; not only the Host in your hand or on your tongue. It's your ceaseless effort to understand different mind-sets, to feel deeply for those who don't attract you naturally, to forgive as the Lord has forgiven you. Because it is the *community* that is the Body of Christ. And the reason why St. Paul could declare that no one of us can say to any other, "I have no need of you" (1 Cor 12:21), is because we Christians are a community. But a community to the extent that we are distinguished for our yearning to understand one another, our compassion for the suffering in our midst, our willingness to forgive not seven times but seventy times seven.

So do you as individuals, you as community, become light. So does "your light shine before others, so that they see your good works and give glory to your Father in heaven" (Mt 5:16). It's not fantasy. It would be fantasy if the light we shed were of our own creation. No. Our light is a gift of God, a grace we cannot earn. And it is always God who gives the increase, who spreads our dim light to our church, to our country, to our world. Yes, the darkness can be disheartening, but only if we forget that the light of the world is Christ— Christ in us, Christ at work in all the world, Christ who died to destroy the darkness.

I leave with you the counsel my dear deceased friend John Courtney Murray often used in farewell to me: "Courage, Walter! It's far more important than intelligence." At times it is; indeed it is.[6]

Holy Trinity Church
Washington, D.C.
March 22, 1998

6
LOVE HEALS
Fourth Week of Lent, Year 1, Monday

- Isaiah 65:17–21
- John 4:43–54

In Cana Jesus heals a child dying in Capernaum. That simple, yet stunning scene sent me scurrying not to Scripture scholars but to a Jewish practitioner of holistic health. About a decade ago Dr. Bernie Siegel authored an intriguing book titled *Love, Medicine & Miracles*.[1] The long subtitle reads: "Lessons Learned about Self-Healing from a Surgeon's Experience with Exceptional Patients." Two provocative passages from that stimulating work continue to haunt me. (1) "I am convinced that unconditional love is the most powerful known stimulant of the immune system. If I told patients to raise their blood levels of immune globulins or killer T cells, no one would know how. But if I can teach them to love themselves and others fully, the same changes happen automatically. The truth is, love heals."[2] (2) "Remember I said love heals. I do not claim love cures everything but it can heal and in the process of healing cures occur also."[3]

Those startling sentences have triggered fresh thoughts on three healers or sets of healers: (1) Jesus, (2) Christians in general, (3) specifically you and your homilist.[4] A word on each.

I

First, Jesus. The Son of God borrowed our humanity, soul and body, spirit and flesh. Why? For one profound purpose: to heal the whole of our humanity—all of us and the whole of each. I find it fascinating how some Fathers of the Church insisted on that. They could not tolerate Docetists who claimed that Jesus only seemed to be born of Mary, did not really have a human body, was not genuinely human. They could not endure a fourth-century theologian named Apollinaris, who argued that Christ did not have a human soul. No, they cried, what was not assumed by God's Son, what in our human nature was not taken by him, was not healed. And the healing was not done from outer space. Jesus healed by living and loving. Living our total existence, mind and heart, seeing and hearing, touching and tasting and smelling—like us in simply everything save our sin. Loving with an utterness and a for-otherness no man or woman can ever equal.

I see Jesus healing on three levels: the physical, the psychological, and the spiritual. The physical: He commanded the paralytic to take up his mat and walk, cured the dying son of Capernaum's royal official, raised from the depths of death the only son of Naim's widow. The psychological: He restored dignity to an adulteress, showed a proud Pharisee at table how a sinful woman could love more than he, persuaded a cured demoniac not to follow him but to return to his dear ones a new man. The spiritual: Over and above all other healing, the reason behind all other healing, Jesus brought in his own person to the world, to all the world, God's favor, God's grace, God's love. For when he died, it was not crucifixion that redeemed us, sheer shedding of his blood. Only love redeemed us, the love that led him to his baptism in blood. "Having loved his own who were in this world," John declares, "he showed his love for them to the very end" (Jn 13:1), loved us utterly, completely, without reserve.

So has Jesus healed us, so are we ceaselessly being healed: by love, "God's love poured into our hearts through the Holy Spirit that has been given to us" (Rom 5:5).

II

But if the gift was not given without cost to Christ, neither is it given without cost to Christians. The gift of healing is indeed given; for Christians are called to be healers. Wounded healers indeed, but all the more Christlike in their woundedness.

Some Christians—I know some—have been graced with healing hands, have excised cancerous flesh, drilled healing holes in brittle brains, brought lasered sight to dimming eyes. There are hands that, within a community that sings and prays, persuade crippled feet to stand and walk, diseased lungs to breathe afresh, depressed spirits to joy and hope once more. And in the Catholic anointing of the sick, physical health may follow, does at times follow, if it will help toward the invalid's salvation.

Others—I know many—have been graced with uncommon insight into obstacles to psychic or emotional well-being, stumbling blocks to wholeness. Pastoral counselors and spiritual directors can heal the broken spirit, and in the process may discover a spiritual bonding that heals counselor and counselee.[5]

In the Christian perspective it is God's grace that makes for wholeness. But, to draw grace from God, only love is all-powerful. Especially a crucified love. Without love, Paul told us, we are nothing. With love—loving God, loving ourselves, loving others without reserve—Christians continue the healing that was conceived in Nazareth, brought to birth in Bethlehem, and consummated on Calvary. Nothing is impossible to love, because nothing is impossible to a God who *is* Love.

III

Third, you and I. Where do we, precisely as priests, discover our healing powers? We do have healing powers, you know; for Paul says God has given us "the ministry of reconciliation" (2 Cor 5:18). And where does that reconciliation lie? Not only with an absolution in the confessional; not only with oils at the bedside of the ailing. Recall what you heard so eloquently this morning from our gifted Scripture scholar.[6] The core of our preaching is a single biblical word: justice. And what is biblical justice? Right relationships: with God, with people, with the earth. Love God above all else; love every human like another self; treat God's "things" with reverence.

In what sense is this a healing? Because it repairs the rupture that sin created in the beginning. For one shining segment of time, all relationships were right: humans one with God, humans at peace with one another, humans in harmony with the creatures of earth and sky and sea. One shining moment...till sin severed us from God, set us at war with one another, made nonhuman creation an enemy we felt we had to subdue.

Read, ponder, God's efforts to set relationships right. Listen to God making one covenant with both humans and animals: "I am establishing my covenant with you [Noah] and your descendants after you, and *with every living creature* that is with you" (Gen 9:9–10). Listen to Hosea expressing God's hope for a return of the original harmony: "I will make for you a covenant on that day with the wild animals, the birds of the air, and the creeping things of the ground" (Hos 2:18). Rediscover in the Hebrew Testament an Israel so linked to its environment that healing for Israel means healing for nature as well. Struggle to understand that in the crucifixion of Christ the single, triadic community becomes possible. Humans with God: "Whoever is in Christ is a new creation" (2 Cor 5:17). Humans with one another: a humanity where no one can say to any other, "I have no need of you" (1 Cor 12:21). In the Synoptic Gospels, the healing miracles reveal that salvation in Christ means the healing of human beings and their environment. God's plan "for the fulness of time" was, Paul says, "to gather *all things* in Christ, things in heaven and things on earth" (Eph 1:10).

The reconciliation we are privileged to preach is salvation within a single, all-embracing community. It's a shivering, exhilarating awakening. Salvation in Christ, the salvation I must preach, depends on fidelity to three relationships: Do I love God above all else? Do I love each sister and brother like another I, as Jesus loves me? Do I touch each "thing" (that ice-cold word) with the reverence God asked of humankind at its birthing? Is this the fidelity I am asking of my people? Is this the fidelity I demand of myself?

You may say we have come a far piece from the royal official and his ailing son. Yes, if all you want is a short story with a happy Hollywood ending. No, if you want to preach the gospel the Son of God took our flesh to proclaim.

Marydale Retreat Center
Erlanger, Kentucky
March 10, 1997

7
I'LL NEVER BELIEVE UNLESS...
Second Sunday of Easter (C)

- Acts 5:12–16
- Revelation 1:9–13, 17–19
- John 20:19–31

Many decades ago, I scandalized a pious aunt of mine. I had to choose a name for my confirmation, and I had chosen...Thomas. "Doubting Thomas!" she cried. "Oh, no!" It was as if I had opted to be infected with the virus of disbelief, a virus passed on internationally a week after Easter in that two-syllable name for ever preceded by "doubting." I could conceivably have countered with theologian Thomas Aquinas, with martyr Thomas Becket, with a score of Thomases who testified to the truth; but no, the Thomas who wasn't where he should have been on Easter Sunday, the Thomas who declared "I'll never believe unless I can touch his wounds," how could I do this to her, how could I break her heart? I don't know, but I did.

Still, my aunt's horrified "Oh, no!" has not been wafted on the wind. Thomas deserves a better press, and his experience can be beneficial to you and me. Two points, therefore: Thomas and we. In each case, by way of two exclamations: "I'll never believe unless..." and "My Lord and my God!"

I

First, Thomas. "I'll never believe unless...." Sounds arrogant, doesn't it? Especially coming from an apostle who had for some reason deserted the community, perhaps wandered downtown to immerse his melancholy in a mug of Manishewitz. But then I put myself in Thomas'

38

sandals; I tried to think as Thomas might have been thinking. Something like this:

> I know I should believe what Peter and John and the other eight of our company have told me, "We have seen the Lord" (Jn 20:25). I've gotten to know them quite well these past three years. Not only are they honest men, wouldn't lie if you paid them. Tricky Judas might have, but he's dead, hung himself. Many of them are down-to-earth fellows—fishermen, a toll collector—not easily taken in by visions. Not likely to see a ghost and mistake it for Jesus. Not all ten of them. Nobody would bet money on that; the odds are off the board.
>
> And still....We've all wanted to believe what Jesus told us so often: that he had to die, but that he would come back to life, that we would see him again. Especially what he said to us the night before he died: "Do not let your hearts be troubled, and do not be afraid. You have heard me tell you, 'I am going away,' and 'I am coming back to you'" (Jn 14:28). And what he said to us after we left the supper room: "You are sad now; but I shall see you again, and your hearts will rejoice with a joy no one can take from you" (Jn 16:22). We have wanted so badly to believe him, wanted so terribly to see him. If I had stayed with them, maybe I too would have thought I saw him.

It could have been so. But even if we find out in heaven that on the first Easter evening there's no excuse for "doubting Thomas," he does come through splendidly a week later. But here be careful. When you hear that joyful cry from Thomas' lips, "My Lord and my God!" (Jn 20:28), don't think it was all very simple. It looks simple. Here was Jesus in the flesh—glorified flesh yes, but still his flesh. What else could he do, with Jesus standing before him, Jesus inviting Thomas to do what he had insisted he must do to believe: "Reach out your finger and examine my hands; reach out your hand and put it into my side. And do not persist in your disbelief, but become a believer"? (Jn 20:27).

Not so fast! Thomas did not say, could not say, "My Lord and my God" simply because Jesus stood before him, because he saw the glorified wounds of Jesus' passion. Remember, Thomas did not say "My Lord and my God!" when Jesus raised Lazarus from the dead. Remember the remark of St. Paul: "No one can say 'Jesus is Lord' except by the Holy Spirit" (1 Cor 12:3). To see *God* in human flesh is not the result of logic, the conclusion of a syllogism. It is an act of *faith*. Thomas' outburst is a gift—a gift only God can offer, a gift Thomas could have refused. Thomas addresses Jesus the way Israel addressed Yahweh: "My Lord and my God!" (v. 28).[1] In the Gospel of John this is the climax of *faith;* to these five words the Gospel has been moving.[2] I like what Scripture scholar Raymond Brown has said: "nothing more profound could be said about Jesus."[3]

II

Second, you and I. As before, so now, there is the doubting and there is the affirming. There is "I'll never believe unless" and there is "My Lord and my God!"

"I'll never believe unless...." It takes many forms: the occasional scientist who won't believe what is not in his lab; the skeptic who lives by the axiom "seeing is believing"; the naturalist or materialist for whom the supernatural is unreal, doesn't exist. What concerns me here is someone else. I mean Christians who feel they must apologize for faith, as for a crutch on which you lean when all the more powerful arguments have dwindled away, a support for the intellectually maimed, a lame excuse.

The genuine Christian lives by the basic declaration in the First Letter of Peter: "Although you have not seen [Jesus Christ], you love him; and even though you do not see him now, you believe in him and rejoice with an indescribable and glorious joy, for you are receiving the outcome of your faith, the salvation of your souls" (1 Pet 1:8–9). I mean what Jesus said to Thomas, "Happy those who have not seen and yet have believed" (Jn 20:29).

But what is this faith, this belief? Faith does indeed include propositions, our Sunday Creed: "I believe in one God the Father, the Almighty, Creator of heaven and earth. I believe in one Lord Jesus Christ. I believe in the Holy Spirit, the Lord, the Giver of life." But to accept a set of propositions, however important, is not enough. The New Testament Letter of James was brutally blunt on this point: "You believe that God is one; you do well. Even the demons believe—and shudder" (Jas 2:19). Faith in its fulness, faith alive, is inseparable from love.

Is there room for doubt in our Christian lives? Some say no, I say yes. We are never too old to doubt, especially as education confuses us and technology bewilders us. What I said here nine years ago, I can repeat all the more humbly this evening: Every so often I wake up at night wondering how the Christian thing makes sense. How can a God even be, a God who is, our philosophy claims, One Eternal Act? How can God die—and for me? How can this wafer be not a wafer but Jesus

Christ, body and blood, soul and divinity? How can I share God's life right now? How can I, this strange creature, live forever—that impossible word? And I shake, I shiver. Till I bend at my bed and beg with the father of the Gospel epileptic, "I believe, help my unbelief!" (Mk 9:24). And, thank God, I do believe. Not because I see. A leap in the dark—but a leap that is God's gift to me.[4] No apologies; only gratitude.

Then, for us too, there is the expression "My Lord and my God!" Here let me confront a contemporary concern for many Catholics. I mean the word "Lord." Lord is not in favor these days. Perhaps acceptable in Great Britain, for prelates and nobles; not in a nation of equals. And surely not for the Jesus who came not to be served but to serve. And so some will not use it of Jesus, omit it in Scripture reading, substitute some other title—brother, friend, companion.

I think I understand. And yet, I dare suggest other factors, factors that take precedence in my theology and worship. If angels could announce the world's best-news-ever by declaring "There has been born to you today a Savior who is...the Lord" (Lk 2:11); if Elizabeth "filled with the Holy Spirit" could ask in wonder, "Why should this happen to me that the mother of my Lord comes to me?" (Lk 1:41, 43); if early Christians used "Lord" to put Jesus on the same level as Yahweh; if a resounding early Christian hymn preserved by Paul could sing "God gave [Jesus] a name that is above every name, so that...every tongue should confess 'Jesus Christ is Lord'" (Phil 2:9–11); if Jesus himself could say to his disciples, "You call me...Lord, and you are right, for that is what I am" (Jn 13:13); if Scripture can end with the heartfelt prayer "Come, Lord Jesus" (Rev 22:20)—why should I hesitate to call him Lord? Yes, Jesus is my elder brother, because he is as human as you and I; but he is more than my brother, because he is as divine as his Father and his Holy Spirit.

It is true, the title "Lord" does express dominion: Paul declares, "You have died to the law through the body of Christ, so that you may belong to another, to him who has been raised from the dead in order that we may bear fruit for God" (Rom 7:4). We belong no longer to ourselves; we have been "ransomed...by the precious blood of Christ" (1 Pet 1:18–19). Still, somewhat as Jesus insisted, "My kingdom does not belong to this world" (Jn 18:36), is *in* this world but not *of* this world, so he could say his lordship is not like earthly lordships. "You know," Jesus said to his disciples, "that the rulers of the Gentiles lord it over them, and their great ones are tyrants over them. It will not be so among you; but whoever wishes to be great among you must be your servant, and whoever wishes to be first among you must be your slave;

just as the Son of Man came not to be served but to serve, and to give his life a ransom for many" (Mt 20:25–28).

Jesus has given a new meaning to "My Lord." Indeed we belong utterly to him; but this Lord washes the feet of his servants; this Lord we serve freely or not at all, serve him who took our flesh to serve us. Let's keep the name, honor it, even (if you prefer) use it of no one now on earth; for Jesus has transformed it.

Thomas started something, didn't he? I think I've learned more from Thomas doubting than from Peter exclaiming immediately, "You are the Messiah, the Son of the living God" (Mt 16:16). Still, what Jesus said to Peter he said in effect to Thomas and he says to you and me: "Blessed are you. For flesh and blood has not revealed this to you, but my Father in heaven" (v. 17). Yes, my friends, blessed are you. Believe it!

Holy Trinity Church
Washington, D.C.
April 19, 1998

8

BY THIS ALL WILL KNOW
YOU ARE MY DISCIPLES
Fifth Sunday of Easter (C)

- Acts 14:21b–27
- Revelation 21:1–5a
- John 13:31–33a, 34–35

"Love one another as I have loved you" (Jn 13:34). The temptation for a theologian is to present a profound lecture, wherein I tell you precisely what love *is,* the different *kinds* of love, and *how* to love as God wants you to love.

No, good friends. A homily is not a lecture, is not abstract knowledge. A homily on love should give you living images of love, bring love to life, reveal people who have loved, who can be patterns of love, models who have loved in ways we should love.

And so I proceed today. Three points, three persons, three loves: (1) the Jesus who commands us to love as he loved; (2) the Mary who marks this month of May as the perfect disciple of love; (3) the mothers we honor today for the kinds of love that make our world go round.

I

First, Jesus. This world has never known, will never again experience, the love Jesus lived, exactly as he lived it. Think of it. God's own Son became what you and I are. He took our bone and blood, our sinews and senses, our mind and muscle, our ignorance and insights, our weakness and worries, our fears and tears, our desolation and death. Why? To save us from ourselves, to make us better than we are, to shape us more like himself, to make our earth a place where love outlasts hate, where peace replaces war, where we can come to see each man, woman, and child as an image of God.

43

No other human has loved, can ever love, so many other humans with Jesus' intensity, his passion. The leprous and the paralyzed, prostitutes and the possessed, Samaritans and Canaanites, farmers and fishermen, Pharisees and a fevered mother, a high priest and a Roman procurator—it mattered not what sex or status, what color or age, how different. None of this mattered. Jesus lived to link each one to his Father in love.

It was not easy. You might think it would be. After all, wasn't he God's unique Son, divine as Father and Holy Spirit are divine? Yes, yes, a thousand times yes; but he was also as human as you and I. That is why he tired and thirsted, why he wept and worried. That is why he sweated blood in a garden, begged his Father, "Don't let me die!" That is why he could feel forsaken by his Father as he was dying in acute agony. The deeper the love, the crueler the pain when love is crucified.

How sum up Jesus' love? A total gift of himself—not only to his Father; to you and me as well. He held nothing back; he kept nothing for himself. He even left us a unique lasting memorial of himself, of his love: what looks like bread, feels like bread, tastes like bread, but is not bread, is himself, his body and blood, his soul and divinity.

Now that's love!

II

Jesus' love we cannot reproduce, just as we cannot reproduce his life. You see, in the lives of all graced persons, in your life and mine, there are realizations of love which in his restricted life Jesus did not and could not experience. He was a man, not a woman; he had close female friends but was not married; he was a teacher, but not a scholar; he did not experience old age or Alzheimer's disease; he never even lived to be a Jesuit! More accurate, then, than "imitate" is "follow," be Jesus' disciple—his disciple in loving. Keep in mind that revealing remark of Jesus in today's Gospel, "By this everyone will know that you are my disciples: by the love you have for one another" (Jn 13:35). That brings us to Jesus' first and most remarkable disciple: his mother.

If you are looking for love, listen to Mary when an angel tells her, to her utter surprise, that the Holy Spirit will overshadow her, a child will be born of her without Joseph's co-operation, her child will be Son of God. Her response? "Let it be with me as you say!" (Lk

1:38). Whatever you want, dear God. However surprising, however unbelievable—whatever God wants. Whatever. Now that's love!

Watch our Lady when she visits her pregnant relative Elizabeth, when she breaks out into the magnificent Magnificat:

> My soul declares the greatness of the Lord,
>   and my spirit finds delight in God my Savior,...
> for he who is mighty has done great things for me,
>   he whose name is holy.
>
> (Lk 1:46–49)

Now that's love!

Picture this mother when Jesus leaves Nazareth for his ministry, leaves home once and for all. Never a plea to come back home, even when his fellow townsmen try to throw him over a cliff, even when his relatives shout "He's mad!" (Mk 3:21). Never "Come back to me, to the carpenter's shop, where it's safe; those fools don't deserve you." Never. Now that's love!

Listen to the woman in the crowd proclaiming Mary's womb blessed for bearing Jesus. Listen to Jesus' response: Even more blessed are "those who listen to God's word and obey it" (Lk 11:27–28). Not a rebuke to his mother, not a put-down; quite the contrary. Mary is indeed blessed because she gave birth to Jesus, but even more blessed because she more than any sheerly human being listened to God speaking and said yes. Now that's love!

Stand with Mary beneath her Son's cross. As Jesus gives her to John and to us, she gives him back to his Father. Silently, without a spoken word. Simply her whole heart murmuring through tears, "You gave him to me, I return him to you." Now that's love!

See, after the Ascension, after Jesus' return to his Father, Mary returning to Jerusalem. Not in isolation. She stays with the disciples. "All these," Luke tells us, "were constantly devoting themselves to prayer" (Acts 1:14). What Luke says of the disciples is surely true of Mary: "Day by day, as they spent much time together in the temple, they broke bread at home and ate their food with glad and generous hearts, praising God and having the good will of all the people" (2:46–47). Now that's love!

III

Finally, turn from Jesus' mother to today's mother. Ever since "Cain rose up against his brother Abel and killed him" (Gen 4:8), mother love has been a tough love. Tougher still today, when mothers must confront a culture of crack and cocaine, an environment of violence; when peer pressure on children can undo a decade of loving; when economics limits the time for mothering; when all too many homes are fatherless. Tougher still when today's headlines are often misleading. They feature a mother who drives into a lake to kill her children; a college student who gives birth in a hotel bathroom, tosses the infant into a dumpster, and returns to the prom; a mother who strangles her child because he never ceases to scream.

True, but dreadfully deceiving. The gospel is *good* news; and the good news today is a daily miracle of love we take for granted. I mean...mothers. Who give birth—even to septuplets? Mothers, of course; who else? Who experience the most intimate nine-month relationship between humans God ever invented? Mothers, of course; who else? Who do instinctively what psychologists have just discovered: develop children's minds by reading to them, arms around them? Mothers, for the most part. Who pick up after infants, scrub them, evacuate them, keep little children from killing themselves in a hundred imaginative ways? Mothers, mostly. Oh, I know, men now help out in wondrous if inept ways. But how many millions of years had to pass before we males, we warriors, evolved to this level of child care? Before we moved from dividing child care to sharing it?

If you need current statistics, know that mothers still spend about four times more than fathers with their children; twice as many moms as dads are involved at school; soccer moms make up a third of soccer coaches; and 83% of mothers stay home with a sick child, compared with 22% of fathers.[1] Not a criticism of fathering, simply a fact of mothering.

Who must have eyes in the back of their heads, see more than they let on, comfort while disciplining, even at times take trash from smart-ass teenagers? Who take such joy in the first steps of a child, in the first word (even if it's Da-da)? Who suffer more intensely from loss, when a son or daughter goes wrong, thinks coke is cool, guns down a classmate, abuses a child? Who still go on with their parenting, who never stop loving?

In a word, who love more obviously as our Lady loved, as disciples of Jesus? Mothers love from their own Bethlehem, from frequent flights into their own Egypts, from the inevitable departure of their Jesus, from their own calvaries—like my mother, burying my father and my only brother within three weeks of each other. From their experience they seem to sense, far more intimately than I, that human living, for all its joy, involves a cross, but that, like Calvary, their cross is grace, their cross is courage, their cross is victory. Now that's love!

As the Amish have it, "we grow too soon old, too late smart." Before it's too late, let's sit quietly for a few moments, sunk in our memories—memories of mothers alive with us, mothers alive with God; mothers who still shake their heads at our follies, mothers up there with Mary and boasting about their children; mothers in good health, mothers musing over their mammograms; mothers happy in their husbands, mothers left to loneliness. Or don't think at all; don't worry about words; simply be, be grateful, be thankful; be a child, your mother's child.

Holy Trinity Church
Washington, D.C.
May 10, 1998

9
LET NOT YOUR HEARTS BE FEARFUL?
Fifth Week of Easter, Year 1, Monday

- Acts 14:5–18
- John 14:21–27

"Let not your hearts[1] be fearful" (Jn 14:27).[2] Don't be afraid. A startling charge of Jesus. Startling to his disciples, startling to us, startling for the reasons Jesus gives. A word on each.

I

First, the injunction of Jesus must have been startling to his disciples. How could it not be? At least two good reasons for his closest friends to be fearful. To begin with, outside that cozy, love-filled room, all through Jerusalem, they were disliked, despised, suspect, perhaps even hated—and this by fellow Jews, from the high priest through the scribes and Pharisees down to some ordinary folk. Why? Because they were disciples of a Nazarene who dishonored their Sabbath, dined with sinners, absolved an adulteress, asserted he was alive before Abraham, claimed to be a Son of God greater than their patriarchs and prophets. They remembered, too, that Jesus' own relatives had thought he was out of his mind; scribes from Jerusalem said he was possessed by demons; his own townspeople had tried to cast him from a cliff. Don't be afraid?

Besides, their Master had told them he was going to leave them. Not for a two-week vacation in the groves of Lebanon or on the shores of the Mediterranean. He was about to die. Not a quiet, natural kind of passing away. No, a gruesome death. Oh yes, he had told them he would come to life again, they would see him again. But at that point they were too slow of mind to grasp a dying/rising

Jesus. And so they were fearful—afraid of life-after-Jesus, life without Jesus. Afraid of being left orphans.

II

Second, the injunction of Jesus may well be startling to us, to you and me, to priests at the edge of the third Christian millennium.[3] It is terribly difficult not to be afraid. In 56 years I have moved from a priestly existence that was stable, secure, respected, to a presbyterate that is worried, nervous, suspect.

Yes, I am fearful. Fearful not for myself; fearful for our Catholic people, fearful for our priesthood.[4] Fearful because churches are closing and parishes have no Eucharist. Fearful because Catholics, individually and in factions, are clawing one another like cats in a sack. Fearful because only 26.5 percent of Catholics worship regularly on weekends, and a fearsome number no longer believe in the real presence of Christ in the Eucharist. Fearful because Catholics increasingly distrust established authority, not only president but pope as well.

I am fearful because all too many Catholics are questioning whether Christ is genuinely God, questioning whether Jesus actually rose from the dead. Fearful because many Catholics see social justice as masking an unrealistic whimper for the lazy on welfare. Fearful when I find Catholics prochoice on abortion, making up their own minds on birth control, on sex before marriage, on living together without marriage. Fearful because Catholics too question whether in our time anyone can say "for ever," whether there are any absolutes at all in moral living.

I am fearful because sociologists such as Robert Bellah tell us that, in today's resurgence of rugged individualism, where the race is to the swift, the shrewd, and the savage, where in the last analysis I am the only one who matters, Catholics are little different from their non-Catholic neighbors. Fearful because Catholics are included in the 76 percent of Americans who accept assisted suicide, and hardly differ in numbers from the 75 percent of Americans who cry for capital punishment.

I am fearful because polls and experience reveal that American Catholics, especially our youth, know so little about their faith, lack a vocabulary to help them form a Catholic identity.

I am fearful because, as we travel about the country in our project Preaching the Just Word, we experience a period of priestly peril without parallel perhaps since the Reformation. Worldwide, more than 100,000 priests have left the active ministry in the last 30 years. In our own dear country, a number of elements have fueled the contemporary crisis within our common priesthood. Our people criticize us as celebrants and celibates, as theologians and preachers, as activists and administrators, as males. One-priest parishes proliferate, expectations from an educated laity rise higher, appreciation is at a premium. Hence low morale, resentment, burnout, even fear of aging.

I am fearful because sex scandals continue to tarnish our priestly image: in one small diocese, 11 cases of pedophilia; in Catholic Ireland public esteem of the clergy only "0.1 points over journalists, normally the most despised category."[5]

Let not your hearts be fearful?

III

The answer, believe it or not, lies partially in a Greek word — the word in John translated as "fearful, afraid." The Greek word has to do with being "timid, cowardly." There is indeed a sensible, prudent fear. It makes sense to be concerned over the future of our country, our church, our priesthood, our selves. Fear can indeed shiver and shake you to your advantage. Ignatius Loyola, in his Spiritual Exercises, tells retreatants that if love isn't powerful enough to keep them from sinning, fear of hell might well do the trick. Recently it was not a bad idea to be afraid to fly in a Valujet.

John's Greek word means: Don't let the fear freeze you, paralyze you, immobilize you, defeat you, make you despair. But why not? For two splendid reasons: Christ Jesus and the Holy Spirit. A Presence and a Power. The real presence of Christ to and in our world, and the incredible power that is the Spirit. In harmony with today's Gospel, let me focus on the Holy Spirit, Jesus' deathless promise to his disciples and to us before his dying.

Look what the Holy Spirit did to the apostles. Contrast the Peter who swore to servant girls and bystanders "I do not know the man" (Mt 26:69–74) with the Peter who announced to hostile Jerusalem, "Let the entire house of Israel know with certainty that God has made [Jesus] both Lord and Messiah, this Jesus whom you crucified" (Acts 2:36). Contrast the Saul who persecuted Jesus with the Paul who died for him.

Come down to our own day. You've heard the bad news; look at the "good news," none of it possible without the Spirit whom the

New Testament sees as *dynamis*, "dynamite." Catholics by the hundreds of thousands feed the hungry and slake the thirsty, clothe the naked and house the homeless, nurse the ailing and pray with the imprisoned. After graduation, Jesuit Volunteers by the hundreds spend two years with the impoverished and neglected, not only in the States but in Micronesia, in Belize, in Chile. A CARA survey "reveals a solid core group of involved young laity" and reports "that youth ministry is highly effective in shaping moral attitudes and that participating youth had a very strong sense of Catholic identity and a high level of admiration for the pope."[6] A March 1996 Gallup poll reported a high degree of Catholic loyalty to the faith.[7] Thousands join the Catholic Church each year through the Rite of Christian Initiation of Adults.

Such data are far-reaching. For you and me, for priests from New York to California, God's injunction is "Let not your hearts be timid, cowardly." Let not the bad news freeze you. Not because you and I are so powerful. Only because the Holy Spirit is all-powerful, is divine Power. Only because, like Paul, "I can do all things through Him who strengthens me" (Phil 4:13).

Still, I am not urging you simply to survive. Our task is to help create the Church, the parish, of the third millennium. It will not be done simply by not surrendering, not giving up. Here a fresh Catholic imagination is imperative. Three examples.

First, mission. Persuade your parishioners, in season and out of season, that by baptism each of them is on mission. Recall for them the simple yet profound insight expressed by Belgian Cardinal Suenens: The greatest day in the life of a pope is not his coronation but his baptism, the day of his mission "to live the Christian life in obedience to the gospel."[8] Gather their charisms—women and men, young and middle-aged and aging, CEO and CPA, lawyer and judge, kindergarten teacher and university researcher, conservative and progressive, poverty-stricken and well-heeled—struggle to shape them into a single body, the Body of Christ.

Second, liturgy. We need a liturgy that is not primarily a head trip. Rather a liturgy that is alive, not so much a matter of words as an awareness, in ourselves and our people, of "an obedient standing in the alarming presence of the living God."[9] Where the sacramental genius of the Church is more obvious in the art and symbols, the poetry and metaphors of our Christian tradition. Where the senses return to worship: not only ashes to smudge our foreheads and crossed candles to cool our throats, but the Litany of the Saints as our Catholic ancestry.

Third, the justice we preach. No longer sheerly ethical justice, giving people what they deserve. Rather the biblical justice of Old Testament and New, fidelity to relationships and responsibilities that stem from our covenant: loving God above all else, loving each brother and sister like another I, touching God's nonhuman creation with reverence. Scores of today's justice issues within your parishes and outside you have scotch-taped to the walls of this conference room: for example, the homeless and the immigrant, child abuse and sexual exploitation, racism and ageism, drug addiction and AIDS affliction, abortion and euthanasia, political corruption and welfare reform, sweatshops and the prison system, injustice within our own dear Church.

It can be done. In justice to the cross of Christ, it must be done. At the Preface, "lift up your hearts." Let them throb with the confidence of Jesus declaring, "When I am lifted up from the earth, I will draw all people to myself" (Jn 12:32).

Fearful? Of course. Frozen with fear? Never!

Don Bosco Retreat Center
West Haverstraw, New York
April 28, 1997

10

IN HER SHORT LIFE NEVER FELT LOVE
Sixth Sunday of Easter (B)

- Acts 10:25–26, 34–35, 44–48
- 1 John 4:7–10
- John 15:9–17

A single monosyllable dominates the passages proclaimed to you from John and 1 John. The monosyllable? Love. A word well worn, overused, misused, at times defiled. With all that, how touch it to the Catholic Health Association of Canada?[1] Three stages: a story, a convention, a prayer.

I

The story stems from a young college graduate. Her name: Kaela Volkmer. She is a Jesuit Volunteer just beginning two years in Arica, Chile. The specific locale: a social-service agency, Hogar de la Niña (Young Girl's Home), founded by a recently beatified Jesuit, Alberto Hurtado. Kaela works with girls abandoned, with girls abused. Twenty-one girls are under Kaela's care. Here is one of her stories, in her own words.

> I was talking with a six-year-old, to get to know her and her situation. I began by asking her if she had any questions for me (the young ones are a bit confused by the gringa that keeps coming in every day and talks funny). The little girl said, "Yes." Then she asked, "Como es el amor?" "What is love?" I wasn't sure what exactly she meant, so I probed a little, and she responded that she hears love talked of all the time, but she didn't know what it meant. I thought at that moment, as I looked into her sincere face with the deep brown questioning eyes, that my heart would break, because love is something we feel, and she had

53

never felt it during her short little life. I struggled to give her Spanish synonyms that ended up being completely useless to her...how does one answer such a tremendous question? The simplest statement I could give her to respond to her question was "Dios es el amor." "God is love."

I told her that because God created her, out of love, she is wonderful, beautiful, special and important, and that no matter what, God will always be there to love her. Maybe over the next two years together we can figure out together what love is and what it feels like....[2]

"Maybe over the next two years...."

II

Can *we*, can Canada's healthcare Catholics, make a fresh beginning now? Kaela began her story of love where the First Letter of John bases its story: "God is love" (1 Jn 4:8), where your own story must focus. For your story is a love story. It began decades ago, when God shaped you not simply of human parents but of divine love, so imaginative a love that each of you images your God in a unique, unrepeatable way. I mean, in your distinctive freedom to love—to love others even as Christ loved and loves you.[3] Your story took a giant step forward when you selected one significant way to express your love: by bringing new life, and therefore new possibilities for love, not simply into ailing flesh, but to that amazing wedding of body, soul, and spirit we call a person. Each person—each man, woman, or child—seeking to be made whole once more, whole enough to love wholly once again or for the first time.

Since that decision for healthcare, your story should be a ceaseless growth: from love of medicine to love of those for whom medicine was born. It responds to what a friend of yours named Hippocrates used to say 2400 years ago: that he would rather know what sort of person has a disease than what sort of disease a person has.[4] It dovetails neatly with his aphorism, "Where you find love of the human person, there you find love of the Art."[5]

It isn't easy to love the ailing. The lovely, lissome young lady with a broken toe, the loving, trusting infant with Down's syndrome, no problem. But when year after year you are surrounded by blood and bone, mucous and metastasis, when you struggle each hour with others' fear or anger, depression or despair, when the bodies you stitch or nurse to health are the drug-addicted and the syphilis-afflicted, it's difficult to summon up the love that is compassion. But somehow you must. Otherwise a vocation turns into a job, a job into routine, routine into resentment.

You know, it's just as hard for a priest. The first 52 weeks after a bishop has oiled his hands, it's almost romantic. The mystery of the Mass, the wonder of God's Word trippingly on human lips, sinners reconciled to God and community, the sparkle in the eyes of communicants, man and maid pledging life and love for life, the dying grateful for food into eternity, even Christ in the beggar at the door—as famed Dominican preacher Lacordaire exclaimed, "My God, what a life!" But 10, 20, 30 years later, the ancient, ever-new peril: routine, rut, resentment, fueled at times by lack of appreciation. "No one," a friend told me, "no one phones the rectory to tell you how well things are going." The glow is gone.

Here is where the Christian gospel, the Catholic vision, must take over. You and I are more than mechanics, service stations. You and I are called to continue the redeeming work of Christ, his healing ministry. And how did Jesus heal? Not by sheer suffering; not by a cross alone. Suffering, a cross, transmuted into sacrifice by...love. A strong love, the love St. Paul commended to the Christians of Corinth: "Love bears all things, believes all things, hopes all things, endures all things" (1 Cor 13:7).

III

Finally, a prayer. Back to Kaela. At the end of a week, Kaela found herself "struggling with the child's question. My prayer at the end of that week is written on a page stained with tears of gratitude, sadness, confusion and joy." It reads:

> Dear God, I thank you whole-heartedly for helping me through this week. Please continue to strengthen me, that I may rise up to the challenges, so that "poco á poco" I will start to understand and begin to see more vividly your face in the faces of each of those precious girls, your daughters. I give them to you to hold, dear God. Please hug them close to your loving heart. Be with them in their moments of sadness, of fear, of loneliness. Be their mother who can't be there, because she is "soltera" [unmarried] and works the land slavishly with her rough, cracked hands—still finding herself in poverty and misery. Be their father who right now is broken by addiction and violence. Answer for each of us "como es el amor" and help me to be a light on the world's journey to healing. Amen.[6]

With very little change, this is your prayer as men and women of medicine. Thanksgiving for the grace of God that gets you through the stress and strain of any week. Without God's grace it cannot be done—not the way you want it done. Not as a job like any other. As God's instrument in the ceaseless task of healing. Not always curing, but always healing. Always seeing on that bed not a number, not a chart, not a wrist tag, not a disease, but a unique person.

With Kaela, therefore, a prayer of petition: to see more and more vividly on the face of each the face of God. The way to do it? The answer lies in that haunting song of Jean Valjean at the close of *Les misérables:* "To love another person is to see the face of God." Here is where you are disturbingly different, here is where you make a difference. Here is where you realize the experience of holistic physician Bernie Siegel. Controversial he has been; but two sentences from a lifetime of medicine continue to haunt me, give me hope. (1) "Remember I said love heals. I do not claim love *cures* everything but it can *heal* and in the process of healing cures occur also."[7] (2) "I am convinced that unconditional love is the most powerful known stimulant of the immune system."[8] Yes, Siegel was thinking primarily of love within those who are suffering. I submit that *your* love can double that healing potential. Not always words; the touch of your hand, the compassion in your eyes, yes the hope in your heart, your conviction that healing is more than the milk of human kindness—healing is a wedding of the human and the divine.

In the spare moments of your ministry, then, don't hesitate to murmur in your own rhetoric the prayer of Kaela for her unloved little ones: "I give them to you to hold, dear God. Please hug them close to your loving heart. Be with them in their moments of sadness, of fear, of loneliness. Help me to be a light on the world's journey to healing.... Amen."

Saint John Hilton Hotel
Saint John, New Brunswick, Canada
May 4, 1997

11
YOU TOO SHOULD BEAR WITNESS
Sixth Week of Easter, Year 2, Monday

- Acts 16:11–15
- John 15:26—16:4a

"You too should bear witness" (Jn 15:27). What did that charge mean for Jesus' original disciples? And what might it mean for you and me?[1]

I

In its fullest meaning, I am a witness not simply if I see something, hear something, not simply if I affirm that something is true. I am a first-rate witness if I do both: if I testify to something I have myself experienced. With my own eyes I have seen John Paul II in the Vatican; with my own ears I have heard Mozart's *Eine kleine Nachtmusik;* I have actually tasted Veal Saltimbocca; I have breathed the aroma of an American rose; I have kissed the Blarney stone upside down. And I tell you about the experience.

A shivering example of what I mean is the sentence that opens the First Letter of John : "What was from the beginning, what we have heard, what we have seen with our eyes, what we have looked upon and our hands have touched, the word of life—this life was revealed, and we have seen it, and we bear witness to it, and we declare to you the eternal life that was with the Father and was revealed to us" (1 Jn 1:1-2).

Such were the apostles to whom Jesus said, "You too should bear witness, because you have been with me from the beginning" (Jn 15:27). Witnesses without peer. They had walked the dusty ways of Galilee with him, had heard the music and thunder of his voice, had fished with him, prayed with him. Peter had clutched Jesus' hand when he began to sink in the storm; Jesus had washed the feet

57

of each. They saw him when the Risen One "showed them his hands and his side" (Jn 20:20), even took breakfast with him.

Little wonder that before he rose to his Father Jesus told them, "You will be my witnesses in Jerusalem, in all Judea and Samaria, and to the ends of the earth" (Acts 1:8). Little wonder that Peter could preach to fellow Israelites, "This Jesus God raised up, and of that all of us are witnesses" (Acts 2:32). Little wonder that thousands upon thousands repented of their sins and were baptized. Little wonder that "day by day the Lord added to their number those who were being saved" (Acts 2:47). They had experienced Jesus *and* they simply had to let the world know.

II

We too are called to bear witness. Witness to what we have experienced. With time pressing, I focus on one experience. Karl Rahner expressed it excitingly when, from profound knowledge, he put these words on the lips of Ignatius Loyola:

> As you know, my great desire was to 'help souls,' as I put it in my day; to tell people about God....I was convinced that first, tentatively, during my illness in Loyola and then, decisively, during my time as a hermit in Manresa I had a direct encounter with God. This was the experience I longed to communicate to others.
>
> When I claim to have known God at first hand, I do not intend here to add to my assertion a theological treatise on the nature of such a direct experience of God....I am not going to talk of forms and visions, symbols, voices, not of the gift of tears and such things. All I say is I knew God, nameless and unfathomable, silent and yet near, bestowing Himself upon me in His Trinity. I knew God beyond all concrete imaginings. I knew Him clearly in such nearness and grace as is impossible to confound or mistake....
>
> God Himself. I experienced God Himself, not human words describing Him. I experienced God and the freedom which is an integral part of Him and which can only be experienced through Him and not as the sum total of finite realities and calculations about Him. This experience is grace indeed, and basically there is no one to whom it is refused. Of precisely this was I convinced.[2]

It was in such statements as those which Rahner put on the lips of Ignatius that, in the mind of his collaborator Herbert Vorgrimler and others, "the aged Karl Rahner spoke about the primal experience which completely captivated him while he was still young and which provides the key to his life and work."[3]

Good for Ignatius! He "experienced God Himself, not human words describing Him." But note what he declared as well, with impressive conviction: "there is no one to whom [this experience] is refused." Certainly not refused to such as have vowed to God, "Take and receive, O Lord, all my liberty, my memory, my understanding, my whole will, all I have and possess. Give me your love and your grace; this is enough for me." It raises a basic question for me, at times a troubling question: What has been my experience of God? Not my theology of God, not what I think and say about God. No, my experience of God, my encounter with a living God, a God dwelling within me in Trinity. How real is it, how close, how absorbing, how thrilling?

III

All of which plunges us into a final question: Granted that I do experience God, that like Ignatius I know God "clearly in such nearness and grace as is impossible to confound or mistake," how should I bear witness to that experience? The apostles *spoke* about it—here, there, everywhere. Especially their experience of Jesus, God's risen Son. And they bore witness unto death, *by* their death—what Jesus predicted immediately after his exhortation to witness: "They are going to put you out of the Synagogue. In fact, the hour is coming when the man who puts you to death will think that he is serving God!" (Jn 16:2). I find it intriguing that the Greek word for witness or testimony *(martyrion)* has given us what we call martyrdom, the ultimate witness.

Such witnesses we have known in our day: Oscar Romero shot to death at the altar, four American women missionaries raped and murdered in El Salvador, six Jesuits horribly assassinated on their University of Central America campus, civil-rights bishop Juan Girardi Conedera savagely slain in Guatemala—the list is growing. But what of us, quite sheltered from martyrdom in the nation's most homicidal city?

I suggest that, in concrete reality for us, witness always has to do with human persons you and I touch: a class at Gonzaga, a congregation in St. Aloysius or Holy Trinity, diocesan priests gathered for a Preaching the Just Word retreat/workshop, the homeless or hungry or unemployed at the McKenna Center, the elderly poor in J. B. Johnson Nursing Center, Hispanics ill at ease in a strange country or an inhospitable Anglo parish, African Americans constantly crossing our campus, immigrants legal or illegal. What do they see in us? From the words we utter or our silent listening, from the way we celebrate Eucharist or serve the disadvantaged, from our attitude when hustled for a handout to reach Hagerstown—do people sense that we host God within us? If they do not see us specifically as tabernacles of the Trinity, do we at least puzzle them, intrigue them, compel them to wonder, to rethink an agnosticism, a pessimism, a cynicism, an antipathy toward authority, hostility toward those who have so much?

A final word. I realize how easy it is to frame such questions, how difficult to shape concrete answers. That said, I suggest we go back to the Jesus of the Last Discourse. In his words to the apostles on witnessing, don't overlook a conjunctive adverb: "You *too,* you *also,* should bear witness." That "too," that "also," was prompted by a sentence that preceded: "When the Paraclete comes, the Spirit of Truth who comes forth from the Father and whom I shall send to you from the Father, He will bear witness on my behalf" (v. 26). But the witness of the Holy Spirit and the witness of Jesus' disciples are not two separate witnesses. The Spirit of Truth, John tells us, "the world cannot accept, since it neither sees nor recognizes Him." The way an invisible Holy Spirit bears witness, the way the Spirit's witness can be heard, is through the Spirit's disciples, through those who "do recognize Him" because He is within them (Jn 14:17).[4] St. Augustine put it pithily: "Because [the Spirit] will speak, you will also speak—He in your hearts, you in words; He by inspiration, you by sounds."[5]

So then, good disciples, not to worry! Our primary task is a close encounter with a God One and Three, "in such nearness and grace as is impossible to confound or mistake." Then it is that we shall hear the invisible Spirit speaking in our hearts, and hearing we shall break forth like Peter and the other apostles in Acts: "We are witnesses to these things, and so is the Holy Spirit whom God has given to those who obey Him" (Acts 5:32).

Our Lady's Chapel
Gonzaga College High School
Washington, D.C.
May 18, 1998

Ordinary Time

12

ORDINARY TIME...OR EXTRAORDINARY?
First Week, Year 1, Monday

● Hebrews 1:1–6
● Mark 1:14–20

For the committed Christian, today marks something of a letdown. With Isaiah we waited expectantly for a Messiah, a Savior. With the shepherds we rushed over to Bethlehem to the song of angels. With Mary we welcomed the Christ Child into our homes, our cribs, our hearts. With astrologers from a far country we too laid our gifts, primarily the gift of ourselves, before God-in-swaddling-bands, Omnipotence in bonds.

But today—today the excitement is over. We are beginning what the liturgy calls "ordinary time." From the extraordinary to the ordinary. The party is over. It's down with the tree, pack up the tinsel and the trains, back to school, back to the office, back to green vestments and parish complaints, back to the humdrum of human existence.

But is it? Yes, life as we experience it must go on, the monotony of ordinary time. And still today's liturgy addresses the ordinary with a resounding challenge. The readings remind us that for the Christian the ordinary is quite extraordinary. This Jesus we caroled yesterday as a baby, this same Jesus comes on the human scene grown up—comes not to Galilee but to Hawaii, and proclaims not to Jews but to you and me three stunning realities: (1) "The kingdom of God has come near." (2) "Repent." (3) "Believe in the good news" (Mk 1:15). A word on each.

I

God's kingdom has come near. It's a thrilling example of a paradox we talked about in theology: the already and the not yet. Here but not all here. God's rule over human hearts, but not all hearts, and not even all of my heart. Still, God's kingdom has come incomparably near, because the king himself has come. Has come not in the guise of an angel but in our flesh. The opening of the Letter to the Hebrews ceaselessly thrills me: "Long ago God spoke to our ancestors in many and various ways by the prophets, but in these last days He has spoken to us by a Son, whom He appointed heir of all things, through whom He also created the worlds. He is the reflection of God's glory and the exact imprint of God's very being, and he sustains all things by his powerful word" (Heb 1:1-3).

Breathtaking, of course—who this Jesus is. But even more of a shocker is what this God-in-flesh did just by touching our earth in our flesh. It is summed up in that final phrase above: He guides and sustains all that has been created through him.[1] A happy coincidence here. Today's liturgy commemorates a fourth-century bishop, Hilary of Poitiers in Gaul. Exiled to the East because he had broken off communion with the Arian leaders who had condemned Athanasius, he learned more profoundly how complex the issues were, learned how to reconcile some positions in a way that had escaped most Westerners. Here a single sentence from Hilary makes my point: "The whole of humanity (totus homo) was in Christ Jesus."[2] That seemingly simple sentence, and others like it in early Christian literature, have exercised the minds of theologians beyond numbering.

Not to turn a homily into a lecture, let me simply say this: A new oneness, a root unity, between humanity and God was conceived in Nazareth and brought to birth in Bethlehem. True, when Mary spoke her fiat to God through Gabriel, and when Mary first held the world's Savior in her arms, humanity was not yet the Body of Christ, alive with his life, thrilling to his divine touch. But humanity was ready, poised on the edge of divinity. No longer was flesh simply the tinderbox of sin. If it had not yet begun to live with the life of Christ, it all but quivered with his breath. For the flesh that the Son of God took is our flesh; in some genuine sense it is my flesh, your flesh, the flesh of every human being born into this world. Little wonder that for authors like Athanasius "the world is so truly one whole that when the Word enters into it and becomes one of our race, all things take on a new dignity."[3]

Once the Son of God touched this earth in our flesh, our world could never be quite the same. Wars still rage, hate severs people and nations, hunger savages infants and the elderly, death never takes a holiday; and still, our planet is different. Why? Because Christ has not only come; Christ is here. Not only in our memory of Christmas; not only in our Eucharist. Christ is active in each and every creature of his creation; otherwise the hills would fall, the thrush could not sing or the shad ascend the waters, the eagle soar or the leopard roam the forest; you and I could not have the mind of Christ or love as Jesus loved.

No, our world is not yet subjected to Christ; and still our world is a new world, because Christ is here, is everywhere.

II

But precisely because our world is not yet totally subject to Christ, because on this earth you and I are never totally Christlike, we have his second proclamation, a single powerful word: "Repent!" A disturbing word, for it means I have to change. Not necessarily a radical change: the "good thief" crucified beside Christ, murmuring for the first time "Jesus, remember me" (Lk 23:42); Augustine in a Milanese garden, in an instant his will no longer prey to pleasure, his prayer no longer "Grant me chastity and continence, but not yet";[4] Dorothy Day, saint of the homeless and hopeless, moving from Communism to Christ.

I am not downplaying such cosmic conversion, such radical repentance. I am suggesting that, for you and me, for us who feed on the Eucharistic Christ each day, for us who preach repentance day in and day out, Christ may be calling for a different kind of conversion. Perhaps a conversion from something quite good, a sheerly human justice, to something much better, God's vision of justice: from ethical justice, giving each man, woman, and child what he or she deserves, to biblical justice.

In the concrete, what do I mean? I mean I am determined to be consistently faithful to all the relationships, all the responsibilities, that flow from my covenant with Christ. I shall actually love God above all else, let no person however seductive, no thing however attractive, replace the one true God even for a moment. I shall actually try to treat each man or woman whose path I cross like another self, another I, another Christ; actually feed the hungry and slake the thirsty, welcome the immigrant with open arms and clothe the ragged from my closet, spend time in hospitals with the cancerous and the depressed, in prisons with "dead men walking."[5] I shall actually see in each "thing," in everything that is not God or a human person, a trace, a vestige, a reflection of the God who shaped it, and I shall treat it, touch it, with reverence. I shall not rape God's earth, pollute God's air, consume as much as I can get my hands on.[6]

III

My third point can be uncommonly brief. For if I live God's justice, I shall be responding to Christ's other command, "Believe in the good news." It is a commonplace now: Christian belief, a living faith, is not a nakedly intellectual act: I accept as true one God, one Son of God made human, the Holy Spirit; I accept as true the holy Catholic Church, the communion of saints, the forgiveness of sins, the resurrection of the body, life without end. Believing in the good news, in the gospel Jesus preached, a living faith, a saving faith, is a faith that does justice. God's idea of justice.

On second thought, more is demanded of you and me than *living* the good news, living God's justice; we are commissioned, commanded, to *preach* it. And for all too long we Catholic preachers have been content to proclaim a justice that gives to others what they can claim as a strict right, because it can be proven from philosophy or has been written into law. Important yes, but not enough. Our Catholic people do not occupy our pews to hear an argument from reason. In the Liturgy of the Word they want to hear, have a right to hear, God's Word. The whole of God's Word. Not simply or primarily what the mind of man and woman can construct. Far more importantly, what God has revealed, what God in flesh has proclaimed. Very simply, right relationships in all we and our people are and do. Concretely, love God above all else; love each human person like another self; touch every facet of God's creation with reverence.

This is what God's own Son took our flesh to preach. This is why he died: to enable us to preach it, to enable our people to live it. This is what Preaching the Just Word is all about. This is the good news, this is the gospel, this is the kingdom of God—indeed here because Christ is here, not yet here because Christ is not yet all in all.

Dear just Jesus, grace us not only to live your justice; grace us to preach it.

St. Stephen Diocesan Center
Kaneohe, Hawaii
January 13, 1997

13

HEBREW PROPHET, CHRISTIAN PREACHER
First Week, Year 2, Tuesday

- 1 Samuel 1:9–20
- Mark 1:21b–28

It may sound strange, but today the springboard for my homily is not Mark but Samuel. Why? For two reasons that dovetail neatly: Samuel tells of a significant change in Israel, the emergence of a prophet, and our contemporary Christian crises call for priests who are prophets in the biblical sense.

I

First, a word on Samuel, on the biblical prophet.[1] The two Books of Samuel deal with a period in Israel when two critical elements came to the fore: the prophet and the king. 1 Samuel opens with the emergence of Samuel as a prophet to all of Israel. His birth portrays a classic situation: the oppressed woman. Barren, childless, she is ridiculed by her rival within the household. "So it went on year by year" (1 Sam 1:7). It reminds us of Sarah in Genesis, childless, looked on "with contempt" by her slave girl Hagar (Gen 16:4). What becomes clear is this: "Samuel is the Lord's gift to an oppressed woman in Israel. His life is God's gift; in return, his life is given to God."[2] Through him Yahweh will fulfil the song put on the lips of Hannah his mother—the song that Mary's Magnificat echoes:

> My heart exults in the Lord;
>   my strength is exalted in my God....
> The bows of the mighty are broken,
>   but the feeble gird on strength.

Those who were full have hired themselves out for bread,
  but those who were hungry are fat with spoil....
The Lord makes poor and makes rich;
  He brings low, He also exalts.
He raises up the poor from the dust;
  He lifts the needy from the ash heap,
to make them sit with princes
  and inherit a seat of honor.

(1 Sam 2:1–8)

But what did it mean to be a prophet in Israel? How did God make use of prophets to work out the divine story of salvation? What were they supposed to be, to do?[3] Not in the first instance to make predictions, to tell their people what was to happen in days or years to come. The prophets were inspired by God to speak in God's name. A twofold function: In the presence of the people they took the part of God; in the presence of God they took the part of the people.

At least five facets distinguish the Hebrew prophets.[4] First, they are extraordinarily sensitive to evil, to injustice. Rabbi Abraham Heschel put it powerfully: "To us a single act of injustice—cheating in business, exploitation of the poor—is slight; to the prophet, a disaster. To us injustice is injurious to the welfare of the people; to the prophets it is a deathblow to existence; to us, an episode; to them, a catastrophe, a threat to the world."[5]

Second, and in consequence, the prophets feel fiercely. In their voice God rages. And so they rarely sing, they castigate; their images do not shine, they burn; their words do not aim to edify, they are meant to shock.

Third, the prophets are iconoclasts. They challenge sacred institutions, sacred beliefs, sacred persons. The temple, they cry, will not save the people; they must amend their ways, execute justice; otherwise the house of God becomes a den of robbers (Jer 7:4 ff.). As long as faithfulness is far from God's people, their sacrifices are not acceptable (Jer 6:20). The kings anointed to shepherd Israel Ezekiel flays: "The weak you have not strengthened, the sick you have not healed, the crippled you have not bound up, the strayed you have not brought back, the lost you have not sought, but with force and harshness you have ruled them" (Ezek 34:4). In the name of God the prophet dares to castigate what is most sacred to Israel, what is awesome and holy.

Fourth, the Hebrew prophet is embarrassed, lonely, frustrated. Embarrassed because, while others are predicting peace and prosperity, he threatens disaster and destruction. Lonely because he alienates simply everybody: wicked and pious, cynics and believers, princes and priests. Frustrated the way Jeremiah was: "For 23 years...I have spoken persistently to you, but you have not listened" (Jer 25:3).

Fifth, the prophets' words are charged with divine power because they have experienced the God of the covenant, a God involved in history, a God intimately affected by events. They have experienced God as "living care."[6] Not only a loving and compassionate God, but a God who is disappointed, indignant, angry. The prophets not only hear God's voice, they feel God's heart. How, then, can they ever speak dispassionately, serene and unruffled? How can their words be ever other than aflame, afire with a God whose living is caring?

II

And now, the priest as prophet. I am aware of Vatican II: "[Besides Christ's priestly office,] the holy People of God shares also in Christ's prophetic office. It spreads abroad a living witness to him, specially by a life of faith and love and by offering to God a sacrifice of praise."[7] All Christians have a prophetic role to play. Here I am concerned with the ordained, with you and me—particularly with the priest as preacher. My point is, the Hebrew prophets can model our own prophetic preaching, should model it as the third Christian millennium opens on a world where justice is terribly at risk.

First, we too must be sensitive to evil and injustice. Hardly a difficulty for those who have experienced firsthand the sorry existence of the poor and the imprisoned, the hungry and the downtrodden. But those of us who experience injustice at a safe distance, in newspapers and on TV, have a problem. Somehow I must refuse to get used to injustice, leave the evening news on Rwanda the way I leave a quarrel on the "soap" *General Hospital.*

Second, to preach with passion, for my words to burn, I too must feel fiercely. I must put a face on poverty, look into a hungry man's empty eyes, cradle a child HIV-positive, listen to blacks as they still clamor to be free, listen to women as they still struggle to be equal, listen to prisoners on death row as they beg to be alive, to immigrants as they argue for the rights of their children.

Third, the Christian preacher, like the Hebrew prophet, must ceaselessly challenge the community. Iconoclasts? Yes, in the sense that our task, in part, is to shatter false images, destroy idols. Pope John Paul does not hesitate to attack them: the way we subordinate real needs to "superfluous church ornaments and costly furnishing for divine worship";[8] the private property that exalts having over being, "especially when the 'having' of a few can be to the detriment of the 'being' of many others";[9] the "civilization of 'consumption' or 'consumerism,' which involves so much 'throwing-away' and 'waste.'"[10] And there is the rugged individualism that sociologist Robert Bellah and others see conquering our culture, pervading our Catholicism.

Fourth, it is the rare preacher who is only rarely lonely and frustrated. A certain loneliness built into our priesthood presses on our preaching. For all the affectionate folk who people our paths, we walk very much alone. Few of us share their lives, save at a respectful distance. Our link to them is our ministry. In a special way, our preaching; for our preaching is a prayer that stems from their hurts, their joys, their hopes, an inspired word that helps them to see Jesus with their own eyes, hear him with their own ears, respond to him with fresh fervor.

Our frustration takes varied forms. We can be discouraged by (1) the gulf that yawns between the high holiness we preach and the soso level of so much of "Christian" existence, including our own; (2) our prophetic inadequacy when matched against the demands of the gospel; (3) how rarely we actually see the increase God alone can give to the seed we sow.

Fifth, our words, like the words of the Hebrew prophets, should be charged with divine power. Not primarily because we have been ordained to preach, but because we have experienced God. A God intimately involved in our history. However difficult it is to reconcile such a God with scholasticism's single, eternal Pure Act, I still must experience and preach a God who, as Heschel expressed it, "not only rules the world in the majesty of His might and wisdom, but reacts intimately to the events of history...does not stand outside the range of human suffering and sorrow [but]...is personally involved in, even stirred by, the conduct and fate of man."[11]

A privilege and a burden, this prophetic priesthood of ours. In the presence of our people we speak the word of God; in the presence of God we plead the hurts of our people. A mission impossible? Not if we love the Lord our God with all our mind and heart, all our strength and spirit. Not if we love this paradoxical people, this struggling, sinning, saintly people of God's special selecting—love them with a crucifying passion.[12]

Kenlake State Resort Park
Hardin, Kentucky
January 13, 1998

14
NEW WINE IN OLD WINESKINS?
Second Week, Year 2, Monday

- 1 Samuel 15:16–23
- Mark 2:18–22

"No one puts new wine into old wineskins...; one puts new wine into fresh wineskins" (Mk 2:22). An intriguing aphorism. A word on Jesus' use of it, a word on its Christian application, and a word on how it might touch you and me.[1]

I

First, what did Jesus have in mind? We know enough about wine to appreciate the literal truth of his remark. "Filling old leather wineskins, which were wearing thin and had lost their capacity to stretch, with the fresh wine that had yet to do its fierce fermenting and expanding"[2]—this makes no sense, oenological, economical, gastronomical. As Jesus said, "The wine will burst the skins, and the wine is lost, and so are the skins" (v. 22).

But what did Jesus have in mind? What is this new wine, and what are these old wineskins? Jesus himself does not tell us; if he did explain at the time, Mark has not bothered to clue us in. Was Jesus declaring that the normative Judaism of his time could not continue alongside his own community? Not likely, if Matthew's version fits that context: "new wine is put into fresh wineskins, and so both are preserved" (Mt 9:17). Did Jesus have in mind the disciples of the Baptist, the spread of Baptistic sects through the Mediterranean world? Possibly. Jesus admired John. "Of all those born of woman," he declared, "no one has arisen greater than John the Baptist" (Mt 11:11).

But if loyalty to the Baptist forced his followers to refuse allegiance to Jesus, that community could not coexist with the new community.[3]

The principle is clear; what compelled Jesus to state it, to whom he applied it, we can only conjecture. For the present at least, certainty is seemingly lost to us.

II

But how might we relate the principle to postapostolic Christian history? Let me suggest one significant application. More than a quarter century ago, Jesuit historian John O'Malley did us all a signal service. He was arguing that we misunderstand Vatican II's reform if we see that reform in traditional fashion simply as correction or revival or development or even updating. Genuine reform is transformation, revolution; it involves creativity; and creativity means something new—in part at least, a rejection of the past.[4] Hear one short paragraph:

> Imagination and creativity must enter every reform if it is not to be utterly irrelevant and dreary beyond human endurance. As a matter of fact, creativity has been at the heart of every successful reform and renaissance, even when men sincerely believed that they were doing nothing else than transposing the past into the present. Creativity, which is radically opposed to slavish imitation, implies both utilization of the past and rejection of the past. The outcome of creativity, in any case, is something *new*.[5]

Take that out of the clouds. Today we celebrate Martin Luther King Jr. His life was a struggle not simply to correct the past, not even to update the past. While using the past, it was in a significant way a rejection of the past. He used the past—the past that is enduringly graven in the words of Jesus: "If you love those who love you, what reward do you have? Do not even the tax collectors do the same? If you greet only your brothers and sisters, what more are you doing than others? Do not even the Gentiles do the same? Be perfect, therefore, as your heavenly Father is perfect" (Mt 5:46–48). And still he rejected the past—the past that enslaved a color. As he addressed perhaps 300,000 between the Capitol and the Washington Monument, as he

> tolled the freedom bells from New Hampshire to California and back across Mississippi, his solid, square frame shook and his stateliness barely contained the push to an end that was old to King but

new to the world: "And when this happens...we will be able to speed up that day when all God's children, black men and white men, Jews and Gentiles, Protestants and Catholics, will be able to join hands and sing in the words of the old Negro spiritual, 'Free at last! Free at last! Thank God Almighty, we are free at last!'"[6]

Something new? Remember Andrew Young? In the sixties he took Joshua seriously. You recall how Joshua captured Jericho. On the seventh day he had the Israelites march around Jericho seven times. The seventh time, after the priests had blown their trumpets, the people "raised a great shout, and the wall fell down flat; so the people charged straight ahead into the city and captured it" (Jos 6:1–22). Andrew Young was convinced that what God had done to Jericho, God could do to the Capitol. If God's people believed. He had thousands, black and white, march around the Capitol seven times. The seventh time, after the trumpets had blown, the thousands raised a deafening shout that seemed to reach to heaven. And yes, the Capitol fell: The bill on equal employment was passed.

Do you remember African-American Sister Thea Bowman? Already advanced in her cancer, she told assembled U.S. bishops in heart-rending, heart-lifting syllables what it means to be black and Catholic and American. She closed with a unique request. She asked the bishops to cross their right arms over their left, clasp one another's hands:

> ...you've got to move together to do that. All right now, walk with me. See, in the old days, you had to tighten up so that when the bullets would come, so that when the tear gas would come, so that when the dogs would come, so that when the horses would come, so that when the tanks would come, brothers and sisters would not be separated from one another.[7]

"We shall live in love," she sang. And all the bishops swayed and sang. The new in her message?

> Listen! Hear us! While the world is full of hate, strife, vengeance, we sing songs of love, laughter, worship, wisdom, justice, and peace because we are free. Though our forefathers bent to bear the heat of the sun, the strike of the lash, the chain of slavery, we are free. No man can enslave us. We are too strong, too unafraid. America needs our strength, our voices to drown out her sorrows, the clatter of war.... Listen! Hear us! We are the voice of negro America.[8]

III

And what of us? I suggest, simply from my own all too lengthy experience, that a ceaseless temptation is to put new wine into old wineskins. The temptation assails not only teachers and pastors but bishops and theologians. "This is the way we've always done it." An argument that proves only one thing: This is the way we've always done it.

Decades ago, at old Woodstock, we faculty ended a year with a week away—a long look at the year, at ourselves. Fortunately, we took with us three professional psychologists to monitor our discussions. We simulated a faculty meeting with real Woodstock problems. Time and again we broke down, helpless before the problem. Time and again one of the psychologists, Fred Flach, would interrupt, "Where's the wild idea?" For we were hamstrung by "This is the way we've always done it."

We've seen what the wild idea, imagination, creativity can achieve. For we are heirs of Ignatius starting a strikingly original religious order in Rome, of Francis Xavier dying with eyes fixed on China six miles away. We've been entranced by Teilhard's vision of the cosmic Christ, have touched in some way the Russian apostolate of Walter Ciszek. We've been fortunate enough to live close to Horace McKenna and John LaFarge, to John Courtney Murray and Gus Weigel. We've seen all sorts of good things happen right here, in school and parish, because brothers of ours saw beneath the surface, beyond the obvious, were willing to take chances to make changes, were ready to risk—literally for Christ's sake.

What am I trying to say? That there is a fair amount of new wine in all of you—fresh ideas, new ways of looking at the things you handle, at the people you serve, at the preaching you do, at the Church, at the Society of Jesus. Especially the Holy Spirit in each of us. The Spirit that almost two millennia ago had the apostles speaking in languages everybody could understand, had the people saying with sneers, "They are filled with new wine" (Acts 2:13). New wine! The people spoke more truly than they knew.

So then, give thanks to God today for Martin Luther King. Not only for the wildest idea of them all—freedom for slaves, in law and in fact, without blood being shed, save his own. With that, thanks for stifling our own very human tendency to rest satisfied with our past, with the way we've always done it. That simply is not why the Holy Spirit, the Spirit of life, the Spirit of light, the Spirit of love, is alive within us.

Our Lady's Chapel
Gonzaga College High School, Washington, D.C.
January 25, 1998

15
WHO ARE WE? WHAT ARE WE TO DO?
Third Sunday of the Year (C)

- Nehemiah 8:2–10
- 1 Corinthians 12:12–20
- Luke 1:1–4; 4:14–21

This evening we are blest. Why? Simply because the two New Testament passages just proclaimed to you fit into a neat package handmade for a homily. St. Paul tells us who we are, and Jesus tells us what we are to do. Christianity in a nutshell. So then, a word from Paul, a word from Jesus, and...a word from me.

I

First, the passage from Paul. God's apostle to the nations reveals in lyrical language who we are. Go back a bit. When a God whose name is Love decided to share that love, our incredibly imaginative God had in mind not billions of isolated humans scattered around a globe, basically independent each of every other. God had in mind a people, a human family, a community of persons, a body genuinely one.

That divine dream the story of Eden reveals. Whether you see Adam and Eve as a real-life situation or as God-inspired fiction, you discover in the Garden of Eden God's plan for human unity. For a brief moment reminiscent of Camelot, four levels of unity prevailed. (1) There was a remarkable oneness, an intimate harmony, between the first humans and God. (2) There was a striking unity within the first humans, an inner poise, a sanity and serenity inside each. (3) There was a unique oneness between man and woman, between person and person, no war between humans, no hate, no "mine and thine," only "I and thou." (4) There was a breathtaking unity, a surprising peace, between the human and the rest of God's creation: Man and woman touched things, nature, with reverence, as a gift of God, lived in concord with the animal world.

Such was God's dream for humanity. You know what sin did to that divine dream. It devastated the human family on those four levels. (1) When love fled from Adam's soul and Eve's, the God of love fled with it. (2) When love fled, a schizophrenia took its place: Man and woman were divided each within, the one person at once image of God and image of Evil. (3) When love fled, humans were sundered from humans: "Cain rose up against his brother Abel and killed him." Cain asked God, "Am I my brother's keeper?" (Gen 4:8-9). (4) Sin shattered the oneness that linked the human to earth: "Cursed is the ground because of you" (3:17).

St. Paul tells us how God's shattered dream was restored in God's own Son. "For just as the [physical] body is one and has many members, and all the members of the body, though many, are one body, so it is with Christ. For in the one Spirit we were all baptized into one body—Jews or Greeks, slaves or free—and we were all made to drink of one Spirit" (1 Cor 12:12-13). The four levels of God's dream are reshaped. (1) "God's love," Paul thunders, "has been poured into our hearts through the Holy Spirit that has been given to us" (Rom 5:5). (2) No longer need we be torn within; from that schizophrenia, Paul cries, we have been rescued, "thanks be to God through Jesus Christ our Lord!" (7:25). (3) Because Christ died for each of us, we can live at peace with one another. In fact, we are commanded to do so: "A new commandment I give you: Love one another as I have loved you" (Jn 13:34). (4) We can, with good will and God's grace, touch the earth and all its creatures with renewed reverence, conscious that the earth and its fulness are the Lord's, aware that we are not earth's despots but its stewards.

All this we can be because we are one body, all of us members of Christ. Different functions, but all of us precious. Of this body alone can we declare, must declare: No one can say to any other, "I have no need of you" (1 Cor 12:21). Not pope to peasant, not rich to poor, not priest to lay, not the bold and beautiful to the raped and ravaged. In fact, to credit St. Paul, "the members of the body that seem to be weaker are indispensable" (v. 22). A mystery, yes; but the divine mystery of grace. In Christ, with Christ, the weaker I am, the stronger I am. Believe it! But stronger because we are a single body.

II

All of which takes me to point 2: If Paul tells us who we are, Jesus tells us what we are to do—what we are to do as the body of Christ.

Today's Gospel declares it. Here is Jesus proclaiming his program as God in our flesh, telling us why he came to earth: "The Spirit of the Lord is upon me, for [the Lord] has anointed me; He has sent me to preach good news to the poor, to proclaim release for prisoners and sight for the blind, to send the downtrodden away relieved" (Lk 4:18). It is a summary way of stating a program we call biblical justice. Matthew had already grasped this, for he applied to Jesus the prophecy in Isaiah: "I will put my Spirit upon him, and he will proclaim justice to the Gentiles.... He will not break a bruised reed or quench a smoldering wick until he brings justice to victory" (Mt 12:18–20; see Isa 42:1–4).

Not simply or primarily the justice we humans stress: Give each man, woman, and child what each deserves, because it can be proven from philosophy or has been written into law. God's justice includes that, but goes beyond it. God's justice is a wondrous word: fidelity. Fidelity to what? To relationships, to responsibilities. What relationships, what responsibilities? To God, to people, to the earth.

Biblical justice is not something we add on to our Christian religion. It focuses our essential Catholic living. What concrete demands does God's justice lay on us? (1) Love God above all else, with all your heart and soul, all your mind and strength. (2) Love each human being like another self, as an image of God, love each as Jesus loves me, especially those who are less fortunate, who share more of Jesus' crucifixion than of his resurrection. How will we be judged? "I was hungry and you gave me food, I was thirsty and you gave me something to drink, I was a stranger and you welcomed me, I was naked and you gave me clothing, I was sick and you took care of me, I was in prison and you visited me" (Mt 25:35–36). (3) Touch every facet of God's creation, in sky, on earth, in the sea, with reverence, as a trace of God, as a gift of God, mindful that we are not despots but stewards of what belongs to someone else. As the Psalmist sings, "The earth is the Lord's, and all that is in it" (Ps 24:1).

Here is our basic spirituality; in fact, on this our salvation depends. Salvation as preached in Scripture takes place within a single, all-embracing community: God, people, earth.

III

From Paul, who we are: members of Christ's body. From Jesus, what we are to do: live biblical justice. Now a word from your homilist. Let me bring Paul and Jesus down to everyday Catholic reality. As I crisscross our country, read our newspapers, listen to different Catholic voices, two impressions will not leave me.

Impression number 1: Paul would be worried about the body of Christ he described. You might recall what Paul wrote to the Christians of Corinth: "It has been reported to me, my brothers and sisters, that there are quarrels among you" (1 Cor 1:11). I realize that in a body composed of fallible humans there will always be disagreement; Catholic history confirms it. Where Paul would be unhappy is (1) where we hurl accusations at one another with little or no foundation in fact; (2) where our disagreement destroys love; (3) where internal, intramural warfare keeps the body of Christ from focusing on its mission outward: "Go and make disciples of all nations" (Mt 28:19).

Believe me, I do not have Holy Trinity in mind; the last thing you need at this point is a Jesuit taking pot shots at you. My concern is more general, as wide as our nation. Examples. An influential Catholic newspaper in Minnesota constantly levels unfounded charges against prominent Catholics who do not meet its ultraconservative criteria. (You may be interested to know that, for the *Wanderer,* my faith is like a weather vane, changing with each passing wind.) Before Cardinal Bernardin's Common Ground initiative got off the ground, it was publicly attacked by three cardinals. One of our most learned and faithful Scripture scholars, Raymond Brown, is picketed when he lectures, was accused by a Catholic columnist of harboring a death wish over the Christ Child. Our differences on burning doctrinal issues give little evidence of the love that should pervade all Catholic disagreements; prochoice versus prolife is simply one example. And the lack of respect for John Paul II's role in the body of Christ can only make the body less effective. And on it goes. I fear that the body of Christ does not yet resonate to Paul's declaration, "If one member suffers, all suffer together with it; if one member is honored, all rejoice together with it" (1 Cor 12:26).

Impression number 2: All too many Catholics live, all too many priests preach, ethical justice alone: Give others simply what they deserve. Important, but not enough. The justice Jesus commanded is to love all others as Jesus has loved and loves us. Not an invitation; a command. Not easy. Many Catholics still see social justice as an option—take it or leave it. Others claim it has nothing to do with the faith. Still others see it as the tears of bleeding hearts for the lazy on welfare. Most Catholics leave it to the Office of Justice and Peace.

Few Catholics realize that it is our faith that is doing justice. Many fail to see that genuine Catholic living is a three-legged stool: believing, worshiping, and loving. Love in action. Take that leg away from the three-legged stool and your faith crashes. Such faith, says the Letter of James, is "lifeless" (Jas 2:17). There are two "great" commandments: Love God above all else, love each human like another self.

May I suggest, paradoxically, that these days are good days for the body of Christ to act like a healthy body? Like a body stimulated by the Holy Spirit? Perhaps once again a child will save us. A swift explanation.

Last year the United Nations Children's Fund issued its annual report, *The State of the World's Children 1997.*[1] It featured one harrowing issue: child labor. Across the world more than 250 million children are little more than slaves, many of them at physical, mental, and emotional risk from hazardous and exploitative labor. In Malaysia children work 17-hour days on rubber plantations, exposed to insect and snake bites. In Tanzania children pick coffee and inhale pesticides. In Portugal children as young as 12 work in heavy construction. In Morocco they hunch at looms for long hours and little pay. In India's Sivakasi, children in the matchstick-making industry, some barely five years old, inhale dust from chemical powders and strong vapors. In Brazil little boys scavenge perilously in garbage dumps, sell waste products for recycling. In Nepal children carry bricks on their heads from fields to trucks, 25 cents for every 100 trips. In the U.S. children are exploited in a garment-industry sweatshop.

In developing countries more than 12.5 million children under five die each year, nine million from causes we have learned to control. In the richest country on earth, our most vulnerable are our children; the younger you are, the poorer you are; 16 million children live below the poverty line; perhaps a million sleep on America's streets each night; 1.5 million unborn are forcibly prevented each year from ever gracing a crib.

Just this new year, can we not reveal to the world a body of Christ that suffers together for each and every child? Twenty-five years after *Roe* v. *Wade,* can this body of Christ not shout in unison that each child, born or unborn, is an image of the Christ Child? Might not each Catholic family reach out in love to one child unloved, one child at risk? Just possibly, such caring may help to heal some wounds in this vulnerable body of Christ.

Holy Trinity Church
Washington, D.C.
January 25, 1998

16
THAT THE POWER OF CHRIST
MAY DWELL IN ME
Third Week, Year 1, Monday

- Hebrews 9:15, 24–28
- Mark 3:22–30

For several weeks today's Gospel baffled me. From Beelzebul, "the lord of dung,"[1] to an unforgivable sin against the Holy Spirit, what can one possibly preach to priests—especially priests come together to discuss preaching the just word?[2] Much mulling, anxious agonizing, prayerful pleas to Jesus' mother—something did break through. It has a great deal to do with Jesus, and it has much to say about you and me.

I

First, Jesus. I tried to put myself in his sandals, to play Jesus for a few moments. I've just come home to Nazareth.[3] Three sets of greetings welcome me home. First, from the folks at large, a shalom, an *aloha* (our last retreat was in Hawaii); they come streaming around me, big crowds for little Nazareth, apparently happy to see me. The local "rag" has trumpeted my preaching; reports of my healing have trickled in. One hometown boy has made it in the big city. Now let the city slickers quote the saying, "Can anything good come out of Nazareth?" Why, they don't give me time and space to eat; but I don't care. It's fun, so many people who have watched me grow, some who have grown up with me, and they are smiling, reaching to touch me.

The second greeting startles me. The voices surprise me; they come from the mouths of relatives. These are people tied to me by blood, tied to my mother and to my father. Some of them were around when I was an infant; they've eaten with us; I've played with their children. I think I see even my mother among them (Mk 3:31).

80

And what are some saying? I'm "out of [my] mind" (v. 21); I'm crazy, *meshugga*[4]; I've lost touch with reality. They want to take me away from the crowd, sit me down, give me something to eat, relax me, maybe get me some Prozac.

The third reaction stems from scribes who have come down from Jerusalem. They aren't happy about me, but neither do they think I'm nuts, off my rocker. Their problem is deeper still. They have figured out how I cast out demons. No doubt about it: I can exorcise because I'm possessed. Within me is a diabolical power, the prince of demons—good ol' Beelzebul, the lord of dung.

My reaction? I can take my relatives. Hard as it is, I feel for them. They are street-smart, but not highly intelligent. More importantly, deep down they love me. They really want to save me from myself. Small town folk, they think I've gotten above myself, a step above "us down-to-earth Nazarenes." Maybe there's even a touch of envy there. It's the scribes, and their counterparts the Pharisees,[5] that cause my bile to erupt. To them, I'm the enemy, a peril to their power over the people. Most of the time I don't pay them much mind. But this—this goes too far; here the people can be lastingly hurt, can be wrenched from my Father's plan for them, can be seduced into questioning who I really am.

When these high-placed people claim, and claim publicly, that I cast out devils as an instrument of Satan, they are not being merely illogical, setting up one of Satan's subjects (me) against his other subjects, dividing his kingdom, destroying Satan in the process. More outrageous still, they are behaving blasphemously. Not only do they fail to discern the Holy Spirit in my ministry; they claim that the spirit responsible for my healing power is "an unclean spirit" (v. 30), Satan. This is literally unforgivable. All other sins—murder, apostasy, whatever—all other blasphemies can be forgiven. Not this blasphemy, not this sin. Never. That is "an eternal sin" (v. 29).

II

A solemn statement, a frightening affirmation. It still puzzles me. I find it difficult to believe that the scribes who sinned against the Spirit were damned at that moment, were doomed for ever, could never repent and do penance for their blasphemy. But that problem will not be resolved in this liturgy. I am concerned indeed with the Holy Spirit, but not with technical blasphemy. My problem

is not with the Spirit within Jesus, but with the Spirit within ourselves, specifically as preachers of God's Word. Let me explain.

Addressing ordained priests, Vatican II insisted that
"priests...have as their primary duty the proclamation of the gospel
of God."[6] And this ministry of the Word, though "carried out in
many ways,"

> is needed for the very administration of the sacraments. For
> these are sacraments of faith, and faith is born of the Word and
> nourished by it. Such is especially true of the Liturgy of the Word
> during the celebration of Mass. In this celebration, the proclama-
> tion of the death and resurrection of the Lord is inseparably
> joined to the response of the people who hear, and to the very
> offering whereby Christ ratified the New Testament in his blood.[7]

And a bit later: "in performing sacred functions [priests] can act as
the ministers of him who in the liturgy continually exercises his
priestly office on our behalf by the action of his Spirit."[8]

By the action of Christ's Spirit. You know, among all too many of
us priests there is a hidden, unspoken, forgivable kind of blasphemy. It
is the protest of Jeremiah when the Lord appointed him a prophet to
the nations: "Ah, Lord God! Truly I do not know how to speak" (Jer
1:6). Unintended blasphemy—to preach, or refuse to preach, as if suc-
cessful preaching depended primarily on me. The blasphemy is the
implication that preaching is effective only when the preacher enjoys
natural gifts: a prominent presence, graceful gestures, sonorous
sounds, assonance and alliteration, paradox and pictures—as enter-
taining as Bob Hope or Seinfeld. Desirable indeed, save for the most
desirable asset. A homily's effect is a matter of grace, and grace comes
through the action of the Holy Spirit—on my people and on me. And
God rarely gives inspiration to the lazy however gifted, much more
often to the humble however limited. If, as the Old Testament story of
Balaam reveals, God can speak through the mouth of a harassed ass
(Num 22:38), God can surely speak through the dullest and most plod-
ding of preachers. Not an ideal, just a fact.

As a young priest preparing to preach, I usually resorted to the
chapel only as a last resort, when my mind was iced over and nothing
emerged. Now my first act of preparation is a prayerful appeal to the
Spirit, the Light that enlightens my darkness, the Power that propels
my passion, the Lord who alone can change the hearts of hearers, the
Spirit who alone can renew the face of the earth. My early sin was not
the sin of the scribes, ascribing miracles of healing to a diabolical

spirit. Still, analogous: ascribing miracles of grace to a very human, woefully weak spirit.

Is this a homily or a lecture? A homily, because I am not telling you how to shape a sermon, I am pleading with you to give room to the Holy Spirit, to let God be God. Not to turn you into an engaging speaker, only into an effective speaker, only into an instrument of the Holy Spirit. Your patron of parish priests St. John Vianney had few of your native gifts and mine; he did have complete trust in what the God of the impossible could do. The powerful rhetoric of Fulton Sheen may seem dated; what is unfortunately even more dated is his hour each day before the Blessed Sacrament.

I end with a consoling reminder. The Spirit that gives the increase to the word we scatter is not some gossamer ghost in outer space. The Spirit is God, God within us—within you, within me, within the people we are privileged to address. Remember that in the New Testament the Spirit is *dynamis*, "power," our "dynamite." Shake that Spirit loose! That's why the Spirit possesses us: not to hide in us, not simply to rest in us—to share divine power, to make it possible for us weak humans to hear the Lord saying not only to St. Paul but to us, "My grace is sufficient for you, for [my] power is made perfect in weakness" (2 Cor 12:9); make it possible for us to conclude with Paul, "So, I will boast all the more gladly of my weaknesses, so that the power of Christ [the Spirit of power] may dwell in me....Whenever I am weak, then I am strong" (vv. 9–10).

Do you believe that?

Cedarbrake Renewal Center
Belton, Texas
January 27, 1997

17
GO HOME, TELL YOUR FRIENDS...
Fourth Week, Year 1, Monday

● Hebrews 11:32–40
● Mark 5:1–20

This evening, a story from today, a story from yesterday, and a story for tomorrow.

I

First, a true story from today. Just before Christmas 1996, *USA Today* had a cover story that refuses to leave me.[1] It told of a married couple, Camille and Mike Geraldi. Camille, 48, is a nurse; Mike, 53, is a pediatrician. They take care of 39 disabled children. Most suffer from Down's syndrome; one boy, 4, was born blind and deaf, with very little brain. None will grow up to live on their own. Thirteen of the children they have adopted; nine more adoptions are pending.

Problems? (1) Money. In one year, $66,000 went for food, $13,800 for formula, $12,000 for diapers, $28,000 for utilities, and there are salaries for 14 care-giving staffers. Income: in 1995, $542,925; expenses, $808,000; Mike makes up the difference from his medical practice. (2) Hostility. Property values down; more than a hundred hostile or threatening letters, vandalism, acid on a car, feces on their doorstep; friends abandoning them. (3) Pressures physical and emotional. It means accepting life and accepting death; 13 of the children have died. Never a vacation. Mike and Camille have two teenage daughters of their own.

Benefits? Says Camille: "There's never a time that I don't look at [these children] and say, 'How could I be so lucky as to have these children?'" Camille and Mike don't hide the children; they celebrate them. "We treat them like they're normal."

Oh yes, Mike and Camille take care of eight retarded adults.

II

Second, a story from yesterday. The story you just heard from Mark's Gospel. A tough story—tough to read, tough to understand. It's the madman possessed by evil spirits, a demoniac who lived among the tombs. How the spirits within him begged Jesus to let them enter a great herd of pigs. And Jesus did. And about two thousand pigs plunged down a steep bank into the sea...and drowned. And the swineherds implored Jesus to leave their territory.

It is a story on which Scripture scholars have spent oceans of ink: How much of it is authentic, how much legendary? How separate the core of the exorcism story from the horrifying details? Is the word "Legion" a hostile hint at the Roman legions occupying Palestine, or is it connected with multiple personality or schizophrenia? Especially, how justify so destructive a Jesus, a Jesus so unjust where the property of others, other folks' pigs, are at risk?[2]

Leave all that to the classroom. What attracts me today is the upshot of the story. The man who had been possessed begs Jesus "that he might be with him" (Mk 5:18),[3] become part of the Twelve, join in their Galilean mission. Surely Jesus, with so few disciples, will respond, "Come, by all means come with me." Unexpectedly, Jesus says...no. What is this man's mission? "Go home to your friends, tell them how much the Lord has done for you and what mercy he has shown you" (Mk 5:19). Go to the Decapolis, the "ten cities" outside the traditional boundaries of the land of Israel. *There* is the field of your evangelizing efforts; *there* you tell of Jesus' power, *there* you tell of his mercy. Back home, where you lived before possessed. As an insightful Scripture scholar has put it, "The cured man..., in his gratitude and admiration, longs to stay with Jesus. Jesus, however, gives him the harder task of staying at home and explaining there the new life that he had been given."[4]

It's Mike and Camille Geraldi two millennia ago. To be apostles, you need not join the Twelve, you need not be ordained, you need not join a foreign legion, you need not even leave family behind. Just...go back home...and do something. At times that can be the harder task.

III

Third, a story for tomorrow. It is no news to you that the Catholic Church in our land is less than flourishing, is hardly "on a roll." Many reasons combine to explain why this is so. Let me focus on one. It has to do with evangelization, bringing the gospel, the good news that is Jesus Christ, to a world, to cultures, to people that do not know him or, knowing him, do not live their lives in his light. That task, that privilege, is not the preserve of the pope, of clergy and catechists. It is rooted in baptism. And baptism not only destroys original sin, not only connects us to Christ, not only makes us members of his Church. Baptism is a call. A call to all the baptized. A call to share, to give generously what we have been given graciously, without any deserving on our part. To play John the Baptist to the less fortunate, to the unbelieving, the uncaring, the stiff-necked. Like John, to go before the Lord to prepare his paths, to pave the ways for his coming.

As with the Gospel demoniac healed of his madness, so with the baptized freed of Satan's chains. Only a relatively few leave home, dear ones, country to spread Christ's gospel. The challenge to the vast majority is to evangelize where they are, where they live, where they work. Precisely here we who preach[5] must confront a frightening Catholic flaw. For the most part, our people leave evangelizing to specialists: to the offices of peace and justice, of education, of ecumenism, Catholic Charities. Oh, not everyone. There will always be a Dorothy Day to live with the destitute, an Ozanam to found a St. Vincent de Paul Society, a Marian Wright Edelman to challenge our President on a child-threatening welfare bill, a Sister McGeady to welcome runaway, angel-dusted, prostituted youngsters into a Covenant House. Still, the bulk of Catholics contribute in two ways: We write a check and we pray.

Good indeed. Without green bills and rosary beads no churches would be built, no schools flourish, no seminaries rise; no missionaries would fly to Africa. Good, but not enough. Where we live and toil, where we play and pray, there each Christian is asked to do what Jesus asked of the demoniac: Go home and tell your friends, tell your neighbors, all that the Lord has done for you.

Among your retreat/workshop materials there is an article on liturgy and justice. The author quotes a director of the Arche community in Mobile, Alabama, Martin O'Malley. O'Malley tells certain people who feel guilty around him "they don't have to go to India to live out the gospel. I ask them, 'What have you done for your mother lately?'" And he adds, "If we would just take care of the people in our immediate neighborhood, even just in our immediate families, the world would be a much better place."[6]

Not to be despised. If biblical justice prevailed in all Christian homes—right relationships among all the members of every family—what a remarkably different world we would enjoy! Something of a paradox, isn't it, evangelizing primitives in the Kalahari Desert while our own families are breaking apart, admiring our missionaries in Micronesia while on the streets surrounding us kids are killing for Reeboks, drugs are maiming young minds, and the younger you are the poorer you are?

My point is, we are selling Christianity terribly short if only a fringe of our faithful are struggling for right relationships in American society; if the majority continue to take with extreme literalness the older catechisms' affirmation that "God made me to praise, reverence, and serve Him in this life and to be happy with Him forever in the next"; if they are satisfied with a me-and-Jesus spirituality and do not realize that Christian living is a ceaseless process of being shaped in the image of Christ *for the sake of others.*

Why belabor this flaw before fellow priests? Because little will change in our people if little changes in us. Because few of our parishes will become centers of social Catholicism if we priests do not proclaim as Jesus proclaimed, "The Spirit of the Lord is upon me; for [the Lord] has anointed me, has sent me to preach good news to the poor, to proclaim release for prisoners and sight for the blind, to send the downtrodden away relieved" (Lk 4:18). Not only preach it—to some extent live it, time and again send someone who is downtrodden, oppressed, send that man, woman, or child away feeling good, feeling loved.

A single example. One day last year I preached on Luke 14:12–14, some remarks of Jesus to his host at the dinner table:

> When you give a luncheon or a dinner, do not invite your friends or your brothers or your relatives or rich neighbors, in case they may invite you in return, and you would be repaid. But when you give a banquet, invite the poor, the crippled, the lame, and the blind. And you will be blessed, because they cannot repay you, for you will be repaid at the resurrection of the righteous.

I was embarrassed then; I have been embarrassed ever since. You see, I've never hosted a meal like that. Have you?

Spiritual Life Center
Wichita, Kansas
February 3, 1997

18
YOU SHALL BE CATCHING PEOPLE
Fifth Sunday of the Year (C)

- Isaiah 6:1–2a, 3–8
- 1 Corinthians 15:1–11
- Luke 5:1–11

A fascinating Gospel. Not because it's another can-you-top-this fish story. Rather because Peter's life experience is so important for Christian living, for you and me. And so, against all my instincts, only two points: (1) Peter and (2) you and I.

I

First, let's talk about Peter.[1] Who is this Jewish man who in the Gospels heads the list of Jesus' special friends? The New Testament tells us much, and still too little. You know Peter was married, don't you? How do we know? He had a mother-in-law; Jesus got her fever below 98.6. Peter's trade? A fisherman, a partner with John and James. In fact, he had just spent a whole night fishing, had just let down his nets again for an unexpected catch, when Jesus said to him, "from now on you shall be catching people" (Lk 5:10).

Peter's apprenticeship as an apostle, his boot camp for catching people, is a maddening mix of incidents delightful and incidents frustrating, a genuine example of human growing under a tough but compassionate teacher. A few episodes from "Peter, This Is Your Life."

Peter is impetuous; his heart speaks ahead of his head. At times it works out well, at times it's disastrous. Remember the apostles' boat on the wind-swept waters? Jesus comes "walking toward them on the sea." Peter cries, "Lord, if it is you [out there], bid me come to you on the water." Jesus says, "Come." Peter starts out, the wind terrifies him, he starts to doubt, begins to sink. Jesus takes him by the hand: "O man of little faith, why did you doubt?" (Mt 14:22–31). Again, when Jesus asks his disciples, "Who am I?," Peter blurts out before anyone else, "You are the Messiah, the Son of the living God" (Mt 16:16). And Jesus reacts: "Blessed are you.... You are Peter, and on this rock I will build my church.... I will give you the keys of the kingdom of heaven" (Mt 16:15–19). But when Jesus predicts his passion, his dreadful dying, Peter takes him aside, rebukes him, "God forbid it, Lord! This must never happen to you." And Jesus responds in unusually harsh language, "Get behind me, Satan!" (vv. 22–23).

Peter is touchingly humble. Take today's Gospel. Tired after an empty night, annoyed perhaps at this landlubber's "Put out into the deep water," he still lowers the nets at Jesus' word. When the fish fill two boats, he sinks down at Jesus' feet and begs, "Go away from me, Lord, for I am a sinful man" (Lk 5:8).

Peter has trouble being faithful. When Jesus tells him, "I have prayed for you that your faith (your fidelity, your loyalty) may not fail," Peter cries impulsively, "Lord, I am ready to go with you to prison and to death" (Lk 22:32–33). And yet Jesus has to reproach him for falling asleep while his master endures a bloody sweat in Gethsemane: "Could you not keep awake one hour?" (Mk 14:37). More sadly still, when Jesus has been captured and a servant girl stares at Peter and says, "This man also was with [Jesus]," his response stuns us: "Woman, I do not know him" (Lk 22:56–57). Three times he denies his master. The Lord looks at Peter, and Peter weeps "bitterly" (vv. 61–62).

Peter loves his Lord. Recall the beach scene after Jesus' resurrection. Seven disciples are fishing, with nary a bite; Jesus appears on the beach, tells them, "Cast the net to the right side of the boat and you will find some" (Jn 21:6). After they've hauled in 153, John says to Peter, "It is the Lord!" Immediately Peter jumps off the boat, swims ashore to greet Jesus and have breakfast with him. But after breakfast Jesus still has something more for Peter. Three times Peter had denied him; three times Jesus asks him, "Do you love me?" After the third time, Peter is hurt: "Lord, you know everything; you know well that I love you" (Jn 21:15–17). And Jesus commits his flock to him.

Peter follows his master to the end. Once Jesus has given Peter full pastoral care of his flock,[2] he utters sobering words for Peter: "Truly, I tell you, when you were a young man, you used to fasten your own belt and set off for wherever you wished. But when you grow old, you will stretch out your hands, and another will fasten your belt around you and take you where you do not wish to go" (Jn 21:18).[3] And

John the evangelist adds, "What [Jesus] said indicated the sort of death by which [Peter] was to glorify God" (v. 19). In perhaps 64 or 65 Peter died a martyr in Rome, a victim of Nero's persecution. Possibly he was crucified.

II

Now how does the experience of Peter touch you and me? One obvious way: the word "apostle." It means, literally, someone who is *sent,* someone on mission. And that summons up a profound program propounded 30 years ago by Belgian Cardinal Léon-Joseph Suenens, a program for coresponsibility in the Church, a program, founded on profound theological insight, to regroup the Church into an organic body with a shared responsibility. Integral to coresponsibility was Suenens' startling statement: The greatest day in the life of a pope is not his coronation but his baptism, the day of his mission, his sending, "to live the Christian life in obedience to the gospel."[4]

By baptism each of us is an apostle, is sent on mission. Each of us is sent to penetrate our culture with the spirit of the gospel, to transform our earth into a realm of justice, peace, and love. Pope and peasant, female and male, young and middle-aged and "third age." Not alone, not each a Lone Ranger. Over these past weeks St. Paul has proclaimed to us a church that is a single body, the body of Christ, a body where each of us is important, where no one can say to any other "I have no need of you," where "the members of the body that seem to be weaker are indispensable" (1 Cor 12:21–22). A body that is effective to the extent that all of us share responsibility, all of us are coworkers in the one mission. What Vatican II phrased in technical language, imaginative Jesuit William O'Malley put in a typically perky paragraph:

> ...we can no longer depend on the comforting simplism of "The Church Teaching" and "The Church Taught"; there are too many Ph.D.'s out in the pews now. The magisterium and the People of God are now like Henry Higgins and Eliza Doolittle at the end of "Pygmalion." He had found a tatterdemalion flower girl and turned her into a lady. But once the metamorphosis took place, neither Higgins nor Eliza knew quite what to do about the new relationship. He was no longer the all-knowing teacher, and she no longer the biddable pupil. Not only does the official church have an obligation to listen more to the people, but the people have the intimidating obligation to speak up....[5]

The point is, my friends in the pews, you are not substitutes for a decimated priesthood, to be returned to the sidelines if and when vocations to the first team blossom again. This is your God-given turf. Take hold of it—with all due modesty if you can, aggressively if you must.

Precisely here dear apostle Peter can help. Your life as an apostle may well mirror his, and so it may be well to keep Peter in mind. He is so much the way you are or are likely to be. Not because he had a mother-in-law. Rather because, to be an effective apostle, you too will have to experience your Christ. Not quite as he did, face to face; but as he did, heart to heart. Will have to speak to Christ, more especially listen to him.

Like Peter, you too may mingle the rational and the rash, find your heart speaking before your head. At times it will work out well, at times it may prove counterproductive. In times of peace and consolation, you too will profess passionately a unique Son of God who borrowed your flesh and died for you; when the storm clouds gather, you just might cry out against a suffering Lord who permits so much pain in his own human images from womb to tomb: "God forbid it! This must never happen to us."

Like Peter, you will sink to your knees in sorrow over your failure to trust your Christ, may well exclaim, "Go away from me, Lord, for I am so sinful." Like Peter, you may glory in your fidelity, your loyalty, assure him confidently, "I am ready to go with you to prison and to death," and suddenly sense how faithless each of us humans can be. But if so, then, please God, you too will weep bitterly and know that Jesus still loves you.

Like Peter, you can protest, hurt because you can say sincerely to your Christ, "You know I love you," yet recognize how far removed our love is from his love who said, "Love one another as I have loved you" (Jn 15:12).

Like Peter, you may have to follow your Christ to a bitter end, may hear words similar to those he heard: "When you are old, you will stretch out your hands, and another will lead you a way you don't want to go." And still you will go, because you love your Christ, and because it is the cross that saves—his cross and yours. And so you will say with St. Paul to the body of Christ, "I am now rejoicing in my sufferings for your sake, and in my flesh I am completing what is lacking in Christ's afflictions for the sake of his body, the Church" (Col 1:24).

What is wondrous about all this is that none of it need be loss; all of it, the highs and the lows, can make for an effective apostle, help to transform the earth on which you dance. Why? Because all of it is human and Christian growing, where grace is more powerful than sin, where you can say forcefully with Paul, "I will boast all the more gladly of my weaknesses, so that the power of Christ may dwell in me.... For whenever I am weak, then I am strong" (2 Cor 12:9–10). "I can do all things through him who strengthens me" (Phil 4:13).

Peter discovered that. I must ask myself: Have I?

Holy Trinity Church
Washington, D.C.
February 8, 1998

19

PEACE IS A WORK OF JUSTICE
Sixth Week, Year 2, Monday

- Isaiah 32:14-20
- John 14:25-29

The substance of my homily? The opening prayer of this evening's Mass for Peace and Justice: "Help us to work without ceasing for that justice which brings true and lasting peace."[1] But those words, though apposite as a prayer, are inadequate as a program. Happily, they raise three questions: (1) What is "a true and lasting peace"? (2) What is "that justice" which brings such a peace about? (3) What does it mean to "work without ceasing" for that justice?

I

First, peace. Within God's story of salvation, peace is a rich, multifaceted concept. Go back a moment to ancient Israel. What was Israel's vision of peace? A state of existence highly desirable. It was a "state of bounty and well-being that comes from God," a state that included "concord, harmony, order, security, and prosperity."[2] In time "peace" became the mark of the messianic kingdom all awaited with such high expectancy. For the prophets, the messianic king sent by God was to be a "prince of peace" (Isa 9:6) who would "command peace to the nations" (Zech 9:10). Jewish religion was not indifferent to the good things of earth; these fell under God's gifts, these were part and parcel of peace.

Go back to Jesus. Remember what the angels proclaimed to the shepherds: "Peace on earth for the people God favors" (Lk 2:14). On Jesus' lips, "peace" at its most profound is associated with salvation: To the sinful woman, "Your faith has saved you; go in peace" (Lk 7:50). To the hemorrhaging woman, "Your faith has made you well; go in peace" (8:48). When the disciples precede Jesus to various towns to preach the reign of God, what they announce first is "Peace to this house!" (Lk 10:5).

Jesus' coming will not always bring peace, "because he realizes that human beings will have to make a decision about him, either for or against him."[3] And you may recognize the play on the name "Jerusalem," popularly translated "city of peace," the pathos in Jesus' weeping words, "Would that you, even you, had recognized this day what would make for peace!" (Lk 19:42).

Central to our understanding of New Testament peace is Jesus' last discourse. "'Peace' is my farewell to you. My 'peace' is my gift to you, and I do not give it to you as the world gives it" (Jn 14:27). Jesus' peace in not the absence of war or a tenuous truce between enemies; not an end to psychological tension; not a sentimental feeling of well-being. Not even a reference to earthly possessions, to order, security, prosperity. Jesus' peace is a gift that has to do with salvation, with our relationship to *God* now and into eternity. It has to do with God dwelling within us, life as God alive in us. "In just a little while the world will not see me any more; but you will see me because I have life and you will have life. On that day you will recognize that I am in the Father, and you are in me, and I in you" (Jn 14:19–20). That is why he could say to his disciples (and to us), "Do not let your hearts be troubled, and do not be fearful" (Jn 14:27).[4] Peace!

It is a peace that exists alongside suffering: "I have said this to you so that in me you may find peace. In the world you find suffering, but have courage: I have conquered the world" (Jn 16:33). Peace flows from believing in Jesus; peace consists in being one with Jesus. In John's Gospel, peace is not possible without effort; it comes from victory over "the world," humanity in its hostility to God. If Jesus conquers the world, each Christian must also conquer the world (Rev 3:21). And this, the First Letter of John tells us, "this is the victory that conquers the world, our faith. Who is it that conquers the world but the one who believes that Jesus is the Son of God?" (1 Jn 5:4–5).[5]

II

Second, justice. The peace God has revealed has two basic levels. At one level, the sheerly human level, it includes concord, harmony, order, security, prosperity. But at its deepest level, the divine level, it is a profound oneness with God, God's dwelling within us—a oneness that can exist even when life is tough, when the going is rough, when human living is not very human and not much alive.

Christianity is concerned with both levels. And here is where justice comes in. It begins with Isaiah, "Peace is a work [an effect, an enterprise] of justice" (Is 32:17). So too Vatican II.[6] But what is the justice that brings peace into being? Ethical justice and legal justice can give us order, security, prosperity. We have to give each man, woman, and child what each deserves, what each has a right to expect, because it has been written into law or can be proven from philosophy. Without this much, life on earth turns into a jungle, where "might makes right," where the prize goes to the powerful, to the swift, the shrewd, the savage. Vatican II recognized this:

> A firm determination to respect other humans and peoples and their dignity, as well as the studied practice of brotherhood, are absolutely necessary if peace is to be established. Consequently, peace is likewise the fruit of love, which goes beyond what justice can provide.[7]

Yes, if by justice you mean ethical and legal justice. What Vatican II did not say, probably did not see, is that love does not go beyond what *biblical* justice can provide. For biblical justice *is* love. Biblical justice is fidelity to relationships, to responsibilities, that stem from a covenant. What relationships, what responsibilities? To God: Love God above all else. To people: Love each human being like another self, as an image of God, especially the less fortunate. To the earth: Treat things, handle each facet of God's creation, with respect, with reverence, as a gift of God.

I am reminded that in the Hebrew Testament kings, as representatives of God's kingship, were obligated to bring peace to their people through God's type of justice. Listen to parts of Psalm 72, the Responsorial Psalm that sounded the keynote of this Mass:

> Give the king your justice, O God,
>   and your righteousness to a king's son.
> May he judge your people with righteousness,
>   and your poor with justice.
> May the mountains yield prosperity for the people,
>   and the hills, in righteousness.
> May he defend the cause of the poor of the people,
>   give deliverance to the needy,
>   and crush the oppressor.
> In his days may righteousness flourish
>   and peace abound, until the moon is no more.

May he have dominion from sea to sea,
  and from the River to the ends of the earth.
For he delivers the needy when they call,
  the poor and those who have no helper.
He has pity on the weak and the needy,
  and saves the lives of the needy.
May his name endure for ever,
  his fame continue as long as the sun.
May all nations be blessed in him,
  may they pronounce him happy.
                              (Ps 72:1–4, 7–8, 12–13, 17)

And the more profound peace, oneness with God, union with Jesus, the Trinity tabernacled within us? That peace is never the fruit sheerly or primarily of human activity, regal or legal; it is the effect of God's love that is at the heart of biblical justice, "God's love poured into our hearts through the Holy Spirit that has been given to us" (Rom 5:5).

III

But justice does not bring peace automatically. Peace comes when enough people "work" for justice "without ceasing." I mean, of course, the parish priest, the permanent deacon, the lay associate, the Office of Peace and Justice, day after day living and proclaiming fidelity to God, to people, to earth. But I mean far more.

I mean the lawyer who struggles "without ceasing" to overthrow *Roe* v. *Wade* or minimize its effects. I mean the legislator who argues "without ceasing" against a legislature's acceptance of physician-assisted suicide. I mean the thousands of ordinary folk who appealed "without ceasing" to the governor of Texas to commute the death sentence against Karla Faye Tucker, not because she was a woman but because she was a human, a person. I mean the pope who calls "without ceasing" for a new solidarity between developing nations and the highly industrialized, challenges the structural forms of poverty, exhaustion of the soil, uncontrolled deforestation, consumerism, and instant gratification. I mean cancer-ridden Sister Thea Bowman telling the U.S. bishops straight-out how difficult it is to be Catholic and American and black.

It's the United Nations Children's Fund publicizing and decrying the slave labor that dehumanizes 250 million children across the world. It's Dorothy Day living with the downtrodden amid vermin and squalor, insisting that the poor do *not* have the gospel preached to them. It's Archbishop Oscar Romero assassinated at the altar, mingling his own blood with the blood of Christ, because he dared to cry out against governmental injustice in El Salvador. It's Senator Patrick Leahy calling our country to restrict land mines that each week kill or maim 500 men, women, and children across the world. It's Martin Luther King Jr. living and dying to "speed up the day when all God's children, black men and white men, Jews and Gentiles, Protestants and Catholics, will be able to join hands and sing in the words of the old Negro spiritual, 'Free at last! Free at last! Thank God Almighty, we are free at last.'"[8]

Yes, I mean the untold thousands of ordinary women who day after day choose life within a culture of death—life in the womb and life near the tomb.

As Jesus predicted, the peace that accompanies such "ceaseless working" for justice often goes hand in hand with suffering; for the evangelist John's "world" is not only hostile but powerful. Witnesses to that power multiply down the ages, from a crucified Jesus to America's King and Africa's Mandela. But the paradox remains: More powerful than the hate that distinguishes John's "world" is the love that flows from a cross—Christ's cross and every cross linked to his. We still proclaim with Paul "Christ crucified,...Christ the power of God and the wisdom of God. For God's foolishness is wiser than human wisdom, and God's weakness is stronger than human strength" (1 Cor 1:23–25).

This we still believe, this we still proclaim. Or do we?

St. Stephen Diocesan Center
Kaneohe, Hawaii
February 16, 1998

20
LET GO AND LET GOD
Ninth Week, Year 1, Monday

- Tobit 1:1–3; 2:1–8
- Mark 12:1–12

Few people have ever read Tobit straight through. For different reasons. Jews and Protestants because the book is not in the Hebrew canon; Catholics because we rarely read any biblical book straight through; I've just done Tobit, at 82. Perhaps we priests could seduce our people into reading Tobit if we told them the truth: Tobit is fiction; it never really happened; still, fascinating fiction. For the fiction is romance; the age-old romantic quest. There is the struggle between the hero and a sea monster; the bride-to-be is afflicted by a demon; there is an exorcism. And what provides the structure for the plot? Two folk tales: believe it or not, *The Grateful Dead* and *The Monster in the Bridal Chamber!*[1]

For our more specific purposes, preaching the just word, Tobit comes at a felicitous moment. Why? Because of Tobit's message. God is both free and *just;* and the message is illustrated through ordinary *faithful* lives. The believer is summoned to trust God and to mirror in daily life God's freedom, God's mercy, God's *justice.* Let's see how it all works out: (1) the human characters in the novel; (2) the God of Tobit; (3) you and I and our people.[2]

I

First, the human characters. Take four. The father, Tobit, is remarkably faithful. Faithful to the temple in Jerusalem, despite captivity in Nineveh and the apostasy of "all the tribes" (Tob 1:5). Faithful to the dietary laws, though all his "brethren and relatives ate

98

the food of the Gentiles" (1:10–11). Faithful to the poor: bread for the hungry and clothing for the naked, burial for the cast-out dead at the risk of life and possessions (1:16–20), to the scornful laughter of his neighbors (2:8). Trusting in God even when blinded by the droppings of sparrows, even when his wife attacks him at his most vulnerable, his justice, when she poses a major question of the book: Does God really reward the righteous, the just?

Then there is Sarah, daughter of Raguel. She has had seven husbands; all have been slain by her demon-lover, Asmodeus, before they could consummate their marriage. Her father's maids taunt her, reproach her: "Do you not know that you strangle your husbands? You have had no benefit from any of them. If they are dead, go with them! May we never see a son or daughter of yours!" (3:9). Sarah is tempted to hang herself, but resists; suicide will bring disgrace on her father. Instead she prays—prays to God to take her life or, if that be displeasing to God, make people show her some respect, compassion, reproach her no more.

Then there is Sarah's father, Raguel. When Tobiah asks him for his daughter in marriage, Raguel is completely honest with him: "It is your right to take my child. But let me explain the true situation to you. I have given my daughter to seven husbands, and when each came to her he died in the night. But for the present be merry" (7:10–11).

Then there is Tobiah. Not only does he pray for God's mercy on his wedding night: "And now, O Lord, I am not taking this sister of mine because of lust but with sincerity. Grant that I may find mercy and may grow old together with her" (8:7). There is a touching scene where Tobiah actualizes his father's instructions: "Do not hold over till the next day the wages of any man who works for you, but pay him at once" (4:14). Before he realizes that the man who has brought him back safely to his father, cured his wife, and "scale[d] away the white films from [his father's] eyes" (3:17) is an angel, is Raphael ("God heals"), Tobiah determines to give him not only just wages but half of all the money he has brought back.

Tobit and Tobiah, Sarah and Raguel—ordinary Jews doing ordinary things in difficult circumstances, living the demands of their covenant day after day, their responsibilities (1) to a God who afflicts and heals, (2) to their fellow Jews in joy and sorrow, (3) to the "things" of God—food and drink, money and possessions, even sheer seeing with human eyes.

II

Second, a staggering question: What of God in all this, God's own fidelity, a just God faithful to God's promises? What of Israel's belief that God rewards the good and punishes the wicked? Then as now, no easy answer, perhaps no human answer at all. The Jews themselves were puzzled. One psalm declares with confidence, "The Lord works vindication and justice for all who are oppressed" (Ps 103:6). Another psalm asks in agony, "How long, O Lord? Will you forget me for ever? How long will you hide your face from me? How long must I bear pain in my soul, and have sorrow in my heart all the day?" (Ps 13:1–2). Why is it that pious Tobit, charitable almost to a fault, obeying Jewish law with his life at stake, is impoverished, struck blind? Is there any good reason why Sarah should lose seven husbands on seven wedding nights? Any divine purpose in this? Wouldn't a single death be sufficient?

Against all the odds, the fact this fiction emphasizes is God's fidelity. Tobit admitted it, even when struck blind: "Just you are, O Lord; all your deeds and all your ways are mercy and truth" (3:2). Not that he had the whole answer—even when he prayed, "Your many judgments are true in exacting penalty from me for my sins and those of my fathers, because we did not keep your commandments. For we did not walk in truth before you" (3:5). Were Tobit's sufferings divine retribution for his sins and the sins of his ancestors? Who knows? Tobit thought so. And the novel has for purpose a basic thesis: Whether God afflicts or shows mercy, God is just, God "is our Father for ever" (13:4)

III

Third, how does this touch you and me, touch our people, committed as we are to biblical justice, some of us to preach it, all of us to live it?[3]

Last year the opinion-research master George H. Gallup Jr. had an interview with *America* magazine. Asked about religion in general in the United States, he admitted that though religion is popular here, it is not necessarily the primary driving force in the lives of most people. But, he added,

> religious faith has done staggering things in this country. The light of Christ is shining through in a number of ways, like the high level of voluntarism [volunteerism?] we see and the many

selfless, heroic acts of individuals. The presence of the saints among us, *ordinary people leading exceptionally good lives,* is another sign of that light.[4]

"Ordinary people leading exceptionally good lives." Here is biblical justice, fidelity to God, to people, to earth, through everyday existence—no headlines, no awards. It's your parishioners, those faithful fathers and mothers whose love for God above all creatures centers on the Eucharist, reveals itself as they carry Christ's cross with Christian courage. It's my own immigrant mother and father slaving to put my brother and me through high school, sharing their love so simply with the Jewish grocer and the Italian shoemaker and the Irish widow. It's the varied folk who touch the things of God with respect: the elderly lady who saves the leftovers instead of trashing them; the CEO who makes technology serve people, not people slaves of the machine; the artist who uses clay the way a creative God did, to shape images or traces of divinity.

It's out there, hidden amid all the viciousness and violence, the sin and suffering, the disease and death. Our task, your task and mine, is to recognize the rich reality, foster the fidelity, encourage the enterprising rather than castigate the corrupt. It demands imagination. See yourself as—don't laugh—an angel Raphael; remember what the name means: "God heals." *God* heals. But through you: your mind, your voice, your compassion, your ... justice.

Our people, "ordinary people leading exceptionally good lives," should transform the way we preach, should give a contemporary face to Scripture. Not only to history like the Exodus, but to fiction like Tobit. Let *today's* Tobit and Tobiah, *today's* Sarah and Raguel amaze and challenge us, titillate and frustrate us, put fire in our belly. Listen once more to George Gallup: "just as when people struggle with all sorts of addictions and forms of bondage, [people are]...looking both horizontally—toward one another—and vertically—toward God, to find understanding in regard to our existence.... The great discovery of many small groups is really the idea of 'Let go and let God.'"[5]

Such, I suggest, is Tobit's message to you and me, for how we are to live and what we are to preach: "Let go and let God."

Mercy Center
St. Louis, Missouri
June 2, 1997

21
"WEIGHTIER MATTERS" OF THE GOSPEL?
Ninth Week, Year 2, Tuesday

- 2 Peter 3:12–15a, 17–18
- Mark 12:13–17

"Give to Caesar the things that are Caesar's, and to God the things that are God's" (Mk 12:17). A difficult Gospel to preach on. For a homily is not the place for a lecture on church-state relationships—especially since Jesus was not delivering such a doctrine. He was indeed side-stepping a broader question: Do we Jews co-operate with Roman government or resist it? By a technicality Jesus avoids trouble with Roman authority *and* doesn't lose face with ardent Jewish nationalists. The technicality? The tax to Caesar had to be paid in Roman currency; and so you can pay the tax because it is the emperor's coinage to begin with; the coin belongs to him.

A first-rate New Testament scholar has solved my puzzlement. He noted that Jesus was not simply avoiding a no-win situation; he was moving the conversation with the Pharisees and Herodians to a higher level. He was issuing a challenge: You should be as careful about your obligations to God as you are about your obligations to Caesar.[1] With this in our minds, let me first talk about Jesus and the Pharisees, move on to what the conversation might mean for us and the people we serve,[2] and end with a most unusual letter.

I

First, Jesus and the Pharisees. Here we have to be very careful. You see, many Pharisees, perhaps most of the Pharisees, were devout men, God-fearing men, devoted to Israel, to its religion, to its Lord. Strict indeed on the precepts of the law; terribly strict. That is why

Jesus could chastise some of them: "You tithe mint, dill, and cummin." You try to extend the tithes demanded in Leviticus, "all tithes from the land, all tithes of herd and flock" (Lev 27:30, 32), extend them even to spices. But "you have neglected the weightier matters of the law." What weightier matters? "Justice and mercy and fidelity" (Mt 23:23).

The weightier matters of the law? Not simply the justice that meant giving to others what they deserve, but the justice the Lord demanded through Isaiah:

> Is not this the fast that I choose:
>   to loose the bonds of injustice,
>   to undo the thongs of the yoke,
> to let the oppressed go free,
>   and to break every yoke?
> Is it not to share your bread with the hungry,
>   and bring the homeless poor into your house;
> when you see the naked, to cover them,
>   and not to hide yourself from your own flesh?
> (Isa 58:6–7)

The weightier matters of the law? The mercy commanding that a cloak taken in pledge from a poor person must be returned before nightfall, "for that is his only covering, it is his mantle for his body; in what else shall he sleep?" (Exod 22:26–27).

The weightier matters of the law? Fidelity, faithfulness, trustworthiness. "I desire steadfast love rather than sacrifice" (Hos 6:6). *Steadfast* love.

Was Jesus too harsh? The prophets were just as harsh. Listen to Zechariah castigating the people and the priests: "Thus says the Lord of hosts: 'Render true judgments, show kindness and mercy to one another; do not oppress the widow, the orphan, the alien, or the poor; and do not devise evil in your hearts against one another.' But they refused to listen, and turned a stubborn shoulder, and stopped their ears in order not to hear. They made their hearts adamant in order not to hear the law..." (Zech 7:9–12). And the famous passage from Micah: "[The Lord] has told you, O mortal, what is good; and what does the Lord require of you but to do justice, and to love kindness, and to walk humbly with your God?" (Mic 6:8).

Indeed, Jesus was raising the conversation to a higher level. This was giving to God what belongs to God, what God had a right to require not only of Pharisees but of all God's people.

II

A second question: What of Jesus and us? I suggest that at least two perils threaten genuine Christian living, threaten those who want to live a Christian life. One peril is a failure to realize that not all Jesus asks of us is on the same level. Simply, there are "weightier matters" of the *gospel*.

Examples? For all our devotion to Jesus' mother, the Eucharist should fashion our Christlikeness more profoundly than the Rosary. The public revelation that is God's Word is far more significant for our spirituality than the most convincing of private revelations, Sinai and Calvary more important than Lourdes and Fatima. Falls of the flesh are not always the most unchristian of sins, not necessarily as serious as pride or greed or consumerism. The Nine First Fridays can help us toward salvation, but only Jesus saves. Helping a friend to die in the peace of Christ can supplant Sunday Mass. Possessing the truth is not a Christian reason for withholding love from the Pentecostal, the actively gay, those in error. Society must restrain evil by punishing the evildoer, but the Christian priority on life makes it difficult to justify capital punishment in our stage of human and Christian development. To struggle for Christian unity is more Christian than preserving our present disunion and hostility. Examples fill the Christian cup to overflowing.

Why these examples? To what purpose? To raise our Christian living, our religious "conversation," to a higher level.

A second threat to gospel living? When we fail to put our emphasis, as Jesus did, on "justice and mercy and fidelity." Justice. Not primarily human justice: punishing the criminal. God's vision of justice: Love God above all else, above all human idols; love each person, each image of God however flawed, like another I, another self; touch all of God's creation, earth and sky and ocean, not with lust to possess and consume, but with reverence for all that God saw "was very good" (Gen 1:31), all that is a trace of the divine.

Mercy. Not pity, which looks down on the unfortunate from somewhere above. Rather, compassion, literally "suffering with." The compassion of Christ, the depth of feeling for others that brought God's unique Son to a feeding trough in Bethlehem and a criminal's cross on Calvary. In a special way, the mercy that St. Paul commended to us: "Bear with one another and, if anyone has a complaint against another, forgive each other; just as the Lord has forgiven you, so you also must forgive" (Col 3:13).

Fidelity. In a culture where few dare to say "for ever" and mean it, where loyalty is temporary service to the highest bidder, where promises all too often include an unspoken "if," the Christian's "yes" is a sacred word—not only to God, but to each man and woman and child, yes to the earth that keeps us alive.

There are indeed "weightier matters" of the gospel. "These," Jesus would say to us, "these you ought to practice without neglecting the others" (Mt 23:23). Without neglecting the others.

III

Finally, the letter I promised you. It appeared back on May 19, in the *Washington Post*. The letter came from a gentleman in Cape May, New Jersey, Lorry W, Post. He was responding to a news story in the *Post* for April 30. The paper had reported that a majority of five of the nine Supreme Court justices had issued a blistering rebuke to the 9th Circuit federal appeals court for temporarily blocking the execution of a murderer. He wrote:

> How dare the court speak for me, my family and my murdered daughter when it says: "Only with finality can the victims move forward knowing the moral judgment will be carried out." It is bad enough when the politicians utter those false banalities in order to get elected, but, as a retired attorney, I am appalled by the statements of our highest court. Who says it is a "moral judgment" to kill someone? As a God-loving people, whatever happened to God's morality, consisting of love, compassion and forgiveness?
>
> Who says that "the victims can move forward" as soon as we execute the killer? What victim? My daughter is moving nowhere. If they are referring to the victims' families, what about all those who are opposed to the death penalty, such as myself and family members belonging to the national organization Murder Victims Families for Reconciliation and those countless others, who remain silent but don't want any more killings?
>
> The five justices in the majority are the so-called conservatives, who are conservative only when it suits their own predilections. They often admonish their liberal colleagues for expressing their personal views in their decisions, and here are these judges talking about their brand of morality and their versions of victims' wishes.
>
> This is an extremely emotional issue, and members of victims' families come down on both sides, as in any other such highly charged issue. This is certainly understandable. However,

my wife expresses it best when she says that this court and these politicians dishonor our Lisa's name when they profess to speak for her.

My daughter would not have wanted to see anyone killed, and especially not in her name. Therefore, I would request that judges and prosecutors and politicians cease and desist in their politicizing about victims' families who need "closure" and begin to have the courage to speak for themselves and not for my daughter.[3]

The father and mother of Lisa Post have raised our conversation to a higher level: "whatever happened to God's morality,...love, compassion and forgiveness?" Let's stop here...and look within.

Highlander Inn
Iowa City, Iowa
June 2, 1998

22

THE PARISH: COMMUNITY OF SALT AND LIGHT
Tenth Week, Year 2, Tuesday

● 1 Kings 17:7–16
● Matthew 5:13–16

This morning we priests and deacons are confronted with a Gospel that touches intimately the ideas and spirituality that engage us this week.[1] Let me (1) explain briefly the two metaphors Jesus uses, (2) link them to your Catholic parishes, and (3) suggest how all this relates to your ministry and mine.

I

First, the metaphors. Jesus uses two: salt and light. In Palestine each item was a must. Salt was irreplaceable. Not yet for Margaritas, but to improve the taste, say, of meat and fish; more importantly, to preserve them. A small thing indeed, a pinch of salt, compared to the meat and fish, yet incomparably important. It changed what it touched, kept it from spoiling, from rotting. That is why, in Old Testament times, salt was used to season every sacrifice. It was a sign, sign of a permanent covenant between the Lord and His people, a covenant that would not corrupt, that would last for ever.

And what of the light? In the one-room cottage of the Oriental peasant, the small dish-like devices in which oil was burned were indispensable. Not a very bright light; hardly our 3-way Sylvania. Yet without it life would have been dark indeed. Once the sun set, I could not have seen you (save by an inconstant moon), could not have read the Torah, could not have walked with sure foot and light heart. So much of life would have stopped—like the evening in New

York City in the 60s, when I saw all the lights gradually go out, and a city of millions sat in darkness, afraid to move.[2]

With these two metaphors Jesus addresses all who claim to be his disciples: "You are the salt of the earth....You are the light of the world" (Mt 5:13, 14).

II

How does that touch the Catholic parish, touch each of your parishes? The bishops of the United States put it powerfully in a document as important as the pastorals on peace and the economy. I mean the extensive statement titled *Communities of Salt and Light*.[3] It stems from, takes its refrain from, today's Gospel. The Appendix, "Reflections on the Social Mission of the Parish," opens with a sentence breathtaking in its implications: "The parish is where the Church lives."[4] The reason for the document?

> ...the local parish is the most important ecclesial setting for sharing and acting on our Catholic social heritage....We see the parish dimensions of social ministry not as an added burden, but as a part of what keeps the parish alive and makes it truly Catholic. Effective social ministry helps the parish not only do more, but be more—more of a reflection of the gospel, more of a worshiping and evangelizing people, more of a faithful community. It is an essential part of parish life.[5]

"More of a reflection of the gospel." Read two passages in the Gospels. Read Luke 4:18, Jesus' summary of his own mission: "The Spirit of the Lord is upon me; for [the Lord] has anointed me: He has sent me to preach good news to the poor, to proclaim release for those imprisoned and sight for the blind, to send the downtrodden away relieved." Then read the mission of all Jesus' disciples in Matthew 25, how we will ultimately be judged: "Come, inherit the kingdom prepared for you. For I was hungry and you gave me food, I was thirsty and you gave me drink, I was a stranger and you welcomed me, I was naked and you clothed me, I was sick and you took care of me, I was in prison and you visited me....[For] just as you did it to one of the least of these my brothers and sisters, you did it to me" (vv. 34–36, 40).

"More of a worshiping community." For worship is not only awe in God's presence. Worship sends the community forth: from church to world, from altar to people, from Christ crucified outside Jerusalem to Christ crucified at the crossroads of our cities.

"More of an evangelizing people." You have only to read Paul VI's remarkable 1975 apostolic exhortation *Evangelization in the Modern World*. After anchoring evangelization in the centrality of Christ, he went on to declare:

> Evangelization cannot be complete...unless account is taken of the links between the gospel and the concrete personal and social life of men and women....In proclaiming liberation and ranging herself with all who suffer and toil for it, the Church cannot allow herself or her mission to be limited to the purely religious sphere while she ignores the temporal problems of the human person....The Church considers it highly important to establish structures which are more human, more just, more respectful of the rights of the person, less oppressive and coercive.[6]

"More of a faithful community." You have only to recall the justice that leaps from the two Testaments. What is it at root? Fidelity, faithfulness. Christians are just if they are faithful to God, love God above all else. If they are faithful to their sisters and brothers, love each human person like another self, especially if they "send the downtrodden away relieved." If they are faithful to the earth that keeps them alive, touch each facet of God's creation with reverence.

This is how the parish is called to be salt of the earth. For it is the task of Christians, as the Body of Christ, small and insignificant as we may seem, to improve the quality of human living, change what we touch, preserve our sin-scarred, tear-stained earth from corruption.

Does that sound "off the wall"? Think a moment. At a time when a culture of death pervades the world—from war in Southeast Europe to violence in an Oregon school, from 50 million annual abortions to 6 million children under five dead from malnutrition, from physician-assisted suicide to an American clamor for the death penalty—the Catholic cries that every human life is sacred, every image of God, however flawed, is to be treasured and loved. When one of every four children in our "land of the free" grows up below the poverty line, the Catholic claims that every human being has a moral right to food, to a home, to an education, to a job, to healthcare. And not mere words. More than any other organization, *we* feed the hungry, *we* shelter the homeless, *we* heal and visit the sick, *we* counsel and console the captive, right to the moment of a court-commanded fatal injection. When the immigrant is a suspect stranger, a potential peril to our precious economy, the Catholic repeats the moving words on the pedestal of the Statue of Liberty,

"Give me your tired, your poor,/ Your huddled masses yearning to breathe free./ Send these, the homeless, tempest-tost to me."

Light to the world? Yes indeed. In a culture imperiled by a rugged individualism where the prize is to the swift, the shrewd, and the savage, we proclaim a philosophy of the common good, where "no man [or woman] is an island," where none may live for themselves alone, where no one can say to any other, "I have no need of you" (1 Cor 12:21), where "the members of the body that seem to be weaker are indispensable" (v. 22), where the option for the needy is a grace for the community. And paradoxically, with St. Paul "we proclaim Christ crucified," the foolishness of God that "is wiser than human wisdom," the weakness of God that "is stronger than human strength" (1 Cor 1:25).

III

Awesome, you say. Till we come to my third point: How does all this relate to your ministry and mine? Specifically, your preaching and mine. The "Catholic" in point two above, the "we," is not our 60 million on the books. It's the Office of Peace and Justice; it's the Campaign for Human Development; it's the volunteers within Share, the Jesuit Volunteer Corps, the Knights of Malta, Mother Teresa's Sisters, groups of business leaders, Gonzaga High School students serving the needy in the District of Columbia, a hundred more operations across the country. Impressive indeed. But, to expand a famous question of Jesus, where are the other 50 million? Were not 60 million baptized?

It is the *whole* parish that is called to be a community of salt and light, not a select group of volunteers. We shall not transform the earth, reshape it in the image of Christ, until the vast majority of our parishes are in their wholeness communities of salt and light. We shall not change the face of America, move power from rugged individualists to those who serve the common good, until we live the charge from our bishops: "The central message is simple: our faith is profoundly social. We cannot be called truly 'Catholic' unless we hear and heed the Church's call to serve those in need and work for justice and peace."[7]

Put simply, to be Catholic is not only to believe, not only to worship. There is a third component that follows from belief and worship: I have to love. And love is shown in action, the action Jesus linked to our salvation: feed the hungry, clothe the naked, house the homeless, comfort the ailing, encourage the captive.

Here is where you and I come in. Only rarely can we share the lives of the downtrodden as Dorothy Day did. Our task, as leaders, is to move the hearts and minds of our people. Not our task to *solve* complex justice issues in a homily: vouchers for education, food stamps for the hungry, work for welfare, the minimum wage. Ours to raise the issues, raise consciousness. Parishioners need to be persuaded that action for the poor is not some left-wing brand of Catholicism. Even more need to be shown that it is not an option, something you can take or shrug off. Catholic action for justice is the *faith* that does justice.

From personal experience, I know there are seminarians who see priesthood in very narrow terms. What attracts some is the liturgy, its solemnity, the music, man's bread made God's flesh, but not the liturgy that does justice. They chant the Psalms enraptured, never noticing the constant refrain: a just God who does justice for the poor. They fast on command, but never hear Isaiah's God:

> Is not this the fast that I choose,
>   to loose the bonds of injustice?
> Is it not to share your bread with the hungry,
>   and bring the homeless poor into your house;
> when you see the naked, to cover them,
>   and not to hide yourself from your own flesh?
> Then you shall call, and the Lord will answer;
>   you shall cry for help, and He will say, "Here I am."
>   (Is 58:6, 7, 9)

Good friends, a new millennium raises a tormenting question: What does it mean to be a priest? A deacon? A Catholic?

The Mid Pines Inn
Southern Pines, North Carolina
June 9, 1998

23

POWER MADE PERFECT IN WEAKNESS
Eleventh Week, Year 1, Monday

- 2 Corinthians 6:1–10
- Matthew 5:38–42

Once again St. Paul rushes to the rescue—the rescue of a homilist. Here we are, ministers of the gospel in a critical period for ordained priesthood,[1] and Paul informs us vividly that our position is not without precedent. Three stages to this reflection: (1) the perils of Paul; (2) the perils of today's priest; (3) the source of his hope and ours.

I

First, the perils of Paul. Meditate a moment on today's powerful text. (I change Paul's plural into a singular, because he is actually talking about his own life.) "As God's servant, I commend myself in every way, through great endurance, in afflictions, hardships, calamities, beatings, imprisonments, tumults, labors, watching, hunger;...in honor and dishonor, in ill repute and good reputation. I am treated as an impostor, and yet I am true; I am treated as someone unknown, and yet I am well known; I am treated as if I were dying, and yet look, I am alive; I am treated as one punished, and yet I am not killed; I am treated as someone sorrowful, yet I am always rejoicing; I am treated as someone poor, yet I make many rich; I am treated as one who has nothing, and yet I possess everything" (2 Cor 6:4–10).

No exaggeration here. You remember how Paul escaped death in Damascus by being lowered over its walls in a basket; how at Lystra he was stoned and left for dead; how he was scourged and imprisoned in Philippi; how a riot forced him to forsake Ephesus.

On and on it goes, summarized in one anguished yet triumphant passage:

> ...imprisonment, countless beatings, often near death. Five times I have received at the hands of the Jews the 40 lashes less one. Three times I have been beaten with rods; once I was stoned. Three times I have been shipwrecked; a night and a day I have been adrift at sea; on frequent journeys, in danger from rivers, danger from robbers, danger from my own people, danger from Gentiles, danger in the city, danger in the wilderness, danger at sea, danger from false brethren; in toil and hardship, through many a sleepless night, in hunger and thirst, often without food, in cold and exposure. And, apart from other things, there is the daily pressure upon me of my anxiety for all the churches. Who is weak, and I am not weak?...If I must boast, I will boast of the things that show my weakness.
>
> (2 Cor 11:23–30)

II

So much for Paul. My point is, in just about every age Christ's ministers have their crises—unpredictable in advance, devastating when they strike. Let me sweep swiftly through eight areas that specify today's crisis of the ordained priest.[2]

1. *Celibacy.* Does celibacy confer "any recognizable strength to the [priest] as a person, any coherence and quality to his life, any effectiveness to his ministry and witness"?[3] For untold numbers of devoted priests (not indeed all), the answer is a decisive if agonizing no; theirs is a forced commitment that belies what should be a gift of the Holy Spirit.

2. *Criticism.* In our immigrant church the priest was the expert in all areas from pulpit to politics. In mid-century priesthood was a respected profession, like medicine and law. Today our people are critical—critical of us as celebrants and celibates, as theologians and preachers, as activists and administrators, as males. Who needs all this flak?

3. *Crossfire.* Today priests more than any other ecclesial body are caught in crossfire. We are trapped in the middle, in a no man's land, between liberal and conservative, between Vatican and laity, between bishop and parish. We make a clear, close, motionless target: at the altar, in the pulpit, in the rectory, by a postcard, local phone call, letter to the editor—lately, e-mail.

4. *Ineffectiveness.* I mean the suspicion that my priesthood has little influence on the lives of my people, that all too often my words are wasted on the wind: abortion, contraception, social justice, the economy. Especially and increasingly, the young.

5. *Closures.* Across the country, schools and churches have been closed. The result? Stress, disappointment, resentment, anger—especially when you have given your lifeblood to a place and/or believe the decision makes no Christian sense, will hurt your people.

6. *Inadequate theology of priesthood.* I mean an undue emphasis on functions and roles, on powers proper to priests, powers that distinguish us from the laity. When we find these—"This is my body," "I absolve you"—these take so little of our time, of our lives; and the rest of our activity is lived in the suspicion that some man or woman in the pews could do it better.

7. *Burnout.* Fewer priests, greater obligations on those who remain, higher expectations from the parishioners, louder outcries when the expectations are not met. Less if any privacy; less time to pray, to relax, to prepare homilies; less time to "fill the cup."

8. *Fear.* No longer pre-Vatican II security. Now we share lay insecurities: how to find and keep a job, how to retire without bitterness, how to age gracefully and usefully, how to die believing, hoping, loving.

III

So much for crisis. Thank you, dear homilist, for turning the dagger in the wound. More seriously, where do we go from here? Is there hope for a renewed priesthood? If so, where do we look? An increase in vocations? A more compassionate congregation? An option for marriage? Ordination of women?

While we are waiting for one or all or none of the above, the same Paul who catalogued his own crises contributed his own formulas, not for sheer survival but for a fruitful, joyful apostolate. Not outside the crisis; rather making the crisis serve the gospel.

Formula 1: Paul's declaration to the Christians of Colossae in Asia Minor: "Now I rejoice in my sufferings for your sake, and in my flesh I complete what is lacking in Christ's afflictions for the sake of his body, that is, the Church" (Col 1:24). It is our Christian calling: follow the Crucified. Not slavish imitation: wearing his sandals, walking his Palestinian paths, eating his lox and bagels. No, sharing his cross through the whole of our lives. Not only physical pain—sinusitis, ileitis, hemorrhoids—but the agonies that are rather psychological and spiritual. Concretely, the agonies that nail you to your priestly crosses today: celibacy, criticism, crossfire, ineffectiveness, closures, burnout, fear. Why? "For the sake of [Christ's] body," for the salvation of your people. But salvation does not stem from your successes. Salvation stems from the grace created by crucifixion—first on Calvary, ever since in large measure on the calvaries that dot the crossroads of our world, of our parishes. Your calvaries, too, and mine.

Formula 2: Paul's confession to the Christians of Corinth: "A thorn was given me in the flesh....Three times I besought the Lord about this, that it should leave me; but he said to me, 'My grace is sufficient for you, for my power is made perfect in weakness.' I will all the more gladly boast of my weaknesses, that the power of Christ may rest upon me. For the sake of Christ, then, I am content with weaknesses, insults, hardships, persecutions, and calamities; for when I am weak, then I am strong" (2 Cor 12:7–10).

How difficult it is for me to believe this, to live it, to see therein the Christian hope, the priestly hope! And yet, there it is, Christianity at its most radical, the saving work of Christ reduced to its core, priesthood summed up in his consecration and mine: "This is my body, [and it is] given for you" (Lk 22:19). Given most grace-fully, most fruit-fully, the weaker we are of ourselves, our strength only the risen Christ within us with the glorified wounds of his passion.

Do you believe this? Is it not here that your hope for priesthood should rest? Is it not thus that you and I love as Jesus loved?

St. John's Seminary
Camarillo, California
June 16, 1997

24

TO HEAL IS TO MAKE WHOLE
Twenty-third Sunday of the Year (B)

- Isaiah 35:4–7a
- James 2:1–5
- Mark 7:31–37

One question Jesus asked of his disciples never ceases to be asked, "Who do you say I am?" (Mt 16:15). The question appears twice in one section of Mark's Gospel: "Who is this?" (Mk 4:41). The Twelve ask it in awe after Jesus rebukes the wind and calms the sea. The people of Nazareth ask it in disbelief after he preaches with wisdom and heals with power.

"Who is this?" The answers are many, if only because no single answer says it all. Jesus is a prophet, a man who speaks to God on our behalf, speaks to us on God's behalf. Jesus is a teacher, a man who wore our flesh, took our tongue, to tell us secrets about God, tell us the way to truth and life. Jesus is God-man, at once unique Son of God and unique Son of Mary. Jesus is Savior, the one mediator between humanity and our Creator, who came to save us from sin, from self, from Satan. And there is so much more—more than a year of homilies could exhaust.

Today's Gospel supplies still another answer. The Jesus who took aside a deaf man with a speech impediment, opened his ears and released his tongue, this Jesus is a healer. The episode is rich, not simply for what it did to one victim of brokenness, but more importantly for what it intimates about Jesus and about you and me. No surprise to you—to reveal this will take three points. (1) What and whom did Jesus heal? (2) Why did Jesus heal? (3) What does a healing Jesus have to say about our own Catholic Christian living?

I

First, what and whom did Jesus heal? The Gospel of Mark is crowded with the stories. There are people possessed: a man convulsed, a boy foaming and grinding his teeth, a little girl. There is Simon Peter's fevered mother-in-law; a leper begging to be cleansed; a paralyzed man let down by his friends through the roof; a man with a withered hand; the dead small daughter of a synagogue leader; a woman hemorrhaging for 12 years; a blind man imploring Jesus to touch him, and the blind Bartimaeus pleading for mercy. In fact, in one instance, "all who were sick or possessed with demons" (Mk 1:32).

The other evangelists are hardly different. Matthew tells us Jesus "went throughout Galilee...curing every disease and every sickness among the people...demoniacs, epileptics, paralytics" (Mt 4:23–24). Luke not only tells of leprosy, paralysis, a withered hand, possession, a dead only son, blindness. There is that striking scene in Luke where John the Baptist sends two disciples to ask, "Are you the one who is to come, or are we to wait for another?" Jesus' answer is not a simple yes. "Go and tell John what you have seen and heard: The blind receive their sight, the lame walk, the lepers are cleansed, the deaf hear, the dead are raised, the poor have good news brought to them" (Lk 7:20–22).

John's Gospel? A Samaritan woman healed of her marital adventures, inspired to preach the Messiah to her townspeople; a man 38 years ill and Lazarus dead four days; an adulteress and a man blind from birth.

So then, Jesus healed. Healed broken bodies; healed savaged spirits; healed mangled minds.

II

Impressive indeed. But why? Why did Jesus heal? On the face of it, often out of compassion: raising to life the only son of a widowed mother. Or to signal that God's reign, God's rule, has come to earth in Jesus: "The time is fulfilled, and the kingdom of God has come near" (Mk 1:15). But there is something more profound. Recall, the very word "heal" has to do with wholeness. Why did Jesus heal? To put the ill, the wounded, the living dead, the sinner on the way to wholeness, to genuine humanness.

At times the beginning was small: cooling the fever of Peter's mother-in-law or eating with Zacchaeus the toll collector. At times more significant: restoring an ostracized leper to family, to community, to friends at worship. Sometimes spectacularly: driving devils out of a mockery of humanity howling among the tombs and on the mountains. But those were the immediate problems, the obvious ailments. At base, why Jesus healed was why the Son of God took our flesh: to destroy the enmity, the hostility, the brokenness that Sin had created. Paralysis and blindness, adultery and dual personality—these could be obstacles to a man's awareness of God's presence, keep a woman from responding to God's love, to Jesus.

In a word, the ultimate healing, the wholeness Jesus had in mind, was reconciliation. To restore harmony, com-munion, on four levels: with God, within each human person, between sisters and brothers, and with the earth. In that way to build up a kingdom of peace and justice and love; to make the Body of Christ whole.

III

And what of you and me? Healing did not stop with Jesus' death, his return to his Father. Within the Catholic body, healing is an ever-present must. Why? Because the Church is human, is com-posed of sinners; because the organization and each of us baptized into it are always in need of reform. Because this Church on earth is not the final kingdom, the perfection of Christ's redeeming crucifix-ion. Because, as long as selfishness and sin, hunger and hate, corrup-tion and conflict, division and distance, distress and despair, disease and death roam our paradoxical earth and infect our Christian body, Christianity is not yet *whole*.

But how does that touch you and me? Because we are part of the problem and we are part of the solution, part of the sickness and part of the remedy. We are wounded healers. Part of the prob-lem, of the sickness. Someone recently wrote: If you are looking for a perfect church and you find it, join it! Then and there it will no longer be perfect. Part of the solution, of the remedy. In sev-eral ways.

First, some Christians are called to image Christ the healer by confronting physical or psychological sickness. Surgeons excise malignant growths; therapists reveal and treat hidden psychoses; believers lay hands on other believers and in the power of the Holy Spirit bent believers stand tall and walk. Not that suffering is incom-patible with Christianity. Only that suffering is not an end in itself. In our imperfect world, in our imperfect Church, all healing is a way to wholeness, and—all other things being equal (which they never are)—the more whole we are, the richer the possibilities of oneness with Christ.[1]

Second, the healing that is reconciliation. *There* is a key word in Christian living, in Catholic spirituality. It sums up the healing for which God's Son took our flesh: to destroy hostility between ourselves and God, within and among ourselves, and between us and the rest of God's creation—our earth. Without reconciliation—oneness with God, with one another, with our earth—Christ is mocked and Christianity is a mockery.

Pressed by time, I limit myself to oneness with one another— to Jesus' command, "Love one another as I have loved you" (Jn 15:12). Fifty-six years a priest, I have seen more conflict in the Church than most of you have read about. Fifty-nine years a theologian, I have engaged in more controversies with other theologians than I can remember. And so I do not condemn conflict. In any human institution conflict is inevitable. In the Catholic Church conflict goes back to the middle of the first century, when Paul had to write to the church in Corinth, "It has been reported to me that there are quarrels among you, my brothers and sisters" (1 Cor 1:11). I castigate only the conflict that destroys love—where, like the ancient Jews and Samaritans, our warring parties will have nothing to do with one another, won't even talk to one another. However alienated, all Catholics must still be reconcilers. Working not necessarily for agreement, but always for oneness in love.

Rather than lose you in abstractions about healing, let me highlight two healers in our time, each a woman, each a nun. First, Sister Thea Bowman. African-American, convert to Catholicism at ten, Ph.D. in English at 35, professor of black theology and the arts, speaker and singer at youth rallies and workshops, diagnosed at 47 with cancer that had spread to the lymph nodes and bones, dead six years later, March 30, 1990. Already advanced in her cancer, she told assembled U.S. bishops what it means to be black and Catholic and American, then closed with a unique request: Cross your right arm over your left.

> You've got to move together to do that. All right now, walk with me. See, in the old days, you had to tighten up so that when the bullets would come, so that when the tear gas would come, so that when the dogs would come, so that when the horses would come, so that when the tanks would come, brothers and sisters would not be separated from one another."[2]

"We shall live in love," she sang. And all the bishops swayed and sang. The U.S. bishops!

As her wheel chair drove her cancerous flesh across the country, Thea's mission in life was never more evident: healing, making whole, "so that brothers and sisters would not be separated from one another." On a September day in 1989, six months before her death, at St. Stephen's Church in Minneapolis, she celebrated healing ministry in a concert for all races AIDS-afflicted. One passage from her message that evening should model our role as reconcilers: "God gave me life, and I want to live as fully as I can live until I die. I want to live my best; I want to love my best; I want to do my best; I want to give my best."[3]

"I want to love my best." I know, from personal experience, you can be in first-rate physical shape and still be far from whole, far from love, far from one with God, with people, with earth. And that is just as true of an institution, of our church. We need reconciliation on so many levels. Important levels—on Eucharist, on hierarchy, on morality. Reconciliation does not mean we always agree, never have arguments. It does mean disagreement will not destroy the love in my heart.

Who are Christians? Healers, wounded healers. For all its high intellectualism, for all its mystery-laden doctrines, Catholicism is not a head trip. Few if any of us will be chastised by Jesus for denying the Immaculate Conception. Few if any of us will be barred by Peter if like a certain little boy we answer the question "How many sacraments are there?" with "Seven for boys, six for girls." We shall be asked, simply, how well we loved.

With Sister Thea, Mother Teresa. Dead only two days, after a lifetime of healing: hugging abandoned children, lepers, the aged; free service to the poor and unwanted, regardless of caste or creed, nationality or race; helping Calcutta's homeless to die in her home, with dignity. Central to her ministry was the healing power of forgiveness. When she visited victims of the chemical-leak disaster in India's Bhopal in 1984, she said, "Forgiveness offers us a clean heart, and people will be a hundred times better after it."[4]

A final word: two questions. (1) Where do I need healing, wholeness? In my personal relationship with God? A schizophrenia of sorts that tears me up inside? A running battle with family, with Catholics I can't stand, prochoice or prolife, feminists or antifeminists, whomsoever? In the way I use God's good earth, the "things" of God, God's rich creation given me not to be clutched but to be shared? (2) Where am I playing Christ the healer, bringing others to wholeness? It is my Christian vocation and yours. Outside these walls and within them, we harbor ills past numbering, ills that keep human images of God from reaching toward wholeness. Where does the healing Christ call *you* to heal? I don't know. Only you know— only you and the Christ within you, the Christ who calls you. Calls you now.

Holy Trinity Church
Washington, D.C.
September 7, 1997

25

WHO IS THIS?

Twenty-fifth Week, Year 2, Thursday

● Ecclesiastes 1:2–11
● Luke 9:7–9

Three verses, three sentences. Short yes, but terribly important for Luke. Important for a question, three small words, "Who is this?" (Lk 9:9). That question is central to Luke's Gospel. Central because it "becomes a christological climax to what has preceded"[1] and it prepares for the all-important travel account. I mean the section where we will see Jesus "authoritatively training the witnesses from Galilee, those who make their way with him to the city of destiny."[2]

Who is he? An important question: important for Herod, important for our world, important for you and me as preachers of the Word.[3]

I

It begins with Herod, the Roman ruler of Galilee. Not Herod the Great; his younger son, Herod Antipas. He has heard much about Jesus, apparently about his preaching and his wondrous works. He has heard that some people think Jesus is John the Baptist risen from the dead. He doesn't believe it: "John I beheaded" (v. 9) period! Immediately he poses the question that dominates this central chapter in Luke's Gospel: "Who is this?"[4]

The last sentence of this passage intrigues me: Herod "was anxious to see" Jesus (v. 9). And he did see him—but not the wonder-worker, not the powerful preacher. He saw Jesus when Pilate sent Jesus to him, because Jesus was "under Herod's jurisdiction" (Lk 23:7) and Herod happened to be in Jerusalem. He saw Jesus with "no

122

form or majesty that we should look at him, nothing in his appearance that we should desire him; despised and rejected; a man of sorrows" (Isa 53:2–3). And Luke tells us:

> When Herod saw Jesus, he was very glad, for he had been wanting to see him for a long time, because he had been hearing about him and hoped to see him perform some miracle. He questioned him at some length, but [Jesus] gave him no answer....Herod with his soldiers treated him with contempt and made fun of him; then [Herod] put an elegant cloak on him and sent him back to Pilate. That same day Herod and Pilate became friends with each other; before this they had been enemies.
>
> (Lk 23:8–12)

How sad! Sad that the Herod who waited so long to see Jesus never found out who he was. Sad that he wanted only a miracle, some superhuman production he could enjoy and boast about. Sad that Jesus' silence provoked not wonderment but contempt. Sad that the promising earlier question "Who is this?" had for final answer: a nobody, a joke, a quack, a pretender he could treat with derision, mock with impunity. Sad that two men of power could become friends because they did not recognize the powerless Power that stood before them.

II

Herod moves us to our own world. "Who is this?" has puzzled just about every century and every continent. Not only Hindus and Moslems, who otherwise have so much in common with us and drew such respect and esteem from Vatican II.[5] Not only the Jewish people, who find it impossible to accept Jesus as Messiah when they see no Messianic kingdom, no Messianic redemption, no Messianic peace. Christians themselves have been consistently puzzled. Early Christians denied that Jesus was genuinely human: Some said he only seemed to be a man, only seemed to suffer and die; some said he did not really have a human soul. Others denied him genuine divinity: Arius called him a secondary deity, the first and greatest of God's creatures; Nestorius, bishop of Constantinople, declared, "It is not right to say of God that He sucked milk." "A born God, a dead God, a buried God I cannot adore."[6]

And so it goes into our own time. Not all Christians who claim Jesus as Savior would welcome the First Council of Nicaea's answer to Arius in 325: In the succinct summary of John Courtney Murray,

"The Son is all that the Father is, except for the name of Father."[7] It takes our breath away; it collides with our logic; it escapes all our experience. But the Catholic Church welcomes it. For,

> from Athanasius onward, the Fathers [of the Church] argue that, if the Son is not God, fully the Pantokrator, wholly situated within the order of the divine power and being, then he is not our Savior and we are not saved. It was clear to the Fathers that there was no salvation in the Arian Son, a time-bound creature such as we are, out of the Father by a making as we are, Son only by a grace that holds no grace for us.[8]

This is what many a Catholic theologian might have said to Herod when asked, "Who is this?" And he would have spoken aright, even if it made no sense to Herod. Correct answer, but not the whole answer. Which compels my third point.

III

Why is the question "Who is this?" so important for you and me as preachers of the Word? Because the question dare not exist in outer space or in academia, dare not be answered only as Nicaea answered it in the context of Arius, or as the Council of Chalcedon answered it in 451: "We confess one and the same Christ, the Son, the Lord, the Only-Begotten, in two natures unconfused, unchangeable, undivided, and inseparable." Important indeed, part of our faith—what Christ is *in himself.* But even more important for effective preaching: Who is Christ *for us?*

Indeed Christ never ceases to be the risen Jesus at the right hand of the Father. But if we focus exclusively on that reality, we place the salvation Jesus mediates in some eternal realm of the spirit.[9] As long as we keep salvation in heaven, as long as we preach redemption as a reality to come, then hunger in Harlem, rape in Rwanda, homelessness in Haiti, injustice in Ireland, savagery in the Sudan, sinful social structures in our "land of the free"—these will have no close connection with God's will to save. And then the humanity of Jesus will provide "the model of patient and uncritical endurance under all circumstances."[10]

Who is "Christ for us"? The God-man we confess each Sunday, "who for us men and women and for our salvation came down from heaven, for our sake was crucified, died, and was buried, for our sake rose from the dead." But we betray the Creed if with the Creed we jump from "He ascended to heaven" right into "He will come again in glory to judge the living and the dead." Between ascension and second coming is Emmanuel, Christ with us. Who is this? The Christ who still calls to us from the hungry stomachs of children and the parched lips of the jobless, from the shivering flesh of the naked and the hopeless hearts of the homeless, from the fearful frames of the bedridden and the despairing eyes of the imprisoned.

Sixteen years ago I published one of my collections of homilies. I titled it *Sir, We Would Like To See Jesus.*[11] The title was taken from a passage in John's Gospel. Some Greeks have come up to worship in Jerusalem. They approach Philip: "Sir, we would like to see Jesus" (Jn 12:20–21).

Such is your fondest wish and mine. Not for Herod's reason: to ask for a miracle. Then why? Because, as preachers of the Word, the Word that above all else is Christ, it is not enough for us to know *about* Christ; we must know *him*. Only if we experience him in his present living reality can we expect to preach him effectively *as he is*. Yes, he speaks to us when the Scriptures are read in the liturgy. But do I actually hear *him* or only the lector? Yes, he lives in us as his grace courses through us. But am I actually aware of something different in me, aware of a power to love as Jesus loved? Yes, we eat his flesh and drink his blood at Communion. But does a thrill run through me? Do I feel, with St. Paul, that "it is no longer I who live, but it is Christ who lives in me" (Gal 2:20)? The danger is, these can remain abstract knowledge, intellectual judgments. Each should be a fresh experience of someone who is more alive than we are.

How? Beg for it, by all means. But more than that, a realistic way of achieving such experience—seeing Jesus—is to touch the living Christ in his images. You remember Matthew 25, "*I* was hungry and you gave me food" and so on? Only recently I was struck by a fresh thought: The men and women who were being welcomed by Jesus into his kingdom never realized till the Last Judgment that they had been feeding Jesus, slaking Jesus' thirst, welcoming Jesus in a stranger, clothing a naked Jesus, caring for a sickly Jesus, visiting an imprisoned Jesus.

A delightful surprise indeed: "When was it we saw you hungry" (Mt 25:37)?. But, I dare to suggest, not a model for Christian imitation. Our people should not have to wait for Judge Jesus to inform them that the drug-infected newborn, the abused baby, the runaway teenager, the HIV-positive, the hungry homeless, the lonely elderly, the illegal immigrant, the convict on death row is Jesus. Here too is the Jesus we must preach.

Not an easy gospel to preach. All too many of these images of Christ are flawed images, fractured, defective, defaced. But aren't we all, to some extent, disfigured images of Christ? Who of us can never say with St. Paul, "I do not do the good I want, but the evil I do not want is what I do" (Rom 7:19)?

Three urgent monosyllables for ourselves and for our preaching: Who is this? Who is, for me, the Jesus Herod was so anxious to see? Only the risen Jesus in all his glory? Or the Jesus "despised and rejected by others, a man of sorrows, one from whom others hide their faces" (Isa 53:3)? And how anxious am I to see this Jesus?

Ursuline Centre
Great Falls, Montana
September 24, 1998

26
PERFECT HOSTESS OR PERFECT DISCIPLE?
Twenty-seventh Week, Year 2, Tuesday

> ● Galatians 1:13–24
> ● Luke 10:38–42

Another Jesus gem. A one-act play in five verses; not a single wasted word. It may sound at first hearing like spiritual pap—"Mary has chosen the best part"[1]—but in actuality it has profound importance for Christian living, indeed for you and me.[2] So then, let me first set the Gospel scene for you, then submit what Jesus was actually saying, and end with its significance for preachers of the just word.

I

First, the Gospel scene. Three actors on center stage: two blood sisters and their good friend, that unpredictable young Jew Jesus. It's Martha's home in Bethany, not far from Jerusalem;[3] and Jesus is her guest, Jesus en route to Jerusalem, to the city of his destiny.

A scene heaven-sent for prime-time TV, perhaps for one of the more believable "soaps." Jesus is sitting quite relaxed in Martha's parlor. Mary is seated next to him, at his feet, like any disciple eager to learn from a teacher. Martha is up and about, constantly on the move, clearly preoccupied by the meal and its details. She too would like to be listening to Jesus, but her task, she feels, is to play the perfect hostess. Still, the least her dear sister might do is to lend her a hand.

Frustrated, Martha can stand it no longer. She complains—not to Mary but to Jesus: "Don't you care that my sister has left me to do all the serving? Speak to her, tell her to help me" (Lk 10:40). Jesus' reply is gentle but firm. Gentle: "Martha, Martha [you can sense the quiet love], you're fretting and disturbed about many things." Firm:

127

"Of one thing only is there need. Mary has chosen the best part, and [for that reason] it shall not be taken away from her" (vv. 41–42).

End of act, end of play.

II

But what is it that Jesus is telling Martha? Equally important, what is he *not* saying? Some have suggested what at first reading seems very plausible: "Not to fret, Martha. No need for a seven-course dinner. Keep it simple. One dish will be enough." Perhaps just the appetizer. Others have suggested that Jesus is instructing women how to show proper hospitality to traveling preachers. Still others have discovered in this episode how Jesus approved of the contemplative life over against the active life.[4]

Sorry, good friends, none of the above. Very simply, what is it that Mary chose to do? Very simply, she chose to listen to Jesus, to the words that fell from Jesus' lips. Martha wanted to play the perfect hostess, and in Jewish hospitality the meal had high importance. For this dear friend, for this prophet, nothing less than an elaborate meal would do. But Jesus reminds her: There is something more important than providing for his physical needs. What is more important? Listening. Listening to what Jesus has to say. Serving Jesus? "The proper 'service' of Jesus is attention to his instruction, not an elaborate provision for his physical needs...."[5]

Listen! Listen to Jesus! It's a lesson that dots the four Gospels. "Everyone who *listens* to these words of mine and acts on them will be like a wise man who built his house on rock" (Mt 7:24). "Blessed are your ears, for they *hear*" (Mt 13:16). "As for what was sown on good soil, this is the one who *hears* the word and understands it" (Mt 13:23). "This is my Son; *listen* to him" (Mt 17:5). "*Listen* to me, all of you" (Mk 7:14). "My mother and my brothers are those who *hear* the word of God and do it" (Lk 8:21). "Blessed rather are those who *hear* the word of God and obey it" (Lk 11:28). "The friend of the bridegroom...stands and *hears* him" (Jn 3:29). "Whoever *hears* my word and believes in him who sent me has eternal life" (Jn 5:24). "Everyone who belongs to the truth *listens* to my voice" (Jn 18:37).

Luke constantly amazes me. Here too. In Luke the story of Martha and Mary comes immediately after the story of the Jew who fell among robbers. We have just been moved mightily by the parable of the Good Samaritan, how important it is to love my neighbor, the stranger, the man or woman in need. Instantly Luke trumps that. He does not retract it; he simply moves to a plane higher still, something even more important: listening to Jesus, listening to the word of the Lord. Not that the word of the Lord replaces love of neighbor; but it is more basic, it is love's motivation, love's driving force. And you know, to listen, to really listen, is itself an act of love. I no longer hear sheer syllables, I give myself to a person. All of which leads smoothly into my third point.

III

What has all this to do with preachers of the just word? Something indispensable. You know now, perhaps have known before we "wise men from the East" and a lady scholar from Chicago[6] invaded your turf, what biblical justice is: fidelity to relationships, to responsibilities, that stem from our covenant with God in Christ. Relationships to God, to people, to earth. Love God above all else; treat every human being as an image of God, like another self; touch sky and sea and earth, God's nonhuman creation, with reverence and respect, as gifts of God. You have sorted out many of the injustices that mar our cosmos, our country, our church. You are part and parcel of a presbyterate that does something about injustices, of a community of believers that is the largest nonprofit organization in the United States committed to social justice.

Why is the Martha-Mary story pertinent for all this, in fact basic to biblical justice? Because biblical justice is not sheer activism. It is not biblical simply because you and your people fill empty stomachs and slake parched lips, welcome immigrants and dole out clothing to the tattered, bring Communion to the housebound and a touch of compassion to the imprisoned.

What makes it biblical? When we have listened. Not only to our people but to the Lord. But how recognize Jesus' voice? Easy enough for Martha and Mary; Jesus was in the same room. Fairly easy for Sunday worshipers; Scripture is proclaimed in the Church, Christ is speaking to them. But actually to live the Christian life, effectively to preach biblical justice, demands a good deal more. To hear consistently what the Lord is saying to us demands a close personal relationship to Christ, living contact with a Lord alive.

Ignatius Loyola was convinced that we can experience God's very Self, not simply human words that describe God. He was convinced that such an experience is grace indeed, and basically there is no one to whom it is refused.[7] In his later years Karl Rahner used to speak of such a primal experience "which completely captivated him while he was still young and which provides the key to his life and work."[8]

To bring this down to earth, I commend to you the Benedictine tradition. It is superbly summarized in the title of a minor classic by Dom Jean Leclercq, *The Love of Learning and the Desire for God*.[9] For scholasticism, theology's aim was knowledge; and the way to knowledge was through the question. In the monasteries the aim was not so much knowledge as experience; and the way to experience was not so much the question as desire. The significant difference was the importance the monastery accorded to the experience of union with God.

I am not trying to change you into monks. I am simply insisting what the Benedictine tradition in study and reflection can do for all of us. For it highlights an inner illumination, a grace of intimate prayer, what Benedict called an *affectus,* a manner of savoring and relishing divine realities. It means that if we want to "know" God, we need to experience God.

It does not demand the contemplation of the mystics, does not ask us to be transported, like St. Paul, to some "third heaven" or to "paradise" to hear "things that no mortal is permitted to repeat" (2 Cor 12:2, 4). It is a down-to-earth spirituality that was illustrated recently by Bishop Robert Morneau of Green Bay, Wisconsin, in a single-page article titled "My Mother's Hidden Prayer Life."[10] He recalled from his childhood how this busy lady, wife, nurse, mother of six, knelt at her "prayer chair" for an hour each morning before dawn, saying her prayers. In that context he has a short paragraph that sums up pithily what I am trying to say:

> Prayer, when reduced to its bare bones, is essentially listening and responding—listening to a God who speaks in scripture, in daily events, in the movements of the heart, in the community, in the needs of our brothers and sisters, in the signs of the times; and then responding appropriately to what the Lord is telling us or asking of us. Prayer is communication in which God takes the initiative, and we are first and foremost listeners.

We talk too much: praise, thanks, contrition, petition. With Morneau, "settle gently into the silence of God's presence, just being with God in the dark and quiet of our souls. This is very difficult. It appears as idleness, maybe even a waste of time. Nothing happens. And yet, something that is really important is happening—an encounter with God."[11] Martha indeed, but Mary before, Mary during, Mary after. Not mere activists, not sheer contemplatives; contemplatives in action.

All that having been said, I suggest we close with our opening prayer, the alternative prayer taken (legitimately) from the Seventh Sunday in Ordinary Time:

> Almighty God,
> Father of our Lord Jesus Christ,
> faith in your word is the way to wisdom,
> and to ponder your divine plan is to grow in the truth.
> Open our eyes to your deeds,
> our ears to the sound of your call,
> so that our every act may increase our sharing
> in the life you have offered us.
> Grant this through Christ our Lord.

New Harmony Inn
New Harmony, Indiana
October 6, 1998

27

WHAT DO YOU HAVE THAT YOU DID NOT RECEIVE?
Twenty-eighth Sunday of the Year (C)

- 2 Kings 5:14–17
- 2 Timothy 2:8–13
- Luke 17:11–19

This morning we gather together within a purpose and a Gospel. The purpose: our response to a Georgetown we treasure. The Gospel: the "good news" of gratitude. To make my homiletic point, I must sketch three related realities that focus on gratitude: (1) the gratitude of one human healed of his leprosy; (2) the gratitude that sparks Catholic existence; (3) the gratitude Georgetown needs to stay alive, to be healed of its scars, to increase, like Jesus, not only in years but "in wisdom and in favor with God and with men and women" (Lk 2:52).[1]

I

First, the "lepers." Ten men, Luke tells us. Was it Hansen's disease? Possibly. More likely, one or several inflammatory or scaly skin diseases: favus, lupus, psoriasis, ringworm, white spots.[2] Whatever it was in this instance, persons so afflicted in biblical times were, for all practical purposes, outcasts, pariahs. They were excluded from normal association with others, could not touch even their nearest and dearest; often they had to live outside of towns and cities. Listen to Leviticus:

> The person who has the leprous disease shall wear torn clothes and let the hair of his head be disheveled; and he shall cover his upper lip and cry out, "Unclean, unclean!" He shall remain unclean as long as he has the disease; he is unclean. He shall live alone; his dwelling shall be outside the camp.
>
> (Lev 13:45–46)

132

That is why these ten "stood at a distance" from Jesus (Lk 17:12), simply called out to him, "Jesus, have pity on us" (v. 13). In harmony with the Mosaic law, Jesus sent them off to the priests for examination;[3] they obeyed. On the way, their obedience, their willingness to trust him, was rewarded; they found, to their amazement, to their delight, that they were healed. They could now return to normal Palestinian society.

Wonderful indeed, but hardly the whole story. Nine of the men cured ran off, disappeared. Why? Probably to surprise their parents, hug their children, make love to their wives; possibly off to the nearest pub for a Manishewitz with old friends. All but one: a Samaritan, a non-Jew, a foreigner, someone who ordinarily had no use for Jews. He not only saw the hideous disfigurements fall away. In the Lucan story this is an awakening; he sensed at some deeper level what had happened, who had healed him. He no longer felt the need to show himself to the priests; he alone returned to Jesus, praised God in ringing phrases, fell at Jesus' feet, thanked him.

Jesus' reaction? Three questions, blunt questions. "Were not ten made clean? The nine, where are they? Can it be that none has been found to come back and give glory to God save this stranger?" (vv. 17–18). The result? The stranger's initial cry for mercy ended in his conversion: "Your faith has brought you salvation" (v. 19).

II

Thanks, gratitude. A constant word in our Catholic vocabulary, a reality that sparks Catholic existence, is central to Catholic living. Just reflect how often we give thanks to God, sometimes spontaneously, at times on cue.

Many of us thank God as we awake, grateful for a new day, the awesome gift of being alive. Alive in a creation shaped by God and reshaped for better and worse by God's creatures, a world that somehow mingles God's rugged Montana mountains and the potholes of our District. We thank God for the food we are about to consume, for the farmer who harvested it, the middleman who processed it, the lady who is serving it. We thank God for the endless miracle of a new infant fashioned of our flesh and God's love. We thank God for the parents without whose caring we might well be "children of another god." We thank God for marriages that mimic the love that flames between Christ and his people, the love that perdures in good times and bad, in poverty and wealth, in sickness and health.

We thank God for the endless graces without which human living would be inhuman. Weekend Catholic golfers thank God for the occasional par. And so much more that only each of you has experienced, each of you alone can tell.

And the climax of thanksgiving? This Eucharist, whose very name means "thanksgiving," gratitude. This sacred hour when Christ speaks to us from God's only Book, when "The Word of the Lord" forces from us the cry "Thanks be to God." As the Preface begins, Father O'Donovan[4] will proclaim, "Let us give thanks to the Lord our God," and all of you will declare, "It is right to give God thanks and praise." Or, as an earlier translation from the Latin phrased it more accurately, "It is a matter of justice to give God thanks and praise." For what? For a Son who out of sheer love was born for us, lived for us, died for us. And so, with St. Paul we "give thanks joyfully to the Father, who has enabled us to share in the inheritance of the saints in light, has rescued us from the power of darkness and transferred us into the kingdom of His beloved Son, in whom we have redemption, the forgiveness of sins" (Col 1:11b–14).

Little wonder that when a God-man rests in the palm of our hands, on our trembling tongues, and in the inmost recesses of our flesh, we shall give thanks. Thanks for the ultimate Gift: Communion, incredibly intimate oneness with our Lord's very self, the pledge and promise that death is not an end, only a beginning; that one day God will wipe away every tear from our eyes, when sadness will not even be a memory, when God will be All in all.

Little wonder I cannot forget Kenneth Branagh's production of Shakespeare's *King Henry the Fifth,* when war has ceased and a resounding song rises to heaven from Psalm 115, "Not to us, O Lord, but to your name give glory" (Ps 115:1). As Paul told the Christians of Corinth, "What do you have that you did not receive? And if you received it, why do you boast as if it were not a gift?" (1 Cor 4:7).

III

All of which moves us to the Hilltop. Not so much a place as a pilgrimage. I mean a progressive movement into womanhood and manhood. Where you concretized the Catholic vision of what it means to be alive, to look, to love, to laugh. Where the life of the mind is an adventure in two closely linked worlds: the world of learning and the world of loving.

In most of you, perhaps in each of you, something of a healing has taken place on the Hilltop. Not from a medical malady, not the leprosy that afflicted the Gospel ten. Still, healing from a comparable affliction. An affliction with two distinct but closely related facets: ignorance and individualism.

Ignorance was healed by learning. Not abstract understanding, but discovery that leads to wonder, to awe in the presence of the multifaceted, myriad miracle that is life, amazement at what breadths and depths there are to being alive. Awe that a time-bound creature can shape an idea, a limited mind cross oceans with the speed of light, the human spirit build skyscrapers and temples, flesh and blood walk in space and on the moon. Awe that you can discover God in God's Word, in God's people, in God's things. A learning wherein, as philosopher Jacques Maritain discovered, the height of human knowing is not conceptual but experiential, not an idea but an experience: Man, woman, feels God. Yes, *feels* God.

If ignorance was healed by learning, individualism was healed by loving. Not some abstraction in outer space. Rather a deepening response to a God-man thrillingly present on this campus: in Dalhgren indeed, in every liturgy from dawn to midnight, but also in thousands of God's images that continually surround us, men and women being shaped in untold ways to a living Christ, to a familiarity with the Lord who lived and died for them.

Here you've experienced a God-man insistently calling for service. Specifically, Archbishop John Carroll's vision of Georgetown: service to the Church, service to society. In a culture sociologists describe as rugged individualism, where the prize is to the swift, the strong, and the savage, the healing is in community. Not primarily a relaxing pub, but a realization that by God's design and initiative human existence is fundamentally social. We are "we" before we are "I" and "thou." Where students touch the ruptures that sever us from our earth, from our sisters and brothers, from our very selves. Not simply in a classroom, but *experience* of rupture. Experience not only of ecology but of an earth irreparably ravaged, not only abstract poverty but the stomach-bloated poor, not only the words "child abuse" but the vacant stare of the child abused, not only a book on racism but the hopelessness and hatred in human hearts.

One striking illustration of community: a true story, a Georgetown story. Perhaps four or five years ago, my good friend Father Raymond Kemp was crossing the campus at night, just about ten o'clock. (Ray not only codirects our project Preaching the Just Word; he teaches a course he calls "Struggle and Transcendence," largely taken by African Americans, including Hoya hoopsters.) Out of the dark, suddenly, unexpectedly, loomed a tall figure, a good seven feet of striking ebony. Ray recognized him: Cheik Dia, usually called Yaya, then a freshman, one of John Thompson's[5] favorite people. Sometimes called "Gramps," because he was somewhat older than his peers.

"Yaya," said Father Kemp, "what are doing here at this hour?"

"I'm on my way to pray," Yaya responded. "I missed all five times of prayer today—so many other things that had to be done. So I'm on my way to the Islamic prayer room."

"How long will your prayer take you?"

"About an hour."

"What happens when you pray?"

"When I pray, I am praising God, thanking God."

"Thanking God for what?"

"Because when I pray, I am connected with my homeland, I am in Senegal. I am one with my family back home, one with my old friends, one with my people."

You know, for us as with the lepers, sometimes it takes a stranger like Yaya to return us time and again to the Real, to link Georgetown to the world John Carroll founded us to love and serve. In his senior year this once somewhat inarticulate son of Islam taught Father Kemp's class, taught Christian students how to approach the All-Holy, the All-Powerful; how to surmount the petty and the paltry, the trifling and the trashy, the isolation that treasures having over being, "me" over "us."

What, more than any other reality, should connect us to the hundreds of thousands who have walked this campus over two centuries, connect us to the world outside these walls, connect us to the All-Holy? This Eucharist, this act of grateful memory, this most demanding of memories: the passion, death, and resurrection of Jesus Christ.

What returns you here? For all its glories, Georgetown is not yet the kingdom of God; hence felicity stuggles with frustration. For Hoyas are not totally Aristotle's rational animals; Hoyas are more like fallen angels with an incredible capacity for beer. The struggle will not end this side of eternity; but the struggle simply must go on.

Georgetown can be better than it has been, more influential than it is. Hence the need for men and women who have come to love her, men and women who are grateful to her, who return to give thanks, who are not content to leave it to strangers like a government to keep her alive, to heal her scars, to help her grow in wisdom, in God's favor, in our culture's appreciation. Hence this weekend. Not lepers; still, men and women with your own scars, but touched by a compassionate Christ, by a Jesus who not only says "Show yourselves to the priests" (Lk 17:14), not only wonders "where are the other" 90 percent, but welcomes you to a Eucharist that should model your own thanksgiving. I mean a gift of your very selves and what you have been given, not to a set of buildings but to a way of learning and loving we dare not let perish.

Gaston Hall
Georgetown University
Washington, D.C.
October 11, 1998

28
SAVE OUR CHILDREN/
INCREASE OUR FAITH
Thirty-second Week, Year 1, Monday

● Wisdom 1:1–7
● Luke 17:1–6

Good sisters and brothers in Christ: This morning your minds are focused on biblical justice.[1] From a top-flight Scripture scholar you learned what biblical justice is: fidelity—fidelity to relationships, responsibilities, that stem from a covenant with God. For a Christian, a covenant with God cut in the blood of Christ. Fidelity on three levels: Love God above all else; love each brother and sister like another self; touch things, God's nonhuman creation, with reverence. You discovered that, if justice is fidelity, injustice must be infidelity, a refusal of responsibility, a no to right relationships. And in your small groups you named the injustices, the rejection of relationships, the irresponsibilities that pollute your parishes.

In that context, permit me a twofold focus. First, one terrifying experience of injustice that sweeps beyond your parishes, envelops the whole of our American landscape. Second, how that experience of injustice, a paradigm of your own experiences, can and must be enriched by the passage just proclaimed to you from Luke's Gospel.

I

First, a frightening experience of injustice across the land we love. I mean our infidelity, our incredible irresponsibility, to our children. The basic fact is a simple statistic, so simple that simply to state it is almost to waft it away on the wind. One of every four children in our country grows up below the poverty line; 16 million. Did you know that "American children are twice as likely to be poor as Canadian children, 3 times as likely to be poor as British children, 4 times as likely to be poor as French children, and 7 to 13 times more likely to be poor than German, Dutch, and Swedish children"?[2]

But statistics do not capture the day-by-day human costs of child poverty. Poverty

> stacks the odds against children before birth and decreases their chances of being born healthy and of normal birthweight or of surviving; it stunts their physical growth and slows their educational development; frays their family bonds and supports; and increases their chances of neglect and abuse. Poverty wears down their resilience and emotional reserves; saps their spirits and sense of self; crushes their hopes; devalues their potential and aspirations; and subjects them over time to physical, mental, and emotional assault, injury, and indignity.
>
> *Poverty even kills....*[3]

I live, I walk, I work in sight of the Capitol. Never have I experienced a million-man, million-woman protest overflowing the Mall, flooding the offices of our representatives, shouting and singing "Save our children!" Many other strident shouts: "Save our guns! Save our endangered owls! Save our capital gains!" Rarely does Congress hear our children crying. And yet, as *Fortune* magazine tells us, "If the well-being of its children is the proper measure of the health of a civilization, the United States is in grave danger."[4] Pope John Paul II challenged us, "in the Christian view, our treatment of children becomes a measure of our fidelity to the Lord himself,"[5] the Jesus who asserted, "Whoever welcomes one such child in my name welcomes me" (Mt 18:5). And it is high time we Christians listened to UNICEF, the United Nations Children's Fund. A powerful paragraph, raw meat for meditation by priest and people, by president and politician:

> ...whether a child survives or not, whether a child is well-nourished or not, whether a child is immunized or not, whether a child has a school to go to or not, should not have to depend on whether interest rates rise or fall, on whether commodity prices go up or down, on whether a particular political party is in power, on whether the economy has been well managed or not, on whether a country is at war or not, or on any other trough or crest in the endless and inevitable undulations [of] political and economic life in the modern nation state.[6]

II

So much for one frightening issue of injustice. It is only a single slice of irresponsibility in relationships, but enough to raise a neuralgic issue for you and me, for your people and mine: How does this touch today's Gospel? Does it touch it at all? Yes indeed! Listen to the final words of Jesus to his apostles: "If you have[7] faith the size of a mustard seed, you would say to this mulberry tree, 'Be uprooted and planted in the sea,' and it would obey you" (Lk 17:6). Two questions: (1) How does this relate to biblical justice? (2) Do you believe it?

First, how does "If you have faith" relate to biblical justice? Very simply: We, our people, are not simply social workers, indispensable as such men and women are. It is not primarily a wonderfully human compassion that sends us to the 16 million American children living in some sort of hell, impels us to clamor for justice. It is our *faith* that does justice. Not a set of memorized words. It is a *living* faith that should move Christians to struggle for right relationships where the most vulnerable in our society are at risk.

Do you need proof? It is a living faith, a faith alive, that is proclaimed in the New Testament Letter of James (2:14–17):

> What good is it, my brothers [and sisters], if you say you have faith but do not have works? Can faith save you? If a brother or sister is badly clothed and lacks daily food, and one of you says to them, 'Go in peace, keep warm and eat your fill,' and yet you do not supply their bodily needs, what good does it do? So faith by itself, if it has no works, is dead.

The inspired text goes on: "Even the devils believe [that God is one]—and they shudder" (v. 19).

Listen to the First Letter of John: "If anyone has this world's goods and sees his brother [or sister] in need and closes his heart against him, how does God's love abide in him?" (1 Jn 3:17).

It is our faith, our living, loving faith, that links us to these children crying in a wilderness. I keep recalling, I keep repeating, Cardinal James Hickey's pregnant line, "We help the poor not because *they* are Catholic, but because *we* are Catholic."

Second, do you, do your people, believe what Jesus told his apostles, "If you have faith the size of a mustard seed, you would say to this mulberry tree, 'Be uprooted and planted in the sea,' and it would obey you"? This is not about mulberry trees; it is not primarily concerned with acceptance of a creed. Jesus' point is this: If your faith is genuine, i.e. if you really listen to God speaking to you, if you listen with an open mind and heart, if you hold on to God's word with persistence and perseverance despite all obstacles, the fruit of your faith will be wondrous indeed.[8] Very little will be impossible, simply because with God nothing is impossible.

Expand your imagination. Just imagine 60 million Catholics listening avidly, greedily, openly, obediently to what God wants of us where children are at risk: where an African-American infant is hungry or born HIV-positive, where a Caucasian child has Down's syndrome or begs a wheel chair, where a Hispanic lass wants to learn English, where a Korean kid needs a baby sitter while his mother works, where a small Salvadoran just yearns for someone to hug. The needs are dismayingly vast, shock our sensibilities on TV and in print. But each need is not an abstract idea; each need is a little image of God, calling to disciples of Jesus to open not only our purses and wallets but even more our arms and hearts.

Biblical justice? Not a concept, always a crucifixion. Right relation? It stares us Christians in the face: "This is my commandment [*Jesus'...commandment*]: Love one another as I have loved you" (Jn 15:12). That's all? Yes, that's all. 16 million of them, 60 million of us.[9] It could give a face lift to a parish, transform the image of America. How? Easy: For each little one, think big.

Do you mind murmuring a prayer with me, the prayer of the apostles to Jesus? "Increase our faith!" (Lk 17:6). *Our* faith. All 60 million of us.

Franciscan Renewal Center
Scottsdale, Arizona
November 10, 1997

A Feast & Memorials

29

GREATER LOVE THAN THIS NO ONE HAS
Trinity Sunday (B)

- Deuteronomy 4:32–34, 39–40
- Romans 8:14–17
- Matthew 28:16–20

Our schedule forbids a wealth of words.[1] Still, sheer silence on a feast that celebrates the Trinity, three Persons in one God, might well be an act of cowardice. And if anything is out of place on Memorial Day, it is cowardice. So then, three swift thoughts, each centered on love: (1) the love that characterizes the secret life of God; (2) the love that marks God's life with us; (3) the love that Memorial Day celebrates, the love we are called to imitate.

I

First, the love that characterizes the secret life of God. Unfortunately, as long as we remain on this earth, you and I will never know what God's intimate life is like; God has not revealed this even to Jesuits! What does God *do* with His or Her time in an existence where there is no time? God's life is so utterly different from anything you and I experience, so different that anything we say about God, even if it's true, doesn't begin to touch the real life God lives.

But perhaps three words from the New Testament come close. They appear in the First Letter of John. Three momentous monosyllables: "God...is...Love" (1 Jn 4:8). Not simply "God loves"; God *is* Love (capital L). Only of God dare we say that. Oh yes, an Englishman might say to his wife, "I say there, luv"; but it's hardly her proper name. Yet it is God's name.

Why? Because the Trinity—Father, Son, and Holy Spirit—is the model without beginning for every love that has ever begun. What

145

do I mean? You have heard the expression "I and thou." It refers to
two distinct persons, to their relationship. And you've heard the
expression "mine and thine." It refers to certain things that belong to
me and not to you; these I have, these you don't; and you'd better not
lay your hands on them. Now, in God there is indeed "I and Thou,"
three distinct persons. The Father is not the Son; the Son is not the
Father; neither Father nor Son is the Holy Spirit. But, wonder of
wonders, there is "I and Thou" but never "mine and thine," those
ice-cold words. No one—Father, Son, Spirit—has anything divine the
others do not have.

Such is perfect love: always "I and thou," never "mine and
thine." Such is God...to perfection.

II

Second, the love that marks God's life with us. You see, God
did not need anything, did not need anyone. Believe it or not, God
was perfectly happy before you and I existed. But perhaps what is
most remarkable about love is that genuine love wants to give, to
share, to communicate. And if you love perfectly, you yearn to give
your whole self, clutch nothing the other dare not touch.

So what did God do? Listen to God's own revealing word in
John's Gospel: "God so loved the world that He gave His only Son, so
that everyone who believes in Him...may have eternal life" (Jn 3:16).
Not some vague "gave." God's own Son was born as we are born,
wore our flesh, hungered as we hunger, was called mad by his relatives, was betrayed with a kiss by a close friend, was lashed with
whips and crowned with thorns, died in exquisite agony such as you
and I will never bear—out of love, so that you and I might share God's
life, God's love, for ever.

Remember, too, your second reading, from Paul's letter to the
Christians of Rome: "You did not receive a spirit of slavery; you
received the [Holy] Spirit of adoption, through which we cry out,
'Father!'...We are children of God, heirs of God and joint heirs with
Christ, if in fact we suffer with him so that we may also be glorified
with him" (Rom 8:15–17).

Little wonder that the reading you heard from Deuteronomy
about the Israelites can be extended to our own experience: "Ask
now about former ages, long before your own, ever since the day that
God created human beings on the earth; ask from one end of heaven
to the other: Has anything so great as this ever happened or has its

like ever been heard of?" (Deut 4:32). That God should give God's own Son to a crucifying death, so that the Holy Spirit might live within us, divine witness that we are God's children!

III

Third, the love that Memorial Day celebrates, the love we are called to imitate. You must remember a remarkable sentence Jesus uttered to his closest friends shortly before he died for us: "Greater love than this no one has, to lay down [your] life for those [you] love" (Jn 15:13). Such is Memorial Day. That is why we honor not only the 529,332 Civil War dead, but also the 1600 white and black casualties it cost to take Santiago in the Spanish-American War; 116,516 military dead in World War I; 405,399 in World War II; 54,246 in the Korean War; over 56,000 in the Vietnam War.[2] "Greater love than this no one has." This is the kind of love Jesus said "is like" loving God (Mt 22:39).

All of this should speak to us, all of this asks something of us. Not only a heartfelt prayer of gratitude for their dying that we might live. Not only a Colbert concert to stir our senses, to help us see the sacrifice and hear the agony, experience what war smells like, touch the tears on unnumbered cheeks, taste the love that inspired such self-giving. In and through this, a tough resolve: If we need not die for our sisters and brothers, can we not at least live for them? We who claim God for Father, Christ for brother, Spirit for inspirer, can we not mimic in our human fashion a Trinity that loves every man, woman, and child shaped in Its image and likeness?

We live in a paradoxical country: indeed "the home of the brave" but not quite "the land of the free." Not when one of every four children grows up in a poverty destructive of mind, body, and spirit. Not when even some Christians see in AIDS God's plague on the promiscuous. Not when thousands of the homeless still rummage in garbage cans for the food we discard so lightly. Not when a disproportionate number of African Americans are poor, work menial labor, rot in prison, are murdered or take their own lives. Not when women still cry out against their powerlessness to shape the world in any but a masculine mold.

The issues are mind-boggling, frightening. On a day when we justly acclaim the brothers and sisters who died to let us live "the American way," how shall we live so that untold sisters and brothers may not, literally or for all practical purposes, die? Those for whom the Son of God died, how shall we help them come alive?

A memorial for the dead lays a burden on the living. Especially when we celebrate their memory with a liturgy which recalls a Trinity that in the crucified love of Jesus made sense out of human dying. "Greater love than this no one has."

Washington Court Hotel
Washington, D.C.
May 25, 1997

30
YOU TOO A SWORD SHALL PIERCE
Memorial of Our Lady of Sorrows

- 1 Timothy 2:1-8
- Luke 2:33-35

During my 56 years as a priest, I have meditated much on the sorrows that afflicted our Lady from the time Gabriel brought her redemption's glad tidings. But until recently I never quite understood what Simeon's prophecy meant when he said to Mary, "Your own soul (your own self) a sword shall pierce" (Lk 2:35). To make this meaningful for our own lives, our priestly spirituality, our more profound preaching,[1] I suggest three questions. (1) What precisely did Simeon have in mind? (2) How much more was there to Mary's sorrow than Simeon suspected? (3) What significance might Mary's sorrows have for our own apostolate?

I

First, what precisely did Simeon have in mind? Much ink has been spilled over it, many sorrows suggested. Was it the rejection our Lady experienced in the public rejection of her Son? Was it the illegitimacy with which Jesus was reproached? Was it the tragedy she experienced in the fall of Jerusalem? Was it, as a learned priest named Origen thought in the third century, doubts about Jesus that pierced Mary during the Passion?[2] Was it, as a bishop named Epiphanius conjectured in the fourth century, her own violent death?[3]

None of the above. To understand Mary's sword of sorrow, we must place it in the context of the whole sentence, *all* the words of Simeon to Mary: "Look, this child is marked for the fall and the rise of many in Israel, to be a symbol that will be rejected—indeed, a sword will pierce you too—so that the thoughts of many minds will be laid bare."[4] The background is the Old Testament sword of discrimination: The sword singles out some for destruction, others for mercy. In Luke's context the sword

> grows out of the idea of Jesus's role causing the fall and the rise of many in Israel. Mary, as part of Israel, will be affected too. In the Gospel proper Jesus will be depicted as one who brings dissension even within families (12:51–53). Thus, with the imagery of the sword piercing Mary, Simeon hints at the difficulty she will have in learning that obedience to the word of God will transcend even family ties.[5]

Examples? Jesus' responses to praise of his mother: "Your mother wants to see you." "My mother and my brothers, they are the ones who listen to the word of God and act on it" (Lk 8:21). Also, "Blessed is the womb that bore you...." "Blessed rather are those who listen to the word of God and observe it" (Lk 11:28). Never did Jesus disparage motherhood. And yet, quite clearly in the Synoptic Gospels Jesus placed even greater value on discipleship.

For Jesus' mother, Simeon hints, discipleship will not be easy. In fact, it will prove extraordinarily difficult. Like a sword of steel, it will cut, it will hurt, it will even pierce our Lady's inmost self. Lady of Sorrows indeed.

II

Second, how much more was there to Mary's sorrow? Call each of them, in Simeon's rhetoric, a sword. There was the charge of adultery that tempted Joseph to "dismiss her quietly" (Mt 1:19). There was the fearful flight into Egypt to shield her child from a king bent on murder. There were the three days in Jerusalem when she lost her preteen Jesus, when on finding him she exclaimed, "Child, why have you treated us like this? Look, your father and I have been searching for you in great anxiety" (Lk 2:48). There was the perilous day his own townspeople "were filled with fury,...took him to the brow of the hill on which their town was built, to throw him over it" (Lk 4:29). There was the shocking day his own relatives "tried to restrain him, for they were saying, 'He is out of his mind'" (Mk 3:21).

Then there were the dreadful final days when one of his closest friends (and Mary surely knew him) betrayed her son with a kiss, when the elders of his own people accused him of perverting their nation, when Herod mocked him and Pilate washed his hands of him, when his back was lashed with whips and his head crowned with thorns, when he was nailed to a cross between two thieves, when she stood beneath that cross and watched him breathe his last with an agonizing cry.

Oh yes, our Lady knew sorrow. And I suspect that only a small fraction of that sorrow has been recorded in our Gospels. Lady of Sorrows indeed.

But here a second thought. I said above that there was more to Mary's sorrow than could be fitted into Simeon's sword. Perhaps not. It may well be that every sorrow in her life stemmed from her effort to live as mother *and* disciple, to balance a mother's protective love and a disciple's "Whatever you want, Lord."

III

Finally, what might our Lady's experience of sorrow say to our own apostolate? Recall the defensible thesis that Mary was her son's first and perfect disciple.[6] Discipleship in Luke links two elements: hearing God's word and living it. Such was our Lady, to perfection. In St. Augustine's well-known dictum: "Full of faith, Mary conceived Christ in her heart before conceiving him in her womb."[7] And her son was not disparaging her when he said "Blessed rather...." For Mary, above all others, listened to God's word all through her life and acted on it. Even so, following her Son in discipleship as he made his torturous way to Jerusalem was costly. The cost? A daily cross that all but crushed her. How could Mary not come close to being crushed when caught between the claims on a disciple and the protective love of a mother?

Somewhat similarly for you and me. A priest, a preacher, who does not experience sorrow is hardly a disciple of Jesus. Sorrow for our people, sorrow for ourselves.

Sorrow for our people. This afternoon you expressed, you listed, some of the injustices that plague your people, that keep them from living lives more human, more Christian. Sorrows that spare no age, no gender, that afflict the haves and the have-nots; sorrows that feed on poverty and prejudice, on abuse and abortion, on hunger and homelessness, on vice and violence, on greed and gluttony, on disease and death, on the scores of infidelities to God, to sisters and brothers, to the earth that sustains us.

Such sorrows it is not sufficient to list, to catalogue, to add up.

Unless the sorrows of our people become our sorrows, we do not resemble the high priest Jesus who was able to "sympathize with our weaknesses" because he "was tested as we are" (Heb 5:15). If our people hurt, we too hurt; where our people hurt, there we hurt. Somewhat like Dorothy Day, who could not consume Communion insensitive to someone's hunger, could not enjoy Eucharistic warmth while brothers and sisters shivered without a blanket, found it difficult to "go to the altar of God" aware that someone was sleeping over a sidewalk grate.

This is not to wallow in grief, wring our hands, curse the darkness. This is simply the compassion of Christ, the compassion he commanded when he told us to love others as he loved and loves us (Jn 15:12). If we, oiled by God to serve, do not "suffer with" (compassion) our people, sorrow when and where they sorrow, to that extent we are not images of the Suffering Servant.

Sorrow for ourselves. This is not to wallow in guilt. Simply an awareness of our own fragility, that we who are ordained to heal are ourselves in need of healing; have to pray ceaselessly "I believe, Lord, help my unbelief"; have to beg forgiveness for the times when, like the priest in Luke's parable, we too have "passed by on the other side" (Lk 10:31).

A final word, good brothers. Today's liturgy is not sheer memory: remembering how our Lady suffered, fingering our own scars. Here is encouragement, stimulus, incentive, grace. Fresh realization that, as with Mary, so with us: Discipleship costs— costs dearly. And so we pray:

Our Lady of Sorrows: Simeon must have startled you. You brought your baby joyously into the temple to present him to the Lord God. And this "just" man (Lk 2:25) not only predicted that this child would be a sign of contradiction. He promised you that your own self too—not only your Son's—a sword would pierce. And indeed it did. Aware of your Son's experience, and your own, we come into God's presence, into your presence, conscious that God's justice will cost us. Help us, then, not only to hear God's justice. Not only to be faithful ourselves—to God, to God's people, to God's earth. Perhaps most costly, help us to preach it. Preach it intelligently, from profound understanding of God's own mind. Preach it passionately, from crucifying experience of it. Preach it courageously, when some of our own people close their ears and tighten their lips. Preach it in season and out of season, trembling with joy or weeping from sorrow, because here lies the gospel in miniature: Love God above all else, love every sister and brother like another self, handle God's nonhuman creation with reverence.

Our Lady of Sorrows: Help us, through our preaching, to turn our paradoxical parishes into islands of your Son's justice.

Tara Hotel
Hyannis, Massachusetts
September 15, 1997

31

YOU ARE GOD'S BUILDING
Dedication of the Lateran Basilica

- Ezekiel 47:1–2, 8–9, 12
- 1 Corinthians 3:9c–11, 16–17
- John 2:13–22

Preach about a basilica? A church building? A building in Rome? It was difficult for me to get excited, difficult to know what to say to get you excited. Yes indeed...until I began to mull seriously over Ezekiel and over Paul. As a result, three stages to my approach. I want to move from the building to those who worship in the building to those who preach in the building.

I

Today's liturgy begins with a building: the Basilica of St. John Lateran. Trivia question number one: Who is the St. John? Surprise: John the Baptist. Trivia question number two: Why the word Lateran after John? Named after the Laterani family, who had a palace on or near the spot where the basilica now stands.

Serious question number one: Why does the official Church celebrate its dedication? Two good reasons. (1) It is the episcopal seat of the pope as bishop of Rome. (2) It is the oldest and the first in rank of the four great patriarchal basilicas of Rome.[1] Serious question number two: What meaning might this particular historical structure have for us, for Catholics ordinary and extraordinary? I suggest it should remind us of two realities: what a church structure can be and do, and what it cannot be and do.

What can a sacred structure be and do? Recall the temple in Jerusalem, for more than a thousand years the most important sanctuary in Israel. It was the proper abode of Yahweh, housed His

154

throne, the ark of the covenant. Therein stood the altar of sacrifices, the altar of incense, the showbread or holy bread always in the presence of Yahweh. It was Yahweh's palace, the dwelling place of divinity, the place of divine intervention.[2] In Jerusalem, the Samaritan woman said to Jesus, "you [Jews] say [it] is the place where people must worship" (Jn 4:20).

Similarly for us Catholics. A church is in a special sense God's house. Each structure is consecrated to God—Father, Son, and Holy Spirit. Here the most significant act of Catholic worship is re-enacted, re-presented: the Last Supper of Jesus; there we replay the death of the Lord until he comes. A tabernacle houses Jesus' sacramental body. Here in blessed waters children become members of Christ's Body, man and woman wed in perpetual love, the dead-in-Christ are entrusted to God's mercy.

What can a temple of God not be and do? The sobering words the Lord told prophet Jeremiah to proclaim to the people of Judah:

> Do not trust in these deceptive words: "This is the temple of the Lord, the temple of the Lord, the temple of the Lord."...Here you are, trusting in deceptive words to no avail. Will you steal, murder, commit adultery, swear falsely, make offerings to Baal, and go after other gods that you have not known and then come and stand before me in this house, which is called by my name, and say, "We are safe!"—only to go on doing all these abominations? Has this house, which is called by my name, become a den of robbers in your sight?
>
> (Jer 7:4–11)

The temple is holy, the basilica is sacred, but neither temple nor basilica ministers mercy by magic; neither sells salvation, what Dietrich Bonhoeffer called "cheap grace."

II

This suggests my second point. St. Paul moves us from a structure of stone to a temple of flesh and blood. "You are God's building. Do you not know that you are God's temple, and that God's Spirit dwells in you?...God's temple is holy, and you are that temple" (1 Cor 3:9c, 16–17).

Here Paul is not concerned immediately with each Christian individually. Oh it's true, Paul wants each Christian to be holy. In fact, as he puts it, God has made Christ our "sanctification" (1 Cor 1:30), that is, Christ is the means whereby men and women are dedicated anew to God, oriented to serve God with awe and respect. To such holiness "God has called us" (1 Thess 4:7). We have been "made holy" by Christ (1 Cor 1:2; 6:11), by the Spirit (Rom 15:16). So real is this for Paul that a common designation for Christians is "saints" (Rom 1:7; 1 Cor 1:2).[3]

But in the second reading today Paul uses "you" in the plural. He is talking directly to the community. The Corinthian community is God's temple. And the community is God's temple to the extent that it is holy. "The community is destroyed by lack of sanctity."[4]

When Jeremiah was urging the people not to place their trust in the structure of stone where God dwelt, what did he urge them to do instead? "If you truly amend your ways and your doings, if you truly act justly with one another, if you do not oppress the alien, the orphan, and the widow, or shed innocent blood in this place, and if you do not go after other gods to your own hurt, then I will dwell with you in this place, in the land that I gave of old to your ancestors for ever and ever" (Jer 7:5-7).

III

All of which leads me to those who preach in the building. Here a happy coincidence: on the same day John Lateran symbolizing where we preach, and biblical justice suggesting what we preach.[5] We preach fidelity to relationships, to responsibilities, that stem from our covenant with God cut in the blood of Christ.

The critical word? "Relationships." If our people are to be just in the biblical sense, they must be in right relationship in all aspects of their lives. Concretely, three relationships: to God, to people, to earth.

First, right relationship to God: Love God above all else. "You shall have no other gods besides [or: before] me" (Deut 5:7). It is "the greatest and first commandment" of the law and the gospel: "You shall love the Lord your God with all your heart and with all your soul and with all your mind" (Mt 22:37-38). It is the vision a gifted Greek theologian named Origen caught and preached early in the third century:

> God...knows that what a man loves with all his heart and soul and might—this for him is God. Let each one of us now examine himself and silently in his own heart decide which is the flame of love that chiefly and above all else is afire within him, which is the passion that he finds he cherishes more keenly than all

others....Whatever it is that weighs the heaviest in the balance of
your affection, that for you is God. But I fear that with very
many the love of gold will turn the scale, that down will come
the weight of covetousness lying heavy in the balance.[6]

Second relationship: to people. It is the second commandment
of the law and the gospel, the Israelite tradition Jesus inherited: "You
shall love your neighbor as yourself" (Lev 19:18; Mt 22:39). It was
partially summed up in the Nazareth synagogue, in what Luke pre-
sents as Jesus' program for his ministry: "The Spirit of the Lord is
upon me, for [the Lord] has anointed me, has sent me to preach
good news to the poor, to proclaim release for prisoners and sight
for the blind, to send the downtrodden away relieved" (Lk 4:18; cf.
Is 61:1–2). For Jesus, too, the just man or woman is not primarily
someone who gives to another what that other deserves. Jesus inaugurated a new covenant, where the most significant relationship is
the monosyllable that says it all: love—and astonishingly, where loving one's neighbor, already commanded in Leviticus, is said by Jesus
to be "like" loving God. To love the other is like loving the Other. It is
the song of Jean Valjean toward the close of *Les Misérables:* "To love
another person is to see the face of God."

But loving your neighbor is not a psychological balancing act:
As much or as little as you love yourself, that much or that little love
shower or trickle on your neighbor. No. I am to love my neighbor
like another self, as if he or she were another "I," as if I were standing
in his or her shoes. Especially the shoes of the disadvantaged, the
downtrodden—those whom Scripture ceaselessly summarizes as "the
widow, the orphan, and the alien." This is what our covenant
demands—what Jesus summed up when he said, "Love one another
as I have loved you" (Jn 15:12).

Third relationship: to earth. I mean all that is not God or the
human person. A problem here, God's summons to humankind in
Genesis: "Fill the earth and subdue it, and have dominion over the
fish of the sea and over the birds of the air and over every living
thing that moves upon the earth" (Gen 1:28). For many a critic, we
Christians see it as God's will that we exploit nature for our own purposes.[7] Our people should hear from us that the text and its context
do not justify exploiting nature for human convenience. The
Hebrew term for "have dominion" is used elsewhere in Scripture to
describe the care that should characterize a king as God's vice-
regent, with especial concern for the most vulnerable and fragile.
The mandate given humanity, given us, in this section of Genesis is

not exploitation; it is reverential care for God's creation.[8] The very context "suggests that this human dominion is to be carried out 'in the image of God,' an image that suggests nurture, blessing, and care rather than exploitation, abuse, and subjugation."[9] Our relationship to nature? We are stewards. And a steward is one who manages what is someone else's. A steward cares, is concerned, agonizes. Stewards may not plunder or waste; they are responsible, can be called to account for their stewardship. As the Psalmist phrased it, "The earth is the Lord's, and all that is in it" (Ps 24:1).

Have we come a long way from the Lateran Basilica, from the temple of stone? Not if we recall what it symbolizes, what it points to. Not if we recall Paul's "You are God's building." Not if we recall that the more important temple is the community to whom we preach, the flesh and blood to be sanctified not only by God's body but by God's word on our lips. Not if we recall that you and I are part and parcel of that temple. Not if we recall that our words are likely to give life only if we too do not "trust in those deceptive words, 'This is the temple of the Lord.'" Not if we recall that we too are called to be holy: I mean, are forbidden to "go after other gods," are commanded to love each temple of flesh and blood as Jesus loved, have for vocation to touch each facet of God's creation, each "thing," with reverence, with awe, as a gift of God.

El Carmelo Retreat House
Redlands, California
November 9, 1998

32

FROM BOHEMIA TO PHILADELPHIA
Memorial of St. John Nepomucene Neumann

- 1 John 3:22—4:6
- Matthew 4:12–17, 23–25

A happy coincidence—or is it more than coincidence? In the first liturgy of our first retreat/workshop for bishops, we celebrate...a bishop.[1] Happily, too, John Nepomucene Neumann has left us a partial autobiography.[2] The manuscript is dated March 27, 1852. The date is intriguing because it is the eve of his ordination as bishop, and the opening words are *Ex obedientia,* "[Written] under obedience," that is, on order of his Redemptorist provincial. Which led his English translator, Redemptorist Alfred Rush, to comment, "Historians will gladly leave to the canonists the discussion whether a Provincial can give a Bishop-Elect a command or *[sic]* obedience."[3] If the answer is no, a *felix culpa.*

There is much I must pass over; a homily is not a history. But there is much I must dwell on; a homily selects from history. And there is a brief bit I dare not neglect; yesterday's bishop addresses today's bishop.

I

There is much I must pass over. There is the family: six children born to devoutly Christian parents in Bohemia (what is now Czechoslovakia), "brought up," he says, "in the old-fashioned school."[4] There is the boy with a thirst for knowledge rather than sports, who acquired from his father a passion for reading, was called by his mother "my little bibliomaniac."[5] There is the lad who felt no early inclination to the priesthood; "it was so exalted that it seemed beyond my reach."[6] There is the young man with enthusiasm for Latin and the humanities, for the natural sciences, for philosophy and theology, who "studied *con amore*" Scripture, Hebrew, and church history.[7]

There is the youngster reading reports from missionaries among the Germans in North America and deciding that there lay his vocation; walking with a fellow student along the Moldau River, after which "my resolution was so strong and lively that I could no longer think of anything else."[8] There is the diocesan seminarian in Prague unhappy with his professors of dogma, moral, and pastoral. "The first was more against the Pope than for him.... The second was far too philosophical for a single one of us to understand him. The third was an out and out Josephinist."[9] With regret I pass over his spiritual progress: temptations against faith, against purity, his high resolve to seek perfection.

There is the young man of 25, whose journey from Bohemia to New York could shape an action movie with special effects: ordination delayed and ecclesiastical foul-ups on his travel, snow 14 or 15 feet high in the Bohemian forest and a rain-soaked walk from Paris to Nanterre, near death from a fallen topmast on an American three-master between Havre and New York. There is the immigrant, lonely, homesick, seasick, a dollar in his pocket, shoes worn, clothes shabby, baggage a few spiritual books, greeted with joy by 78-year-old Bishop John Dubois, himself a refugee from the French Revolution. There is the subdeacon, deacon, and priest ordained by Dubois in New York in June 1836 at Old St. Patrick's Cathedral on Mott St., and giving First Communion to the children he had prepared.

I pass over the diocesan priest in western New York. His ceaseless journeys: Williamsville, North Bush, Niagara Falls, Batavia, Rochester, Buffalo. Trustees to reckon with; long periods of disgust and aridity; doubts about his state of grace, his salvation. With reluctance I pass over his passsage from diocese to religious order, to the Redemptorists, a circuit missionary to the Germans all through Maryland, a traveling pastor in Pittsburgh and its environs, a self-giving that all but ruined his health. I pass over the gifted writer: two German catechisms, a Bible history in German, articles on theological issues.

II

But there is one Neumann I dare not pass over: the fourth bishop of Philadelphia. His diocese: the eastern half of Pennsylvania, the entire State of Delaware, the southern part of New Jersey. What problems confronted him—this short man, just over five-feet-two, about 150 pounds, deep-set penetrating eyes, light brown hair, sallow skin, wide mouth, pleasant smile?[10]

Money: parishes in serious debt; institutions and social agencies to be kept solvent; building programs, like finishing the cathedral. *Immigration:* thousands, mainly Irish and German, streaming into the diocese, often desperately poor. Needed in consequence: more churches, more schools, more priests, more sisters and brothers, more hospitals, more orphanages. *Ethnic* issues: Germans feeling isolated in English-speaking churches, demanding their own parishes. Their slogan: Language saves faith. *Education:* Catholic schools to provide the Catholic education denied in the new public-school system. When Neumann came to Philadelphia in 1852, only about 500 children attended Catholic schools.

Neumann's response? Never easy. He had no chancery force to assist him in administration. "A bishop in America," he wrote to relatives back home, "has to do everything himself and by his own hand."[11] Still, a pastoral letter ten days after his arrival urged support of parish schools. Three meetings of lay and clergy ended in a Central Board of Education for the Diocese of Philadelphia, "the genesis of the present diocesan system of parochial schools prevalent today throughout the United States."[12] He is justifiably considered the father of the parochial school system as we know it.

Here was his key project as bishop, arguably Neumann's most distinctive achievement; this he preached and promoted day in and day out. Catholic school life in Philadelphia grew as never before. In 30 months the number of parish school children rose from 500 to 9000. Besides, in 34 months he completed six churches started by his predecessor, rebuilt six others, added 30 new ones; 80 parishes in less than eight years.

Nothing came easily. Parish finances agonized a man admittedly unskilled in matters of money, perhaps even in the art of government, raised questions in Philadelphia and Rome. Some of his clergy found him "rather taciturn and cold,"[13] a small group never warmed to him. Trustees vilified him, brought him to court. Antiforeign bigotry from the Know-Nothings found in foreign-born Neumann an obvious target for abuse. Disaffected German Catholics placed a railroad tie on the tracks to wreck the train on which he was to leave their town; the train stopped in time.[14]

Profoundly pastoral, Neumann never stopped visiting his parishes—at least five months in each of the first three years—"traveling on one-track trains, on foot, on bumpy stagecoaches or lumbering omnibuses."[15] He had a way with children, in orphanages, in Sunday school, on the streets. Very simply, he loved children. His favorite gimmick? A microscope revealing to youngsters life in a tumbler of water. He not only could read Latin and Greek; he spoke German and Bohemian, French and Spanish, Italian and English; as a bishop, he learned enough Gaelic to hear confessions of the Irish.[16]

Profoundly spiritual, Neumann radiated simplicity: He slept three or four hours, ate sparingly, lived in a small room, gave his best clothes to the poor. He was impressively faithful to meditation, Mass, thanksgiving. He was open to all, but especially to the poor. Neumann had a tender devotion to our Lady, went to Rome for the papal definition of the Immaculate Conception in 1854. He introduced the devotion of the Forty Hours throughout his diocese. Unexpectedly revealing is a backhanded tribute from Archbishop Gaetano Bedini, reporting to Rome after a short stay in Old Philadelphia:

> The Bishop of Philadelphia seems a little inferior for the importance of such a distinguished city, not in learning nor in zeal nor in piety, but because of the littleness of his person [five feet two] and his neglect of the fashions [e.g., the proper way to dress]. He is indeed very holy and full of zeal, but more as a missionary than a bishop. He is not able to forget the very humble customs of the Order to which he belongs [Redemptorists], but the populous City of Philadelphia, rich, intelligent, full of life and importance, surely merits a bishop of another type. He himself, I am sure, would be delighted to be transferred to a new diocese, one entirely poor, because this is much more in accord with his habits and his true and great humility.[17]

III

Finally, what might yesterday's bishop say to today's bishop? Short of eight years as ordinary, not yet 49 when he collapsed on Vine Street near 13th in Old Philadelphia, what might Bishop Neumann stress if he wore your miter in your territory in your time? Knowing your territory as intimately as you do, each of you can answer that question far better than I—and I trust that you will. Two suggestions from a high perch of ignorance. They stem from Neumann the missionary and Neumann the preacher.[18]

First, the missionary. John Neumann was a missionary to a land he knew not; to hundreds of thousands of immigrants often poor and unemployed, in peril of abandoning their faith; to ethnic groups, German, Irish, and Italian Catholics, frequently at war with one another; to sworn enemies of the foreigner.

I suggest that most bishops are missionaries. Without crossing oceans, most come to territories unknown. You too have your Catholic strangers—strangers not only to you but at times to one another: Alaskan natives (Eskimos, Indians, Aleutians) and whites in Anchorage, Asians and Hispanics, Japanese-Americans. The square miles you cover rival, at times exceed, Neumann's experience. The unchurched number 60 percent of your vast Northwest. You are, by episcopal ordination, the top reconciler in your diocese. Reconciliation means that, like Jesus, you cement biblical justice in your area. You above all are ordained to bring your people to love one another as Jesus loves them. To love in action the most vulnerable: the unborn and the lowborn, the drug-addicted and the HIV-afflicted, the sexually abused and the elderly alone, the immigrant and the stranger. You must symbolize in your own person, in your lives, the Catholic social tradition: each person an image of God, the dignity of work, option for the poor, the one human family, reverential care for God's creation. In your lives. The picture of Mother Teresa cradling an orphaned infant in devastated Lebanon is worth a thousand words.

Second, the preacher. Neumann knew the affirmation of Trent, "The principal task of bishops is to preach the gospel."[19] And so he did. Often—on feast days and at High Masses, at retreats and Forty Hours, in religious houses and during visitations. Not with natural eloquence, not with inborn oratory. Rather, the simple style advocated by Alphonsus Liguori—profound thoughts yes, but expressed with clarity and simplicity. The same Alphonsus who had urged a new bishop, "I recommend to you not to spare yourself in preaching in all the places of your diocese. The voice of the bishop reaps harvests far more abundant than that of other preachers."[20]

May I presume on your presence to voice a vision of mine for bishops in our fair land? I want your voice to be heard throughout your territory. The way the bishops of California were heard on Proposition 187 that denied education benefits to children of illegal immigrants. Not only through your priests; your own living voice. Such were bishops in the early Church: liturgical leaders, primary preachers. Not necessarily gifted orators; Augustine had a weak voice, tired quickly, was not very orderly. But what he preached he preached passionately, because he lived in Scripture, because he believed what he preached with all his heart, and because he loved the people in front of him as if they were his blood children.

Let your people hear your voice, hear your heart. Not like a dreadful experience of mine. I mean the bishop I heard preach at Catholic University's school-opening Mass of the Holy Spirit. Before several thousand young students, he sat with his miter on, read quietly from the text in his hands, never lifted his eyes. Rubrically correct, utterly orthodox, and...boring beyond belief.

Neumann moved hearts. A century and a half later, bishops can still move hearts. I've experienced it; I've heard you. The grace is there, the Holy Spirit within you. Let's hear it: God's justice proclaimed with the fire of Isaiah, with the love of Jesus.

Mount Angel Seminary
St. Benedict, Oregon
January 5, 1997

33
THE KING'S GOOD SERVANT
BUT GOD'S FIRST
Memorial of St. Thomas More

- 2 Kings 17:5–8, 13–15a, 18
- Matthew 7:1–5

Four decades ago in America, Thomas More was little more than a name. Yes, he had been canonized in 1935, after Pius XI dispensed with the customary miracles. Yes, Chambers' authoritative biography of More had appeared in 1949.[1] Yes, he has become the patron of Catholic lawyers and university students. And a favored few history buffs may remember that on the scaffold More "moved his tangled gray beard carefully out of the way...he said it should not be cut in two because it had done no treason."[2]

But Thomas More is a household name in America today thanks to theater—because a British playwright, Robert Bolt, staged him as *A Man for All Seasons.*[3] Untold thousands can quote "Man [God] made to serve Him wittily, in the tangle of his mind!" Thousands more repeat or revise More's pained, yet amused response to his betrayer, the perjuring friend Sir Richard Rich: "For Wales? Why, Richard, it profits a man nothing to give his soul for the whole world....But for Wales!"

A play can penetrate to the hidden heart of a human; it's alive, it's vivid, it's imaginative, it puts a face to a name. A homily is more difficult; you hear but you do not see. Still, the man that was More must appear. I mean the More who speaks to us forcefully because his life is peppered with paradox and his death defies dying. Three questions: (1) What was Thomas More? (2) Who was Thomas More? (3) Why and how did Thomas More die?[4]

I

First, what was Thomas More? A humanist. A Renaissance humanist who knew Greek and Latin, believed that the best way to write and speak effectively was to study the ancients. England's outstanding humanist, a leader among humanists then centering in London. Bosom friend of Erasmus, "instrumental...in directing Erasmus toward the great works of Biblical and patristic scholarship that were to become his life work."[5] Dear friend of John Colet, who called More "England's only genius."

What was Thomas More? An author. Hundreds of poems and epigrams, a *History of Richard III*,[6] the first *Utopia* in the English language, a treatise on the *Four Last Things,* polemics against English Protestants.

What was Thomas More? A lawyer. Highly competent, a skilful orator, with a reputation for justice and fairness, defender of citizens and guilds, champion of the people in the May Day riots of 1517, royal counselor under Henry VIII, speaker of Parliament, lord chancellor of England. During his two-and-a-half-year tenure of the realm's highest office, more than 4000 cases are on file in the public record office.

What was Thomas More? A devoted family man. He wanted the love of his wife and children, and he received it. His home was a strict academy. Erasmus tells us that no one ever quarreled there and that More never let anyone leave in anger. He educated his children and both his wives mercilessly, made his first wife, Alice, "thoroughly miserable by his dogged insistence that she improve her mind."[7] At meals one of the daughters read from Scripture; Thomas conducted a colloquium on the passage; everyone had to speak.

II

Humanist, author, lawyer, family man—but *who* was Thomas More? Here his biographers are not at peace. One searching researcher finds in him "contradictions stark and numerous" that "at times make him a disappointing hero."[8] He claims that

> No one can sit, as I have done at times, in the New England twilight looking at that strong, sad face [Holbein's portrait] and believe that Thomas More will ever be anything but a stranger to those who study him—this divided man who believed in miracles as long as they happened in the remote past, who wore a

rough hair shirt next to his skin and made his way steadily in a world of ermine and velvet, a man who flagellated himself with whips and made charming talk at dinner, a man who extolled virginity and married twice, who longed for the monastery and became Lord Chancellor, a man who laughed much in public and nursed a private melancholy, a man who died for an ethereal vision of the sacred that has faded quite away in the electric glow of our modernity.[9]

As early as 12, the world was a stage for Thomas. He had a "natural talent for adopting a role, for entering into a situation and yet remaining curiously detached from it."[10] He was ambitious, but did not want anyone to know. He loved people, but never overcame his early longing for the monk he might have been.

The law intrigued him; he rose steadily in his profession. And yet a career in the Church attracted him; he lived for four years with Carthusian monks. He thought of being ordained, but could not shake off his desire for a wife, decided finally, and surely agonizingly, to become a good husband rather than a bad priest. His spirituality was intense, while his nature was closely connected to the senses. Not for him retirement from the world; he would seek God through and in the world. How? In the law and in marriage; in four children by his first wife, in a second marriage six weeks after the death of his first wife. At one hand, love for literature and the life of the spirit; at the other, legal business and royal missions. Here and elsewhere a ceaseless tension.

Some oppose his "lifelong sensibility and repugnance to physical pain" to his ability to send "heretics to a flaming death with alacrity" and afterwards to mock their torments.[11] Others deny that the charges of intolerant cruelty in heresy cases can be supported; he himself insisted he played no role in the ecclesiastical courts where heretics were tried.[12] From his earliest days he brooded over death. At times he was so fearful of death and hell that his life became a prison from which he yearned to escape, worldly pleasures a trap for the soul. And yet, he loved life with profound passion; in the Tower of London he lamented that he had enjoyed the world so thoroughly. More was a complex spirit, some say a haunted man.

III

Why and how did Thomas More die? One historian concludes that "even his death was irony—he a layman offering his head in witness to the unity of the English church with all Christendom, a unity quickly forsaken by all the English bishops save one, his fellow martyr John Fisher."[13]

But Thomas did not yearn for death, did not ask for martyrdom. He would not have echoed the passionate plea of Ignatius of Antioch to the Christians of Rome on his way to the Colosseum 14 centuries earlier:

> I am writing to all the churches and state emphatically to all that I die willingly for God, provided you do not interfere. I beg you, do not show me unseasonable kindness. Suffer me to be the food of wild beasts, which are the means of my making my way to God....Then only shall I be a genuine disciple of Jesus Christ when the world will not see even my body. Petition Christ in my behalf that through these instruments I may prove God's sacrifice.[14]

No, Sir Thomas did not greet death with a resounding welcome. He found it difficult to face death when his wife did not understand, when he had to leave his dear daughter Meg: "You have long known," he told her, "the secrets of my heart." And given the breadth and depth of his professional life, given the thousands he had known and served, even loved, "He parted with more than most men when he parted with his life."[15]

More loved his church. It was for him a ceaseless miracle, its saints a living presence, its unity over centuries and cultures a stupendous reality—all this "robbed death of its victory, and granted a splendor to life."[16] When Parliament passed the Act of Succession on March 23, 1534, an act that declared Henry's marriage to Catherine null from the beginning and his marriage to Anne lawful matrimony; when all of England had to swear an oath to observe and defend not only this act but also the recognition of Henry as Supreme Head of the church in England, Thomas More was left no legal hiding place. His conscience would not allow him to swear. To the great council of the realm, Parliament, he opposed the sacrosanct council of Christendom, the venerable, unbroken tradition of the Catholic Church.

Somehow during these months in prison, Thomas wrote his last great work, *On the Sadness of Christ;* it has survived in his own hand. It is "art brought to the service of life, a literary discipline to strengthen his mind against the horrors of his imagination...a stunning display of More's calm spirit at a time when he was both terribly afraid and indomitably resolute."[17] The theme is pain—the sorrow and fear Christ felt before his death, a Christ who does not demand that we be fearless in death's face. "The brave man bears up under the blows that beset him. The senseless man simply does not feel them when they strike."[18]

I close with parts of a prayer Thomas wrote in the Tower; it reveals the "man for all seasons" simply and economically.

> Give me thy grace, good Lord,
> To set the world at nought;
>
> To set my mind fast upon thee,
> And not to hang upon the blast of men's mouths;
>
> To be content to be solitary,
> Not to long for worldly company;
>
> Little and little utterly to cast off the world,
> And rid my mind of all the business therof;...
>
> Gladly to be thinking of God,
> Piteously to call for his help;
>
> To lean unto the comfort of God,
> Busily to labor to love him;...
>
> To bewail my sins passed,
> For the purging of them patiently to suffer adversity;
>
> Gladly to bear my purgatory here,
> To be joyful of tribulations;
>
> To walk the narrow way that leadeth to life,
> To bear the cross with Christ;
>
> To have the last thing in remembrance,
> To have ever afore mine eye my death that is ever at hand;
>
> To pray for pardon before the judge come,
> To have continually in mind the passion that Christ suffered for me;
>
> For his benefits uncessantly to give him thanks,
> To buy the time again that I before have lost;

Recreations not necessary—to cut off,
Of worldly substance, friends, liberty, life and all,
 to set the loss at right nought for the winning of Christ;

To think my most enemies my best friends,
For the brethren of Joseph could never have done him so
 much good with their love and favor as they did him
 with their malice and hatred;...[19]

John XXIII Pastoral Center
Charleston, West Virginia
June 22, 1998

34

MOHAWK *AND* CHRISTIAN OR MOHAWK/ CHRISTIAN?
Memorial of Bl. Kateri Tekakwitha

- Isaiah 7:1–9
- Matthew 11:20–24

Among the figures immortalized in bronze on the main entrance doors of St. Patrick's Cathedral in New York City, six were chosen to reflect the cosmopolitan character of the Catholic Church in America. There is a Jew, St. Joseph; a Celt, St. Patrick; a Frenchman, St. Isaac Jogues; an Italian, St. Frances Xavier Cabrini; an Anglo-Saxon American, St. Elizabeth Bayley Seton; and an aboriginal, Bl. Kateri Tekakwitha.[1] To celebrate today's memorial of the first Native American to be beatified, a word on Kateri, then a word on us.[2]

I

For all that she lived only 24 years (1656–80), Kateri was an extraordinary Mohawk woman. Since a homily is not a history, let me simply select four significant facets of her life—significant especially for what they can say to you and me.[3]

First, an epidemic. When Kateri was only four, smallpox swept through her village—what is now Auriesville in upstate New York. Not only did the epidemic destroy all her immediate family—her father, her mother, her baby brother; it left Kateri permanently shattered in health. She was nearly blind, could never again endure bright sunlight; her face was scarred by pockmarks. With both parents dead, an uncle and two aunts adopted her.

Second, a conversion. When Kateri was 20, Jesuit missionary Jacques de Lamberville visited her long house, found her eager to hear stories about Jesus and Catholicism, stories that filled out what she had heard while growing up. "For her, it all suggested a new way of being."[4] Christened Kateri, or Katharine, on Easter Sunday 1676, the young convert found local life difficult. Opposed by her family, harassed and ostracized by the villagers, she fled 200 miles to Canada, settled for good with a Christian Mohawk community in a new Caughnawaga, near Montreal. She gave up some Indian activities like hunting, gave herself to daily Mass and Communion, to prayer and fasting, to the sick and elderly, to penances perhaps extreme—barefoot in snow, a bed of thorns, hot coals for burning.

Third, a vow. At 23, Kateri gave heself completely to Christ with a private vow of chastity.[5] She refused marriage in Caughnawaga as she had in Auriesville, declaring now that she would have "no other spouse but Jesus Christ." And this in the midst of breathtaking sexual excess, in a culture where a woman's survival ordinarily depended on a husband.

Fourth, a symbol. What explains Kateri's increasing appeal to contemporary Native Americans of all tribes? Her "heroic survival in situations of human suffering and its evidence of spiritual transformation and personal spiritual power."[6] Native Americans find parallels between her experience and their history. What parallels? Separation at an early age from so much that was familiar—her own family, loss of her father, her mother, her younger and only brother. Misunderstanding, cruel treatment, and persecution by her own relatives after smallpox disfigured her. Courage in the face of adversity, of ridicule for a virginity alien to the Mohawk way of life. Joy in the rituals that bound her ever more closely to the earth. Special concern, in the spirit of the Five Nations, for the orphan, the aged, and the ill.[7] The way she lived her feminine qualities, insisted on being her own person, a Native American Christian woman, no matter the consequences. And so she has become a dynamic symbol, a model for linking Native traditions with the Catholic reality.

II

An epidemic, a conversion, a vow, a symbol—how might they speak to us? Since time is precious, I focus on the vow and the symbol.

The vow. Chastity is not in favor these days. A well-known entertainer names her baby "Chastity," but that's about it for the headlines. TV's *Dawson's Creek* destroys the virtue for teenagers once a week. HBO floods the night hours with raw sex. Hollywood still calls a one-night stand an act of love, looks to see how far it may dare to go tomorrow. Everywhere a little more each year: more flesh, longer sex scenes, hard Rock with its blatant lyrics.

With our commitment to celibacy and to the chastity it involves, we take a radical risk. John Courtney Murray put it pungently in a conference on the religious vows given a half century ago at old Woodstock College in Maryland. The risk in celibacy? Refusing to enter the world of Eve. We risk a premature senility (sex is dead), thinking ourselves whole when we are not. We risk remaining the proverbial bachelor, "crotchety, emotionally unstable, petulant, and self-enclosed."[8]

A persistent question will not go away. Catholic University professor Roger Balducelli put it succinctly 23 years ago: "The questions that now come to occupy center stage are whether celibacy confers any recognizable strength to the religious as a person, any coherence and quality to his life, any effectiveness to his ministry and witness."[9] Put concretely, has celibacy released me for warm human relations that draw people not only to me but to Christ? Has celibacy freed me from a confining absorption in any one person *and* from a "play the field" mentality? Has this surrender to the divine made me more human? Has this particular yes to God become a yes to the world and to life, to spirit and sexuality, to pulsing persons?

I do not mean that the vow or the promise destroys the struggle. The struggle, for most of us, will never end this side of eternity; for the commitment to celibacy demands a ceaseless effort to transcend, to go beyond yourself; you leap with fearful faith into God's unknown. You live it by God's grace, or you do not live it at all. It was true of Kateri; it is equally true of us.

And what of us as symbols? I suggested earlier that Kateri wedded in her life the best of the Native American and the hard core of Catholicism. The new demand on our faith is summed up in a large polysyllable: inculturation. When I was doing doctoral studies at Catholic U. in the 40s, I was fortunate enough to study under an expert in patristics, Johannes Quasten. Under his influence I became aware of a neuralgic missionary concern that confronted the Church as early as the Jewish-Gentile problem in Acts 10 and 11: the attitude of the Church to a foreign culture. In those days Bishop Paul Yu-Pin was pointing out that, although the 17th century saw close to 300,000 Catholics in China, Christianity "could not succeed," because the Church, in striking at ancestor "worship" and reverence for Confucius, was, in the eyes of the people, the cultural invader of China.[10] If the nations that do not know Christ are to accept him in their corporate fulness, accommodation to culture without compromise of creed is a missiological necessity: "the Church must prove that she can engraft the supernatural upon a naturally good tree and can be a profitable foster mother of any genuine culture, no matter what its origin."[11]

Have we strayed from Kateri? Hardly. This young Mohawk was graced by God to live in singular fashion not two lives, Mohawk and Christian, but a single existence that wedded the newness of her faith to what was best in her ancient culture. Such, increasingly, is the missionary task we face in our country. Do you know that the Archdiocese of Los Angeles harbors more than 55 different ethnic groups? Do you sense the problem a diocese named after Our Lady of the Angels faces as it tries to incorporate more than 55 ethnic Madonnas in its new cathedral? Surely your pastoral experience has opened the problem to many of you: not only how to make (say) Mexican immigrants feel at home with *bollitos y café* (coffee and cakes) after a Mass in Spanish; more importantly, how to integrate two or more cultures so as to shape a single Catholic congregation, to make sure there are no strangers among us, to keep "the others" from hastening to a storefront that not only speaks their language but speaks to their deepest needs.

Blessed Kateri, two graces we commend to your powerful intercession. First, pray God that we may value our celibacy, not only as a sign or symbol to a sex-saturated society, but as a God-given way to give ourselves more fully to a whole little world. Second, pray the God who "has given us the ministry of reconciliation" (2 Cor 5:18) to fashion us anew for our time, mediators between cultures, creators of a new type of community, where colors and tongues, smells and styles, weave a Catholic symphony that gives ceaseless praise to a Creator infinite in imagination, limitless in love.

San Alfonso Retreat Center
West End, New Jersey
July 14, 1998

35
ALWAYS GIVEN UP TO DEATH FOR JESUS' SAKE
Memorial of North American Martyrs

- 2 Corinthians 4:7–15
- Matthew 28:16–20

Eight saints, eight martyrs. Six of them Jesuits, two lay associates. Happily for this native New Yorker, three of them shed their blood in our own New York State, near Auriesville: Isaac Jogues, René Goupil, and Jean de la Lande. The other five were martyred in then New France, now Canada: Jean de Brébeuf, Antoine Daniel, Gabriel Lalement, Charles Garnier, and Noël Chabanel.

Each of these eight is a fascinating character in his own right, each worth a special homily. But time is our enemy. So then, this evening not eight words but three: (1) a word from Jogues; (2) a word on Chabanel; (3) a word for today's priest in the United States.[1]

I

Jogues came to the New World twice. Assigned to the Huron missions in Canada in 1636, he was captured by the hostile Iroquois. Rather than be bored by cold statistics, listen to snatches from Jogues's own experience in a graphic letter to his provincial superior in France:

> [Surrounded by Iroquois,] I, who was barefoot, would not and could not flee, not willing to forsake a Frenchman and the Hurons. After the Hurons had been instructed in the faith, I baptized them. [The Iroquois] burned one of my fingers and crushed another with their teeth; and the others they so twisted that even at present, although partly healed, they are crippled

175

and deformed. Hunger accompanied us always; we passed three days without any food.

It would have been easy for René Goupil and me to flee, with the hope, if not of returning to ours, at least of dying more easily in the woods. But he refused to do so, and I would rather suffer every pain than abandon my French and Huron Christians to death.

Two nails had been left me; they tore these out with their teeth. René, who was not very nimble, received so many blows, especially in the face, that nothing was seen of him but the whites of his eyes. A woman, a Christian slave, was ordered to cut off my thumb. At first she refused, but then was compelled to do so. Then I, taking with my other hand the amputated thumb, offered it to you, my living and true God.

[At another village] they led us into a cabin, where they commanded us to sing. It was necessary to obey and to sing, "but of the canticles of the Lord in a land of exile." From singing they came to torments; they burned me with coals and live ashes, especially on the breast; and they bound me upright between two stakes. In that torture, being almost left to myself alone, I wept.

For seven days they had been leading us from village to village, made a spectacle to God and to the angels, when finally we were notified of death by fire, news assuredly full of horror, but softened by the thought of the divine will and by the hope of a better life.[2]

A prisoner among the Mohawks, an apostle in slavery, in constant peril of death, he was ransomed by the Dutch of Fort Orange (Albany) in 1643. Against his wishes, at least in the beginning. As he wrote to his provincial,

Who in my absence would console the French captives? Who absolve the penitent? Who remind the christened Huron of his duty? Who instruct the prisoners constantly brought in? Who baptize them dying, encourage them in their torments? Who cleanse the infants in the saving waters? Who provide for the salvation of the dying adult, the instruction of those in health? Indeed I cannot but think it a peculiar interposition of divine goodness that...I should have fallen into the hands of these Indians.... Since the time when I was taken, I have baptized seventy persons...of five different nations and languages, that of "every tribe and people and tongue they might stand in the sight of the Lamb."[3]

Jogues escaped to New York, sailed from New York to France. Though his hand was mutilated, Pope Urban VIII granted him a dispensation to celebrate Mass, saying, "It would be shameful for a martyr of Christ not to drink the blood of Christ."

Enough is enough, you say. But not for Isaac Jogues. One spring later, early in 1644, he was back in Canada, entrusted with a peace mission. To whom but...the Iroquois! On September 24 he departed for Ossernenon (our Auriesville), determined to return to the Mohawks as missionary. Waylaid two days before his arrival by Mohawks who blamed their poor crops and epidemic on his box of pious articles, he was stripped and maltreated. Invited to a meal on the evening of October 18, he was tomahawked as he entered the cabin. His head was cut off and put on one of the palisades, facing the route over which he had come.

II

A brief word on Noël Chabanel, if only because he has attracted me mightily for half a century. Picture him: a brilliant professor of rhetoric in France, apparently very sensitive, transported to a wilderness. He detested the Huron way of life: the smoke and the vermin, the filth in the food and the utter absence of privacy. The noise around the lodgefire, the howling dogs, the screeching children—no way could he study. He had no gift for learning the Huron language; five years of tortured effort had little effect, ended pretty much where he had begun. A seductive temptation assailed him: Quit these hostile woods, leave the Hurons to their savage ways, return to France where people will appreciate you. When the temptation refused to go away, Chabanel took a vow of stability, bound himself to remain in Canada to the day of his death. His own words: "I do vow, in the presence of the most holy sacrament of your precious body and blood,...to remain perpetually attached to this mission of the Hurons."

Naturally timid, Chabanel found himself wholly indifferent to danger. He had expressed a desire to be "a martyr in obscurity," unknown, forgotten. And so, for a time, it happened. His fate was shrouded in mystery, until an apostate Huron admitted that he had murdered Chabanel, had robbed him of his clothes and books and papers, had thrown his body into a river. Why? Because he hated the Christian faith.[4]

III

Amazing, breathtaking, sobering. But have these North American martyrs anything significant to say to priests in North America today? To you? Edifying, of course, inspirational. But today's Native Americans are hardly a threat to our parish priests; your consecrated thumbs are not at risk. New York State's perilous forests have been paved over for New York State's Thruway, drums rarely beat along the Mohawk, and Ossernenon the camp is Auriesville the shrine.

Given this transition, let me suggest one area for your reflection. In my long love affair with early Christianity and the Fathers of the Church, one historical development caught my fancy more than most. I mean the movement from martyr to monk. After the year 313, with peace a fresh blessing for the Church, martyrdom in blood became a rare way to God. In its place came bloodless martyrdom. And here pride of place rested with the monk.[5] Total self-giving to Christ out of love; complete sacrifice of self; constant ascetic practices; few if any creature comforts; the cross over and in the monastery; "no pain, no gain." Not the blood of teenage Agnes but the asceticism of centenarian Anthony. Not 86-year-old Polycarp burned on a pyre and stabbed to death but Jerome and Paula building a monastery and a convent in Bethlehem.

> The ascetic ideal, the challenge of complete severance from the world, of surrender to Christ in poverty and chastity, had haunted [Jerome] ever since he had glimpsed it at Trier. To be a monk was for him to possess the Lord and absolutely nothing else, and in return to be himself possessed by the Lord. He saw the monk, like the martyr, undergoing a second baptism, a total immolation of self which cleansed him from all the sins committed since the first.[6]

As I crisscross our country month after month, the reality of the parish priest as martyr ceaselessly intrudes. Not the monastic martyr; the martyr on the front lines. I realize that the word "martyr" can conjure up weird connotations: self-pity, neurotic lust for immolation. But the genuine Christian reality is strikingly different. The martyr, by definition, is a witness. A witness whose actions speak much louder than words. A disciple who, like his Master, takes up his cross daily.

Such, I insist, is today's parish priest. For you not only follow the Crucified at the close of your earth-bound existence; you share in

Jesus' dying by sharing in his cross through the whole of your priestly existence. Not only physical pain—sinusitis or ileitis, angina pectoris or terminal cancer. I mean, concretely, the agonies that nail so many of you to your crosses today: the challenge of celibacy, constant criticism from the pews, loss of status and respect, unrealistic expectations, a gnawing feeling of ineffectiveness, closing of schools and churches, burnout from too much ministry and too little prayer, the insecurities now associated with priestly aging. My point is this: The crosses that constitute our calvaries are not negatives, to be avoided at all costs. The cross of Christ was not defeat; the cross of Christ is the feast we celebrate each September 14: The *Triumph* of the Cross. Our acclamation after the Consecration is crucial: "Dying, you destroyed our death." Jesus' resurrection did not change defeat into victory; it simply put God's seal on the cross as victory: victory over sin, over self, over death. The cross itself.

And so for you and me. The crosses that characterize priestly ministry today are terribly real, have forced thousands from our fraternity. Not my place to pass judgment on any of them. My point is, it is primarily through our crosses, through apparent defeat, that the Church inches toward the kingdom.

A striking example: the Jewish convert Edith Stein gassed in Auschwitz and canonized nine days ago. Her life as a Carmelite reflected the name she requested: Teresia Benedicta a Cruce, Teresa Blessed by the Cross. "More and more she would be drawn into what she would later call *Kreuzewissenschaft,* the 'science of the cross,' the mystery of joy in suffering, of victory in failure, of dying and rising with Christ."[7]

> Certainly there is no denying Edith Stein's gifts and accomplishments.... Still more striking are the innumerable separations, setbacks and disappointments she endured and the countless unexpected turns her journey took.... Scarcely anything turned out exactly as she anticipated except, ironically, her death at the hands of the Nazi regime.[8]

For Edith Stein, what was the life of a Christian? "To suffer and to be happy although suffering, to have one's feet on the earth, to walk on the dirty and rough paths of the earth and yet to be enthroned with Christ at the Father's right hand, to laugh and cry with the children of this world and ceaselessly sing the praises of God with the choirs of angels."[9]

Such, my brothers, is the demand on today's parish priest. To borrow from Jogues's letter: Who in your absence would console the captives? Who absolve the penitent? Who remind the christened of their duty? Who instruct the prisoners? Who cleanse the infants, baptize the dying, instruct the healthy? And in memory of Chabanel: Amid so much that repels, that discourages, that causes priests to cry "Who needs this?," that tempts so many to return to greener pastures, a God-given courage, perhaps even a promise, to remain with your people. Paradoxically, precisely because of the cross. Because it is the cross itself that saves. On this score Paul's emotional address to the Christians of Corinth leaves no room for doubt:

> We are afflicted in every way, but not crushed; perplexed, but not driven to despair; persecuted, but not forsaken; struck down, but not destroyed; always carrying in the body the death of Jesus, so that the life of Jesus may also be made visible in our bodies. For while we live, we are always being given up to death for Jesus' sake, so that the life of Jesus may be made visible in our mortal flesh.
>
> (2 Cor 4:8–11)

Amen, my brothers. So was it for eight North American martyrs. So be it for you and me.

Don Bosco Retreat Center
West Haverstraw, New York
October 19, 1998

Wedding Homilies

36
IT TAKES SO MUCH MORE
TO HAVE A MARRIAGE
Wedding Homily 1

- Song of Songs 8:6–7
- Colossians 3:12–17
- John 15:9–17

Thirteen days ago I was still struggling. What of significance might this celibate male say to this man and this woman about to link their love for life? Restless, frustrated, I was punching my remote control from channel to channel. For some reason—coincidence or providence—I stopped in the middle of..."Touched by an Angel." The scene: only minutes before a wedding ceremony. The bride-to-be had panicked, was paralyzed by anxiety. How could she possibly say "for ever"? All her experience protested, "Nothing lasts for ever." Especially when her own mother and father had divorced.

At that moment the efficient lady in charge of all arrangements suddenly remembered, uttered aloud, the one thing she had forgotten: one invitation. An invitation to...God. Taking up on this, the angel (Della Reese, I believe) said to the bride, "Anybody can have a wedding, but it takes so much more to have a marriage."

Touched by an angel, I turned from tube to IBM Word. How expand on those two insights: an invitation to God, and the "so much more" it takes to have a marriage? Three ideas swept swiftly in—reflections based on three passages from God's own Book— the passages carefully chosen by David and Jill and just proclaimed to you. A word on each.

I

"So much more." First, a verse from the Song of Songs. The Song, author unknown, is a set of love songs. They sing of human loving. Not love on Cloud Nine, not love in theological abstractions. No, sensuous, erotic, the thoughts, the language, the feelings of a man and woman passionately in love.

Some Christians are embarrassed: How dare we sing such songs in a sanctuary, in God's presence? Happily for us, God is not embarrassed. It is God who inspired the author to sing of a love that pervades the whole person, all of a man and a woman—a love that refuses to see the flesh as something evil, a thing of shame.

Specifically, one swift sentence from one of those songs may have escaped you when you heard it moments ago: "Love is a flame of the Lord" (Cant 8:6). The fire of love is a fire of Yahweh; human love is a sharing in the Lord's own white-hot love.[1] Jill and David, the love that flames between you is indeed human, wonderfully and fearfully human. Still, that love is not sheerly your own creation. In shaping you, God made you images of God, fashioned you in the likeness of God's own loving, each capable of loving somewhat as God loves, with your total self, with something of the flaming intensity with which God loves. And your love, at its best, should sing to you what God's love must be like.

David and Jill, treasure those inspired songs. Make them your own. They pose a loving challenge to Elvis Presley's "Love Me Tender," add a depth to Andrew Lloyd Webber's "Love Changes Everything." For they tell you why genuine love, tender love, changes everything: True love is a flame of the Lord; true love is divine love in a human heart.

II

"So much more." A second facet is the passage from Paul. The apostle Paul brings the lyrical Song of Songs down to everyday reality; he confronts love with the chilling challenges to love. And one ceaseless challenge to love comes in one tough demand: "If anyone has a complaint against another, forgive each other; just as the Lord has forgiven you, so you also must forgive" (Col 3:13). Do you remember the film *Love Story*? Hollywood sent a sentence pulsing through romantic America: "Love means never having to say you're sorry." Sorry, good friends. Love on earth, love among humans, is an endless "I'm sorry." You cannot live in close quarters year after year without irritation, without misunderstanding, disagreement, conflict. And love on earth, if it is to last, is an endless response, "And I, dear heart, forgive you."

If you would see the problem in celluloid, watch the "soaps." Forgive? That's for weaklings, for losers. "The bold and the beautiful" curse and scream; "the young and the restless" refuse to listen, respond savagely or with ice-cold silence; those with "one life to live" turn their backs on excuses, explanations.

David and Jill, your model of forgiveness is another human, a flesh-and-blood like you in almost every way. Your model of forgiveness is a man who beyond anyone else had a right to condemn, a reason to refuse forgiveness. A man who was whipped like a dog, crowned with thorns, pinned to a cross between two criminals. And from that cross, from tortured lips we hear a whisper that no one of us should ever forget: "Father, forgive them, for they do not know what they are doing" (Lk 23:34). To forgive is not primarily a work of reason; it is an act of love. The poet was on target: "to forgive is divine." It is a sharing in God's own love, Christ's own forgiving.

To forgive is for weaklings? Quite the contrary. Forgiveness stems from strength, because it leaps from love, a type of love made possible by a God-man crucified because he dared to love against all reason.

III

"So much more." A third facet is the startling command of Jesus, "Love one another as I have loved you" (Jn 15:12). The sentence falls trippingly from our lips; the final phrase should jolt us. I am to love as Jesus loved.

Jill and David: From what I've said thus far, it should be clear that wedded love, your wedded love, is a unique union of two persons turned totally to each other and together turned tenderly to God. But wedded love, your love, has to have a third turning. It will be symbolized in the recessional, when together you turn...outward. That turning is not, in the first instance, a swift movement to Longwood before we thirsty folk get to the liquid refreshments. The recessional is a movement: from church to world, from altar to people, from Christ crucified on Calvary to Christ crucified at the crossroads of our country. A woman psychologist stressed this strongly a decade and a half ago:

> A love that is not for more than itself will die—the wisdom of
> Christian tradition and the best we know from psychology both

assure us of this truth. It is often very appropriate at the early
stages of a relationship that the energy of romance and infatua-
tion exclude the larger world from our vision. But over the long
haul an intimate relationship...which doesn't reach outward will
stagnate.[2]

Outside these sacred walls, almost anywhere you go, there will
be a "tale of two cities." There is the area of peace and prosperity, of
life and love, of work and play, which most of us are privileged to
inhabit. And there is the area where other images of God are living
in various forms of hell. One example. In my own back yard, the
District of Columbia, children are preparing their own funerals—
where they will be waked, how they will be dressed, how they will
look. Why? Because in one five-year period more than 200 of their
playmates have been killed by gunfire. In consequence, the survivors
do not expect to live very long, do not expect to grow up.

David and Jill: I cannot, I dare not, tell you precisely where your
recessional ought to take you. I only know that somewhere out there
is a child physically or sexually abused, a teenager dreadfully drug-
addicted, an HIV-positive begging for blood or crying for compassion, a grown man grubbing in garbage cans for scraps of food, an
elderly widow lonely for the touch of a caring hand, the sound of a
human voice.

The needs are endless—political and personal, economic and
educational. But, believe it or not, this is not a sad coda to today's
glad symphony. Rarely will your two-in-one union feel so close, be so
expressive, as when you have brought love to a child who has never
experienced love. Rarely will you realize your calling as committed
Christians more realistically than when together you have given
hope to the hopeless, the homeless, the helpless.

This it is to love as Jesus loved—the love Jesus spelled out when
he told us how we will be judged: "*I* was hungry and you gave me
food; *I* was thirsty and you gave me drink; *I* was a stranger and you
welcomed me; *I* was naked and you clothed me; *I* was sick and you
visited me; *I* was in prison and you came to me" (Mt 25:35–36). Such
is your calling: not to lay down your life for sisters and brothers, only
to live for them. Such is your role in the mission of Jesus as John the
Evangelist summed it up: Jesus was to die not only for his nation but
"to gather together the dispersed children of God" (Jn 11:51–52).

Allow me, Jill and David, a swift summary. (1) You are turned
to each other in a love that is a flame of the white-hot love of the
Lord. (2) You are ready to express your love as Jesus did: forgiving
each other as he has forgiven you. (3) You are challenged to open

your love outward: indeed to the dear ones who surround you in love today, but also to the unnumbered who are mutely begging for your love to make them whole. And so you are singularly gifted to make your marriage a threefold gift for ever: to God, to each other, and to a whole little world.

Come, then, Jill and David, proclaim to the world what is already spoken in your hearts.

Trinity Episcopal Church
Upperville, Virginia
June 14, 1997

37
A MIRACLE, A MYSTERY, A MIND-SET
Wedding Homily 2

- 1 Corinthians 14:1, 6–12
- Ephesians 5:21–33
- John 2:1–11

In a Catholic wedding ceremony such as this there is a particular peril. The gathering of so many friends from distant places, relatives of all ages reunited, your very joy in the joy of Ellen and Joe— so much can distract you from the words uttered from a pulpit, from the Word of God proclaimed ever so powerfully. Understandable. And yet regrettable. Why? Not only because you may have missed a message from your Creator. Also because these three readings were chosen by Joe and Ellen with uncommon care—chosen not because they were compelled to select three readings, but because the readings they chose tell us in an unusual way, in inspired language, what their marriage means to them. So then, let me focus a few moments on each of those inspired readings; for each has a depth, says something precious for wedded love, that may not be immediately apparent.

I

I begin with the marriage feast at Cana. Like Joe and Ellen, I find it a fascinating story. (1) It's a wedding, and almost everybody loves a wedding. (2) The guests are unusual, if not unique: God's very own Son in flesh, his mother, even his disciples. (3) Another surprise: The wine runs out. Too many thirsty disciples? (4) A genuine Jewish mother. Her Son has shrugged off her delicately phrased suggestion, "They have no wine" (Jn 2:3). She says to the waiters: "You see that good-looking fellow over there, talking to a couple of fishermen? That's my boy, and he can do things you won't find in your wine books." (5) The water-made-wine tastes better than what the bride's father had provided.

Cana is more than a promise that today the wine will not run out. If you know John, the Gospel's author, you know there's more here than meets the eye. Symbolism is the air John breathes.[1] For John, this is the first of Jesus' "signs," the first of his miracles. And what was its effect? "His disciples believed in him" (Jn 2:11). Water-into-wine had the same purpose all his other miracles had: It told them something about Jesus.

I trust that this wedding celebration, in the context of a bread and wine changed into the body and blood of God's Son, will tell you something about him. About his care for you. For I see your adventure not as coincidence but as providence. Oh yes, it looks like chance: that New Orleans and Milwaukee should come together; that you should meet on St. Patrick's Day and start dating on St. Joseph's Day; that on July 12 Louisiana State University and Notre Dame should meet here in endless love before they attack on November 15; that New Orleans jazz should link its sounds with the rock 'n' roll of The Who. No, our good Lord did not play you like pieces of chess. But clearly his grace has been your guide, has directed you to decisions you could not have predicted, has helped fashion your freedom so that shortly you will stand before him together to utter a yes for ever to each other and to him.

You know, the changes in both of you over the years, the changes that have shaped you into your "two in one flesh," these changes are a miracle more difficult than changing 120 gallons of water into just as much wine. For the miracle at Cana changed water that could not possibly resist the power of God's Son. Today's miracle has shaped a unity between a man and a woman who were always free to say no to God's gracious offer of human loving. Believe it! Believe what you have experienced: It is in the power of Jesus Christ that you are able freely to share your love totally, without reservation, till life itself leaves you.

Ellen and Joe: Shift your admiration from Cana in Galilee to Washington in the District of Columbia. Thank God not for water made to blush into wine; thank God for a party that transformed a cool handshake into endless love.

II

Second, I focus on Paul's letter to the Christians of Ephesus. The passage is not a favorite among even moderate feminists: "Wives, be subject to your husbands as you are to the Lord" (Eph 5:22). Not a favorite even though Paul has just said, "Be subject to *one another* out of reverence for Christ" (v. 21). The deeper problem is not the cultural problem—family relationships in the time of Jesus. The deeper problem is a later sentence in the passage from Paul: "[Marriage] is a great mystery, and I take it to mean Christ and the Church" (v. 32). Very simply, this union in one flesh between two Christians, on what should it be modeled? On the union between Christ and the Church, between Christ and the People of God.

What can this possibly mean? Look at the link between Christ and the Church. It is so close that St. Paul calls Christians the "body" of Christ. Recall Paul's startling statement to the Christians of Corinth: "Just as the [human] body is one and has many members, and all the members of the body, though many, are one body, so it is with Christ. For in the one [Holy] Spirit we were all baptized into one body—Jews or Greeks, slaves or free—and we were all made to drink of one [Holy] Spirit" (1 Cor 12:12–13). For this body, for this church, for all of us, out of sheer love, Christ died. And because he died for us, all of us should live for him.

Such is the oneness that should link Ellen and Joe. To the extent that it resembles its model, it is a union not for today and tomorrow but for ever, a love that will not end, will only grow stronger with the years. And to the extent that it imitates its model, it is a sacrificial love. I mean a love that deepens with suffering, the love Jesus described when he said, "Greater love than this no one has, to lay down one's life for those one loves" (Jn 15:13). The love Jesus not only described but modeled when, all but naked on a cross, he gasped out his life for every human from Adam and Eve through Magdalene and Judas to the last man and woman who will touch this earth with their love or their hate.

In all probability, neither of you will be called to die for the other. It may be more difficult still to live for each other; for this involves a ceaseless dying to your self, to your way of doing things, your way of loving, your way of understanding the relationship between Christ and his church. Always remember that both of you have been shaped in the likeness of Christ; each of you is to work out that likeness in his or her way. Not become more like the other, only more like Christ. Not identical clones of Christ, only Christlike as the Christ within you shapes you.

III

Third, I resonate to St. Paul's advice to the Christians of Corinth, "If in a tongue you utter speech that is not intelligible, how will anyone know what is being said? For you will be speaking into the air" (1 Cor 14:9). I know from Joe that this counsel confirms his conviction and Ellen's that a marriage will not endure if a husband and wife do not communicate effectively. And those of you who know Joe as I do know that for him communication is not effective if clarity is absent, if the sounds are not clear, if he does not know what the person across from his favorite hamburger is saying—coworker, Jesuit, wife. Joe's point is well taken. Joe and Ellen share a recent history where only open, utterly clear sharing of their problems made this glorious day possible. I can only hope, half-humorously, that Joe is not linking too literally to his marriage another sentence of St. Paul in the same context: "If the bugle gives an indistinct sound, who will get ready for battle?" (v. 8).

But surely Joe suspects that clarity alone is not enough for effective communication. Joe and Ellen realize that clarity itself is "speaking into the air" if the other person is not listening. Most conversations, I insist, are not conversations at all. Either they are monologues: I wait patiently until you have finished—since civility demands it—and then I say exactly what I would have said had you not spoken at all. Or they are debates: I do indeed listen, but only for that inept word or false phrase at which I proceed to intercept and destroy.

A prime example? The "soaps" that seduce college students and busy housewives five early afternoons a week. If "The Bold and the Beautiful," "The Young and the Restless," "One Life to Live" reflect family life in America, reproduce "communication" between man and woman, we are in deep trouble. The bugles sound for battle; voices are raised together in boiling heat; shoulders are shrugged and backs are turned; a stinging retort and he or she bursts from the room in angry triumph.

No, listening is an arduous art. Why? Because to really listen is to give yourself totally, for that moment or that day, to another, to put yourself into the other's mind, yes the other's heart. It means that you never hear naked words, always a human person. Listening is an act of love.

Remember Helen Keller? Blind...deaf...mute. "Listening" by sheer touch to Annie Sullivan. Listening in sheer desperation, because her life depended on it. Yes, Ellen and Joe, your life, your love, depends on your ability, your willingness, your longing to listen, to actually hear what the one you love is saying. Not always to agree with it; more importantly, to hear the love so often hidden in it.

Good friends all, let me sum up. Today we are privileged to share a miracle, a mystery, and a mind-set. Today we marvel at a miracle—not of water made wine, but of two made one. Today we bend low in awe before a mystery—not an intellectual puzzle, only two splendidly ordinary people symbolizing in their self-giving the sacrificial love that links God's Son with God's people. And today we pray for an ever-deepening mind-set: that with the gift of clarity and the art of listening—words that are clear and hearts open to hear—this marriage will send a message to a culture that all too often puts "me" before "we," claims as America's virtue "prudent self-interest." No, dear Lord, let Ellen and Joe reveal to their world, reveal to us, how each word spoken, each word heard, can be, must be, an act of love.

Come then, Joe and Ellen, come and in the loving presence of the Lord you love, join your hands and your hearts now and for ever.

Church of St. Aloysius Gonzaga
Washington, D.C.
July 12, 1997

38

IN GOD'S IMAGE, TO GOD'S LIKENESS
Wedding Homily 3

- Genesis 2:18–24
- Colossians 3:12–17
- John 15:9–17

Some moments ago something momentous happened to you and me. It happened so swiftly I'm afraid some of us missed it. What happened? God spoke to us. Yes, God...spoke...to us. Oh it's true, we did not see God; I at least did not. But God did speak. God spoke to us three times—from the only book God ever wrote. And what God said was not simply something "real nice" for a church service. What God said was terribly important for Liz and John, for every couple that has ever thought of saying yes to each other for life, every couple that has actually said yes. Interested? Then mull with me over those three divine utterances: (1) God speaking in a garden, (2) God speaking through an apostle, (3) God in flesh speaking with human lips.

I

First, listen to God in a garden—a garden we call Paradise. On some depressed evening, when you're tempted to wonder why God made you or anyone else, listen to a single sentence from that garden, one of the most significant sentences about yourself you'll ever hear: "God said: 'Let us make humankind in our image, to our likeness'" (Gen 1:26). Ever since then, ever since humanity's birth, every human person has come into this world like God. Not always looking divine. But in point of fact, like God.

Whatever might that mean? For centuries we strange creatures called theologians have struggled to understand what God meant, struggled at times unto frustration. One explanation among many makes special sense to me, rich sense for today's celebration. You and I are like God because we have the capacity to love: to love God, to love one another.[1] The First Letter of John is strong on this:

> Whoever does not love does not know God, for God is Love.
> ...In this is love, not that we loved God but that God loved us and sent His Son to be the atoning sacrifice for our sins. Beloved, since God loved us so much, we also ought to love one another.... If we love one another, God lives in us, and His love is perfected in us.
>
> (1 Jn 4:8, 10–12)

That gift reached new meaning when God said, "It is not good that the man should be alone; I will make him a helper as his partner" (Gen 2:18). For God did not make male only, or female only, or something in-between. "Male and female [God] created them" (Gen 1:27). Our imaginative God shaped not one human, but two. Similar, but not the same. Shaped each of you, shaped Liz and John, in such a way that through your love each of you might become more and more like God. Not more and more like each other; more and more like God.

Liz and John, you differ so much—in flesh and spirit, in piercing blue eyes and easygoing brown, in the way you think and the things you like. Thank God you are not the same. Why? Because God wanted each of you to reflect God's wondrous beauty in different ways. What God said to you thousands of years ago was simply and strikingly this: Let your love for each other fashion the other more and more like God. A God whose name is Love. Such is your vocation. Such is one profound meaning of marriage. Two become one so that the more dearly you love each other, the more deeply will each of you resemble God.

II

Second, listen to God speaking through an apostle. Listen because a fiery little fellow called Paul takes what God said in a lovely, sinless, peaceful garden, "Let us make man and woman like God," and brings it to life for John and Liz on a lusty, hyperactive, sleepless island where they will live their love for now. Paul is speaking to Christians of Colossae, a little town in Asia Minor; but his charge reaches out to the Big Apple. "Put to death whatever is earthy in you: impurity, greed, anger, malice, slander, abusive language. Do not lie to one another." Why not? "Because you have stripped off the old self, have clothed yourselves with the new self, which is being made new in the image of [your] Creator" (Col 3:5–10).

What does that mean in concrete living? Listen to Paul: "As God's chosen ones, holy and beloved, clothe yourselves with compassion, kindness, patience. If you have a complaint against the other, forgive, just as the Lord has forgiven you" (vv. 12–13). And then the clincher: "Above all, clothe yourselves with love, which binds everything together in perfect harmony" (v. 14).

Liz and John, it is not on some idyllic island in a paradise that your love for each other must not only survive but come alive. The Big Apple is today's tree of good and evil. Without the words, Paul admits that love is indeed in the wine and the roses. But day after day love lives or dies in what you do where you live and breathe, what you do with your awfully human anger, your impatience over little things like snoring in sleep or socks in the shower, your resentment over the shrugged shoulder, the birthday forgotten, the casual kiss. And whether, as time goes on, work becomes your home, home your work. Not so much Walker Percy's *Love amid the Ruins;* rather love amid the routine, where the magic and mystery of the other disappears, where you take each other for granted, where "like God" gets lost in the "real" world—the demands of Paine Webber, a classroom of devilish angels at Marymount, or just the asphalt jungle.

The "peace of Christ" Paul wants to "rule in your hearts" (v. 15), the peace you will need in the paradox of New York, comes not from a high IQ or a Brite smile, not from a stiff upper lip or TV's "Guiding Light." The peace of Christ is Christ's alone to give; for, Paul tells us, "Christ *is* our peace" (Eph 2:14). Peace is a oneness with Christ that grows as you come to be more and more like Christ. Christ within you, Christ all around you, Christ in your sisters and brothers.

III

Christ in your sisters and brothers. It forces on you God's third word. Listen to God in flesh speaking with human lips, Christ our Lord commanding, "Love one another as I have loved you" (Jn 15:12).

Two weeks ago I revisited Manhattan. I walked the streets of my adolescence, dined in Gallagher's, breakfasted in Lindy's, taped a video in the HBO building. And I thought: St. Paul could never have imagined the redemption wrought by Jesus being played out on an island where eight million people hustle, rustle, and muscle each day. More colors, more sounds, more smells than Jesus ever experienced. Billboards have you repeating "I love New York." Now "I love New York" is a potentially powerful phrase. But it's more than a way of saying "New York has everything anybody could possibly want": Broadway and Lincoln Center, bagels and bread pretzels, the *Daily News* and *Rolling Stone,* Madison Avenue and Madison Square Garden, Wall Street and the Staten Island ferry. New York is a place where deaf Mexican immigrants live and work under slave conditions; where 12,000 runaway youngsters flee to Covenant House each year, pimped, prostituted, angel-dusted; where schools resemble armed camps and drug stops; where elderly men and women dig for food in garbage cans.

What has all this to do with your love? Listen to an experienced woman psychologist:

> A love that is not for more than itself will die—the wisdom of Christian tradition and the best we know from psychology both assure us of this truth. It is often very appropriate at the early stages of a relationship that the energy of romance and infatuation exclude the larger world from our vision. But over the long haul an intimate relationship...which doesn't reach outward will stagnate.[2]

"A love that is not for more than itself will die." I will never cease insisting how splendidly symbolic the recessional of a wedding is. When Liz and John move down the aisle to the strains of Handel's *Water Music,* it will not be a swift run to the Kelleher bar before we selfish folk get there. The recessional is a movement from church to world, from altar to people, from Christ crucified on Calvary to Christ crucified in the slums and on the sidewalks of New York.

John and Liz: God has gifted you in so many wondrous ways— love from parents and grandparents, stimulus from siblings, minds that opened to God's creation at Georgetown and Bucknell, support from friends, work that pleasures you. You are gifted indeed. Still, God's gifts are given not to be clutched but to be shared. It's not an invitation; it's a command: Love others as Jesus has loved and loves you. Love others. Not only such as surround you today, those who are like you and who like you; rather the less fortunate, those who share more of Jesus' crucifixion than of his resurrection. I dare not predict who these might be; I leave it to the Lord to show you. I do commend to you America's children, God's most vulnerable images; for in the richest nation on earth one of every four children is living in poverty, living in some form of hell. Bring hope to the eyes of one hopeless child, bring love to one little image of God who has never known love's touch, and your own love will grow a hundredfold.

Let me sum up. Yes, Liz and John, God has spoken to you, spoken to your life together, spoken three times. (1) Let your love for each other shape the other more and more like God. (2) Let your linked love for our Lord bring the peace of Christ into your hearts. (3) Let your love for others expand your horizons, touch you to the troubled, befriend the less fortunate, bring the compassionate Christ to the crippled in flesh and spirit.

A final word. Earlier this week, in Arles in France, the world's oldest person died. Her age? 122. At 85 she took up fencing; at 100 she was still riding a bicycle; at 121 she released a rap CD, "Time's Mistress." What intrigues me most? Blind, almost deaf, in a wheelchair, she could say, "I have never been bored."[3] Liz and John: Focus on God's vision of marriage, live the way God has spoken to you today, and I promise you—what? Not a hundred wedded years. I promise you, your marriage will never be boring. You won't have *time* to be bored!

Holy Cross Church
Rumson, New Jersey
August 9, 1997

39

YOU CANNOT LOVE LIKE JESUS UNLESS...
Wedding Homily 4

- Romans 12:9–21
- 1 Corinthians 12:31–13:1-13
- John 15:9–12

Good friends all: A wondrous thing has just happened to all of you; you may not have noticed it. Christ our Lord has just spoken to you. Not in a vision, not in a dream. Still, he has spoken to you. The Second Vatican Council said so in one striking sentence: "Jesus Christ is present in his word, since it is Christ himself who speaks when the holy Scriptures are read in the church."[1] Believe it! And Jesus has spoken through three passages that Susie and Gerry have selected—selected because in these three passages Christ speaks eloquently to the union, the oneness, they are about to vow for life.

One word holds all three texts together; not surprisingly, that word is "love." But each text has its own special way of talking about love. Together they reveal God's mind on three questions: (1) Why is love so all-important for Susie and Gerry? (2) What does genuine love demand of them? (3) How should Jesus enter their married love?

I

First, why is love so all-important for Susie and Gerry? The answer lies in St. Paul's extraordinary tribute to love, what was read to you from his first letter to the Christians of Corinth. The problem is, the passage is read so often at weddings that it becomes trite, hackneyed, a cliché. And yet, it expresses in high rhetoric a principle basic for Christian living, a truth essential for every Christian, a reality that must be lived if a marriage is to endure. Let me rephrase what Paul says as we might put it today:

If I can speak with the rolling thunder of Jesse Jackson, if I can preach with the passion of Martin Luther King's "I Have a Dream," but do not love, I am only a harsh, terribly loud noise raping our planet. If I can tell you, predict to our world, what the next century will be like, if like another Einstein I can disentangle the deepest mysteries of science from DNA to cloning, if I have a faith as strong as Jesus' faith, strong enough to move the Rockies, but do not love, "I am nothing" (1 Cor 13:2), a cipher, zero. If I give everything I own to the poor, if I rot in prison a political prisoner for three decades like Africa's Mandela, but do not love, it will do me no good whatsoever; it's all sheer waste.

That is why this evening's celebration is so significant. Not only for you and me; significant for this dear couple's varied worlds, for Columbia and New York City, for Louisville and Mexico City.[2] You see, when Susie and Gerry look at each other and murmur those momentous monosyllables "I do," they will murmur more than a business contract, more than a list, in large letters and fine print, of what each must do and may not do if the contract is not to be broken. It is more than a guarantee against loneliness in old age, more than an approved way of producing little images of themselves, cute Susans and handsome Gerardos. Wedded love is a gift a man and a woman offer to each other, a gift for ever, not of diamonds however precious but of their total selves. "All I am I give to you, in good times and bad, in joy and sorrow, in sickness and health, in poverty and wealth, till death do us part."

II

A second question: What can this love be, this love without which I am nothing even if I have everything? What in the concrete does wedded love demand of Susie and Gerry? In two of the passages you heard, St. Paul brings love down to earth. You heard him rhapsodize to Corinthian Christians: "Love is patient, love is kind, love is not irritable or arrogant, love is not resentful or rude" (1 Cor 13:4–5). Very simply: Unless they are schizophrenic, a man and woman in love will not cut each other with the harsh language of the "soaps," where the bold and the beautiful rarely listen, slash with syllables of sharp steel, turn cold shoulders to the one they love, rush from the room in self-righteous wrath.

You heard Paul charge the Christians of Rome, "Let [your] love be genuine" (Rom 12:9). The Greek word means, literally, "Let [your] love be without hypocrisy." Hypocrisy means playing a part. I am a hypocrite if I pretend to be what I am not, if I feign to feel what I do not feel. And few words are as abused, used with such hypocrisy, as the word "love." Hollywood's *Love Story* made millions on one silly sentence, "Love means never having to say you're sorry." TV's *Dawson's Creek* identifies love with whatever turns you on. A host of novels call a one-night stand a night of love. Today a cool way of saying "Good-bye" is "Luv' ya."

Not so for Paul. If your love is genuine, he tells Susie and Gerry, you will "extend hospitality to strangers" (v. 13). Not only with the word "Peace" at worship; not only doughnuts and coffee after church. Gerry and Susan begin their life together with an uncommon gift: They link in love two cultures, where their love for each other should be a symbol for Anglos and Hispanics who are still learning with difficulty to live their love in our multilingual parishes, a symbol in a land that once welcomed immigrants and now looks on them with suspicion, with anger, some even with hatred.

If your love is genuine, Paul tells Gerry and Susie, you will not curse those who make life difficult for you; "you bless them" (v. 14). Not only a prayer. "If your enemies are hungry, you feed them; if they are thirsty, you give them something to drink" (v. 20). Ever tried it? I don't believe I have. If your love is genuine, you will "associate with the poor, the lowly, the undistinguished" (Rom 12:16), those who have no power, no influence, are just ordinary folk, trying to live each day generously, contradicting W. C. Fields's cute comment, "Every morning start the day with a smile, and get it over with." If your love is genuine, Paul declares, "Never avenge yourselves" (v. 20). A difficult injunction when 75 percent of Americans applaud capital punishment. This even though New York's district attorney tells us from his years of experience, "The death penalty actually hinders the fight against crime."[3] And as a Christian I should never forget the firm affirmation in the Old Testament and the New, "Vengeance is mine, says the Lord" (Deut 32:35; Rom 12:19).

It makes no sense, you say? Yes, unless you recall the passage Susie and Gerry selected for their Gospel.

III

"This is my commandment: Love one another as I have loved you" (Jn 15:12). A command from God's Son in flesh. Not an invitation; a command. Eight words from God to be scotch-taped to your refrigerator. An ideal, of course; an ideal tough to attain. And still, an ideal that takes a marriage *between* Christians and makes it Christian.

Susie and Gerry: Just reflect a moment. Imagine what your marriage will be like if you try to love as Jesus loved. To love each other as Jesus loved you. It will mean imitating the Son of God who, Paul says, "did not regard [his] equality with God as something to be exploited, but emptied himself, being born in human likeness; humbled himself, became obedient to the point of death, even death on a cross" (Phil 2:6–8). Neither of you will ever use your gifts to lord it one over the other, to show yourself superior, to win an argument—only, like Jesus, to serve the one you love; never to make the other more like you, only to help shape the other to reflect Jesus in his or her special way.

When things turn bad, when clouds gather, when problems shake you, you will not retire into yourself, away from the one you love: "Leave me alone, I'll be all right." Not so Jesus; one striking example. On the eve of his death, knowing that the end was near, he gathered his 12 closest friends...for a farewell supper...for conversation...to give them himself under the appearance of bread and wine, to promise them his peace, a peace the world cannot give.

When suffering comes, illness, anxiety, frustration, let your love become a love that heals. Try to remember the experience of a holistic medical doctor: The most powerful known stimulant of the immune system is unconditional love.[4] Love, he insisted, may not always cure; but it always heals.[5] For healing is broader than curing. Love heals when you reconcile enemies. Love heals when you give courage to the discouraged, heart to the downhearted. Love heals when you listen to the lonely, hold an aged arthritic hand, perhaps like Mother Teresa caress an AIDS-afflicted infant. More than three centuries ago St. Vincent de Paul summed up your love for the downtrodden in a single sentence: "Unless you love, the poor will not forgive you for the bread you give them."

That's the way Jesus loved—a healing love. It snatched sinners from their enslavement to sin, transformed a despised tax collector, mended the moral sense of a woman caught in adultery, intrigued a

Samaritan woman five times married, converted a robber on his cross.

Here a warning: The love I have drawn for you from God's one Book, a love like Jesus' love, is not something you can manufacture by yourselves, from your high intelligence and your sparkling personality, from Gerry's brilliant blue eyes and Susie's more subtle blue. It is a gift. It comes, Paul says, "because God's love has been poured into [your] hearts through the Holy Spirit who has been given to [you]" (Rom 5:5). That is why you are joining your hands and your hearts in a church. Not because it's so lovely here; not because the Ruethers have been parishioners here for years. Rather because a church consecrated to God reminds us forcefully of what Jesus told his disciples: "I am the vine, you are the branches. Those who abide in me and I in them bear much fruit, because *apart from me you can do nothing*" (Jn 15:5). Oh yes, you can make millions apart from Jesus; you can rise to political power apart from Jesus; you can be famous apart from Jesus; you can be reasonably happy apart from Jesus. I've never forgotten a warning proclaimed in class a half century ago by a remarkable Jesuit, John Courtney Murray: "Never let anyone tell you sinners are not happy!" My point is, you cannot love like Jesus unless Jesus lives in you. This is not pretty poetry; this is Christian realism.

A final word. A half hour from now, Gerry and Susie, husband and wife, will waltz hand in hand down the center aisle, waltz from church to world. The choir will raise alleluias in a hymn titled..."The Strife Is Over." A strange recessional; for the wedded among you can tell Susie and Gerry that the effort to keep love alive is a ceaseless struggle. It is strikingly symbolized in the Genesis story of the first man and the first woman and the first sin. Strikingly symbolized when Adam cries out to God, "The woman you gave me, she gave me fruit from the tree" (Gen 3:12). Not "my wife," not "the love of my life," but "the woman you gave me." She did it, and it's your fault. And Eve? "The serpent tricked me" (v. 13).

No, the struggle is never over. But the struggle we expect from Susie and Gerry is not warfare. It is the struggle to be first in loving, first in confessing "I'm sorry," first in forgiving. Then it is that choirs of angels can shout "alleluia," the alleluia that means "Praise God." The God from whom all blessings flow.

So then, good friends, before Gerry and Susie say "yes till death," let's sit quietly, prayerfully, for a few sacred moments. In particular, dwell gratefully on two gentlemen, two fathers, not here in flesh and blood, but in God's goodness surely aware of what their children are vowing—fathers without whose loving and caring this sacred hour would not have come to pass. Dwell gratefully on two ladies, two mothers, smiling here through their tears—mothers whose self-sacrifice, total gift of themselves to these dear children, makes this evening's celebration of love uniquely their very own. Ask our all-loving God, the God who at this moment rests within Susie and Gerry, to preserve them in St. Paul's "genuine" love: for each other, for us who love them so dearly, for the less fortunate children of God who will cross their paths in the years ahead. And, for our special wedding gift, join me in promising Susie and Gerry that from this day forward our own love will burst into new life: for them, for those dear to us, for the unnumbered men, women, and children who share more of Jesus' crucifixion than of his resurrection. Do that, and when Susie and Gerry stroll forth from this sanctuary, our own fresh love will swell the alleluias of the angels.

Sacred Heart Church
Columbia, Missouri
August 15, 1998

40
LOVE THAT GIVES LIFE
Wedding Homily 5

- Song of Songs 2:8–10, 14, 16a; 8:6–7a
- 1 Corinthians 13:1–13
- John 15:12–16

Good friends: Today we celebrate! In the midst of an American presidency that saddens us, at a moment when terrorism at home and abroad frightens us, we celebrate. Why? Once again a wedding tears us away from a fearful front page, gives us reason to rejoice, new cause for hope. For Danielle and Jonas foretell a future, symbolize a season, promise a way of life where love is more powerful than hate, where divine grace triumphs over human folly, where the peace of Christ dwells in our hearts despite all manner of war and violence, cynicism and scandal outside.

How do Jonas and Danielle tell us this? One wondrous way is the love wherewith they look at each other. But they also tell us this in the words they chose from God's own Book. In your joy you might have missed those life-giving texts from the Song of Songs, from a letter of Paul, and from the Gospel of John. These passages were not picked blindfolded. They were plucked by this dear couple because they wanted to tell us something of what wedded love means to them, and in the telling they suggest to us what our own love should be like. Three passages that send at least three messages you and I dare not disregard. (1) Love at its best gives life. (2) Love that gives life is love as Jesus loved. (3) Love like Jesus' love ripples out to a whole little world.

I

First, love at its best gives life. Were you surprised to hear the Song of Songs from a Catholic pulpit? Some Christians are shocked because these poems are so sensual. God was not shocked. God not only inspired these love songs; God inspired the Church to put them in the same collection with Genesis and the Gospels, with the Psalms and the Prophets. It is God's imaginative word to us that the body He shaped is not evil, though it can be dangerous; God's word that passion stems from God. It is God's word near the end of the Song, "Love is a flame of the Lord" (8:6b); genuine love between lover and beloved is a sharing in God's white-hot love.[1] The kind of love that gives life, literally, to the one who is loved *and* to the one who loves.

This is not some pious abstraction. In 57 years as a priest, I have experienced time and again how genuine love can give life. Not only to the person loved, but to the lover as well. I discovered it in the musical *Fiddler on the Roof,* when the political activist falls in love. While dancing, he sings enthusiastically, "I [already] have some-*thing* to die for; [now] I have some*one* to live for, too!" I have seen it on hospital beds, seen with my own eyes what holistic physician Bernie Siegel declared from decades of medical experience, "I am convinced that unconditional love is the most powerful known stimulant of the immune system."[2] Not only to the immune system; new life to the whole person. I experienced it when an aging black lady, legless and sightless, dazzled us from her bed of pain with a smile of sheer joy, with her amazing "How wonderful to see you!" Despite the darkness, despite the helplessness, each day for her was new life, a fresh creation, sheer delight in being alive. New life for us as well, for us who surrounded her with new love.

I have experienced it in ever so many marriages of dear friends, marriages with ups and downs, ecstasies and agonies, breakups and make-ups, the whole range of human emotions. And so I stress to Danielle and Jonas: The more total your love, the more you give of your deepest self to the other, the more your love is not an "I" but a "we," the more often you can take the first step and murmur "I'm sorry," so much deeper will be the life in the one you love, so much deeper the life within you. Believe it! Believe Bernie Siegel: "Love heals."[3] It will not always cure a disease; it can always bring new life, richer life, to both of you.

Not surprisingly, you have already begun to experience it. Danielle calls it your six years of long-distance romance. Distance: Blair Academy and Pope John High, Notre Dame Indiana and

Washington and Lee Lexington, Italy and Paris, the Navy and CNBC, a submarine in Norfolk and multimedia in Fort Lee. What was growing within you distance could not destroy. Danielle will, I hope, forgive me for quoting her word for word:

> Despite all odds, we somehow could not let go of our relationship; we were in love. Family, friends, and strangers were all skeptical of such young love. Yet it was the difficulty of growing into young adulthood, with the forces of separation opposing the closeness of our love and friendship, that makes our love eternal. When common sense said it was time to quit, we persisted...and won. Enduring the transition into adulthood was not easy, but the trust and love and closeness we cemented are breathtaking.

Jonas and Danielle, what you were giving each other was...life. Slowly, yes; gradually, yes; but ever so surely, giving each other new life. And, please God, it has just...begun.

II

But what, concretely, in down-to-earth language, is this love? What is the life love gives? Genuine love, the Song of Songs told us, is a sharing in God's own love. The Jewish poets who wrote those inspired poems on parchment could not have imagined how they would be realized in our Christian days. I mean the sentence Jonas and Danielle have borrowed from the Gospel of John, "This is my commandment: Love one another as I have loved you" (Jn 15:12). As Jesus has loved us. Your love at its best is a sharing in the love of God's unique Son. Your love is to imitate, reflect, resemble Jesus' love. "I came," he said. "that [you] may have life, life overflowing" (Jn 10:10).

How did Jesus love us? Think! God's own Son took your flesh and mine, took our flesh as his own, became what you and I are. Not for his own sake; not to get something better for himself. Recall the early Christian hymn St. Paul quoted to the Christians of Philippi:

> Though his condition was divine,
> he did not regard equality with God
> something to exploit for selfish gain.
> Rather, he emptied himself,
> adopting the condition of a slave,
> taking on the likeness of human beings.
> And being found in human form,

he lowered himself further still,
becoming obedient unto death,
even death on a cross.

(Phil 2:6–8)

Why? Listen to the evangelist John: "Just as Moses lifted up the serpent in the desert, so must the Son of Man be lifted up, that whoever believes in him may have eternal life" (Jn 3:14–15). Life now and life hereafter; life for a time and life without end.

You know what it means to be alive, humanly alive. Not just breathing. I mean when you are so excited you can scarcely stand it. Mark McGwire as he rounds the bases with his record-breaking 62nd home run; Sir Edmund Hillary standing atop Mount Everest for the first time; Alexander Fleming discovering penicillin in a test tube; the British Olympic runner in *Chariots of Fire,* "When I run, I feel God's pleasure"; Jonas and Danielle, when you first realized that you were in love, knew beyond any doubt that for you to be alive is to be with and for each other.

Now raise that to the nth degree and you will sense what this sacred ceremony promises you. Not 24 hours of ecstasy each day; neither the Navy nor Dow Jones leaves room for that. But a joy in living that is even deeper and more lasting. You see, Our Lady of the Lake is not just a lovely setting for a wedding, with decades of memories for one branch of bouncing Burghardts. This setting should remind you, remind all of us, that marriage was invented not by Judge Judy[4] but by God. Remind us that when you murmur "I do" each to the other, a third party will enter your wedded life. The same Jesus who lived within our Lady, who has lived in both of you since baptismal water flowed over your brows, now has a new vested interest in you: He wants your love to give life. But, as he told his disciples the night before he died, "Apart from me you can do nothing" (Jn 15:5). Apart from him your love might very well die. Together with him, aware of him deep inside you, in love with him, working with him, you can shape your every wedded day into a new creation: the dull days as well as the delightful, yes frustration and irritation, pain of flesh and pain of spirit. The heart of the matter is this: The Jesus who lives within you died that you might have life, that you might give life. When you receive him on your tongues and in your hearts, his body and blood, his soul and divinity, join your promise to his promise. Make your first Communion as man and wife a commitment to life, to all that is life-giving, a pledge of fidelity to him and to each other. For only with him and in him are all things possible. "One hand, one heart."[5]

III

A final point. Jonas and Danielle: This life you share with each other and with the Lord of life dare not remain a small private party. A love that is only for you, a love that is not shared, will die. In a vivid way, you are already sharing it. With parents whose own love has given you life, a life that still lives within you; with siblings who secretly think you're "the greatest" since sliced bread; with a gathering of relatives and friends whose hearts are bursting with joy in your joy—some have even made the supreme sacrifice, Saturday golf.

A splendid beginning; but no more than a beginning. Your gifts, of nature and of grace, are too rich to be restricted to those near and dear to you. What precisely a loving Lord has in store for you I dare not predict. I do pray that wherever God leads you, not only will your success grace the Internet or the *Wall Street Journal,* but your love will lend life-giving meaning to the word "work." Beyond that, I trust that, with your interests and talents, your love will touch some of the Americans who experience little of your exciting life because they experience little of any energizing love. I mean the little child drug-infected in the womb, mutely pleading for bread and love; the lonely elderly, yearning for a face that cares, a word that encourages, the touch of a warm hand; the million youngsters sleeping on America's streets each night; so many imprisoned behind bars or within their tortured selves. Blessed so richly, your love will be measured by Jesus' own standard: "*I* was hungry and you gave me food, *I* was thirsty and you gave me something to drink, *I* was a stranger and you welcomed me, *I* was naked and you gave me clothing, *I* was sick and you took care of me, *I* was in prison and you visited me" (Mt 25:35–36).

Come then, Danielle and Jonas, and with Jesus' hands clasping your hands, speak the solemn syllables that will shape for ever the life-giving love you share with each other.

Our Lady of the Lake Church
Sparta, New Jersey
September 19, 1998

Medley

41

COME, HOLY SPIRIT, KINDLE IN ME...FIRE
Homily on the Holy Spirit as Fire

- Acts 2:1–17
- John 14:15–17

An age-old prayer refuses to leave me: "Come, Holy Spirit, fill the hearts of your faithful and kindle in them the fire of divine love. Send forth your Spirit, O Lord, and you will renew the face of the earth." Those two sentences suggest three significant facets of your spirituality and mine, three statements at the core of Catholic living. (1) The Holy Spirit is alive within you and me. (2) The Holy Spirit within us is like a fire. (3) With the fire of the Spirit within us, we can help transform our earth. A word on each.

I

First, the Holy Spirit is alive within you and me. This is not some pretty piece of poetry; this is Gospel truth, God's revelation to us. If you are in what we call "the state of grace," if you love God above all else and live as God commands, the Third Person of the Blessed Trinity actually lives deep inside you. Don't take my word for it. Listen to Jesus in his final discourse to his apostles: "If you love me, you will keep my commandments. Then I will ask the Father, and He will give you another Advocate, to be with you for ever. He is the Spirit of Truth, whom the world cannot accept, because it neither sees Him nor recognizes Him. You recognize Him, because He remains with you and is within you" (Jn 14:15–17). Believe it!

Then read what St. Paul wrote to the Christians of Rome: "God's love has been poured into our hearts through the Holy Spirit that has been given to us" (Rom 5:5). "You are not in the flesh," he tells them. He means, you are no longer men and women "alienated from God and hostile to him," no longer "weak and earthbound, the human creature left to itself."[1] You are "in the Spirit, since the Spirit of God dwells in you....If the Spirit of Him who raised Jesus from the dead dwells in you, He who raised Christ from the dead will give life to your mortal bodies also through His Spirit that dwells in you" (Rom 8:9–11). And Paul goes on:

> All who are led by the Spirit of God are children of God. For you did not receive a spirit of slavery to fall back into fear, but you have received a spirit of adoption. When we cry "Abba! Father!" it is that very Spirit bearing witness with our spirit that we are children of God, and if children, then heirs, heirs of God and joint heirs with Christ....
>
> (Rom 8:13–17)

Little wonder that Paul could put it so bluntly, so excitedly, to the Christians of Corinth: "Do you not know that you are God's temple and that God's Spirit dwells in you?...God's temple is holy, and you are that temple" (1 Cor 3:16–17). Not only the Christians of Corinth; the Christians of Our Lady of Victory. Does it "grab" you, does it excite you, does it make you tremble that you are as truly a temple of the living God as the tabernacle in your church is a temple of the risen Christ?

II

But the Holy Spirit does not live in you lifelessly; the Holy Spirit is alive in you, active within you. One metaphor Scripture applies to the Spirit is...fire. You may remember the first Pentecost, Luke's narrative in the Acts of the Apostles:

> [Jesus' disciples[2]] were all together in one place. And suddenly from heaven there came a sound like the rush of a violent wind, and it filled the entire house where they were sitting. Divided tongues, as of fire, appeared among them, and a tongue rested on each of them. All of them were filled with the Holy Spirit and began to speak in other languages, as the Spirit gave them ability.
>
> (Acts 2:1–4)

"A tongue, as of fire, rested on each of them" (2:3). Fire is, of course, an image; at the first Christian Pentecost, a physical image of something spiritual: the igniting, inspiring, illuminating, inciting presence of God the Holy Spirit. In the concrete, it tells of the first Christian community: fearful disciples in hiding transformed to confident proclaimers of God's word; Peter standing before "all Israel" and preaching Jesus crucified and risen. It summons up charismatic gifts that the Spirit breathed into the infant Church: miracles and ecstasies, wondrous insights and exalted speech. It tells of the Spirit as the prime mover of the Church's mission to the Gentiles; for surely it is the Spirit that spoke to Peter and had him understand that "God shows no partiality, but in every nation anyone who fears Him and does what is right is acceptable to Him" (Acts 10:34-35). Yes, this is the Spirit that was "poured out even on the Gentiles," so that Peter could say, "Can anyone withhold the water for baptizing these people who have received the Holy Spirit just as we have?" (Acts 10:45-47).

Little wonder that the "devout Jews from every nation under heaven living in Jerusalem" (Acts 2:5) were "bewildered"; for they heard, in their own languages, the earliest Christians "speaking about God's deeds of power" (v. 11). The skeptics sneered, "They are filled with new wine" (v. 13). Peter responds, perhaps with a soft smile, "These are not drunk, as you suppose, for it is only nine o'clock in the morning" (v. 15). But in a very true sense these Christians were intoxicated. Possessed by the Spirit, they couldn't help shouting like lunatics, perhaps dancing in happy circles. Remember, one of the "fruits" of the Spirit is "joy" (Gal 5:22). And you must have experienced at some time how a joy you feel deeply—your wedding day, a newborn baby, a remission of cancer, parents finding a lost child, a soldier son returning safe from war, a hundred more—your joy cannot always be contained, it bursts the bounds of your body, despite you it has to be shared, it's too much for one fragile frame to keep inside.

That's what the Holy Spirit did to Jesus' friends. They could no longer sit around; they had to tell what a risen Jesus meant to them—had to tell even Jews who disliked them, despised them, threatened them. They had to do something. They were on fire.

Race through early Christian history. Possessed by the Spirit, early Christians transformed the values of their Greco-Roman world. They stressed sharing rather than possessing. They insisted that the rich must give up not their riches but enslavement to riches. They protested that while God has made the earth as the common possession of all, greed has made it a right for the few. They attacked not private property but its misuse. They preached the presence of Christ in the impoverished and disadvantaged. They proclaimed the

Church of Christ as a community of support and sharing. Inflamed by the Holy Spirit, thousands of Christians in the first three centuries stood up against the power of the Roman State, suffered the sword or the headsman's axe rather than forgo their faith. And their blood became the seed of Christian growth.

III

It is in this spirit that the Holy Spirit is given to you and me. You see, the Spirit rests in us not only to sanctify us individually, to make each of us holy, an image of Christ, a sister or brother of Jesus. The Spirit is God's Gift to us, not to be clutched possessively but to be shared generously. Listen to St. Paul: "Now there are varieties of gifts, but the same Spirit; and there are varieties of services, but the same Lord; and there are varieties of activities, but it is the same God who activates all of them in everyone. To each is given the manifestation of the Spirit for the common good" (1 Cor 12:4–7).

For the common good. Look how the Spirit transformed the life of our Lady, and through her transformed the humanity of Jesus. Listen to the angel Gabriel addressing our Lady: "The Holy Spirit will come upon you, and the power of the Most High will overshadow you; *therefore* the child to be born [of you] will be holy; he will be called Son of God" (Lk 1:35). Not primarily for her own sake did the Spirit overshadow Mary; it was the whole of humanity God had in mind, every man, woman, and child in need of her Son.

So too for us. The Holy Spirit transforms us, makes us holy, so that we can transform our acre of God's world. On this Vatican II was emphatic. Read its Decree on the Apostolate of the Laity, your apostolate: "The laity must take on the renewal of the temporal order as their own special obligation. Led by the light of the gospel and the mind of the Church, and motivated by Christian love, let them act directly and definitively in the temporal sphere" (no. 7).

In less technical terminology, your task, your burden, your privilege as Christian laity is to change what is less than human around you, to make your segment of God's world a place where hate gives way to love, war to peace, injustice to justice, rugged individualism to selfless community. It begins where you live; it spreads out to where you work; it touches where you play. No homilist, not even a Jesuit, can tell you specifically how. So much depends on who you are, the gifts you have. You have to let God speak to you, you must listen to the Lord.

But one fact, one theological truth, I can indeed tell you with confidence: All by yourselves, by your naked human powers, by your high IQs and your powerful personalities, all Christians together cannot bring about God's kingdom of justice and peace and love. Only if God's Fire kindles your own fire can you light candles that pierce this world's darkness.

The miracle is this: The Power to change things is closer to you than you are to yourself. The Pentecost gospel declares that inside of you is a Fire just waiting to spread. That Spirit within you makes it possible for you to love with something of the fire wherewith God loves. The Hebrew Testament's Song of Songs suggests it strongly: "Love is a flame of the Lord" (Cant 8:6). The fire of love is "a participation in the Lord's white-hot love."[3] That Spirit within you makes it possible for you to love God above all else, despite the endless seductive idols in our culture. That Spirit within you enables you to love each man, woman, and child as Jesus loves them; to love each and every person like another I, another self, especially the poor and the downtrodden, the stranger and the alien, even the unbelieving and the unattractive, the evildoer and the enemy. That Spirit within you empowers you to touch things, God's material creation, everything God made and "saw was very good" (Gen 1:31), with reverence, as a gift, a trace of God; empowers you to avoid the greed, the consumerism, the itch for more and more that John Paul II saw contaminating our culture. Fifteen hundred years ago Pope St. Leo the Great preached this in one of his Christmas sermons:

> ...Recognize the dignity of your nature. Remember that you were made in God's image; though corrupted in Adam, that image has been restored in Christ.
>
> Use creatures as they should be used: earth, sea, sky, air, springs and rivers. Give praise and glory to their Creator for all you find lovely and wondrous in them....
>
> Our words and exhortations are not intended to make you disdain God's works or think there is anything in creation contrary to your faith; for the good God has Himself made all things good. What we do ask is that you use reasonably and with moderation all the marvelous creatures which adorn this world.[4]

Some of you are already on fire. For simplicity's sake, let me sum it up under a word familiar to Our Lady of Victory: hospitality. Hospitality is a virtue that marks Old Testament and New: the Jew and the Christian as guest and as host.[5] "For Jesus, 'neighbor' is coextensive with 'humanity' to such an extent that the stranger becomes the neighbor."[6] In line with that tradition, hospitality is a word that characterizes your parish in its outreach. Not simply coffee and doughnuts before or after Mass. On your feet you feed the hungry poor; on wheels you feed parishioners imprisoned in their homes. Your Clothing Closet warms the shivering naked; your personal presence lights the eyes of the sick and the lonely. You help your disadvantaged young to break the bonds of crack and coke, help families to find low-cost attractive housing. You see to it that no parishioner of Our Lady of Victory is a stranger, feels unwanted, remains unloved. You network with other faiths to house the homeless and resettle the displaced. And yes, you march and you vote, you pray and you protest, for a Christian prochoice: Choose life. In the womb and near the tomb, you choose life. Where abortion is no longer rare and physician-assisted suicide is on the rise, you choose life. In a culture of death, you choose life.

There is so much more you do that is hidden from me. Let me close with two words you might call words of warning; I prefer to call them a raising of awareness. First, what you are doing at Our Lady of Victory is not simply social action, social service, prompted by a very human compassion. It is that, but it is so much more. It is a work of the Holy Spirit. What has been kindled in you is a fire of divine love. You are continuing the mission that moved the Son of God to take and wear your flesh, the mission he expressed in part when he unrolled the scroll of Isaiah in the synagogue of his hometown Nazareth and declared, "The Spirit of the Lord is upon me, for [the Lord] has anointed me; He has sent me to preach good news to the poor, to proclaim release for prisoners and sight for the blind, to send the downtrodden away relieved" (Lk 4:18). Yes, good friends, the Spirit of the Lord is upon you; the Holy Spirit has anointed you.

Second, this mission, Christian hospitality, is not simply the function of a committee. No more than Sunday Mass is something a committee does for us. Hospitality is an extension of the Eucharist: "All who partake of the Eucharistic meal are challenged to serve others as they have been served."[7] Hospitality, service, self-giving is a demand on each of us, if only because the Holy Spirit rests on us, is within each of us, like a tongue of fire.

I know, for many of you the very human problem of making ends meet can make Christian hospitality, service of sisters and brothers, an added burden all but beyond bearing. A job, a family, four or five children in school, taxes and mortgages and health insurance—there's hardly time even for "Seinfeld" or *Titanic*, surely not for Meals on Wheels.

It's true, tragically true: In the richest nation on earth, the technology that was expected to save us time leaves us with less time. And still the Holy Spirit implores each of us to do *something* for others, to be *someone* for others. Lent is a "tempting" time to begin. Somewhere not far from you is a child who needs a hug or a brace or a McBurger; a bedridden man or woman who feels forgotten and forsaken by the human race; a legislator who needs prodding not to cut funds for Head Start, not to support our President on abortion issues. The needs are endless. Your Social Concerns Ministry has all the information just a local phone call away.

But this evening focus for several quiet moments on Someone *you* need, Someone already given to you, Someone who at this very moment pervades your whole being, Someone who can change your life and through you the lives of those you touch, Someone you may have forgotten in the hurly-burly, the hustle and bustle, of life in a zoo. And close with the age-old prayer with which we began, but much more personal, much more your own prayer: "Come, Holy Spirit, fill the hearts of your faithful—fill my heart—and kindle in me the fire of your own love. Kindle your divine love in me."

Our Lady of Victory Church
Washington, D.C.
March 11, 1998

42

COVENANT WITH THE LAW, COVENANT WITH THE LORD
Homily for a Red Mass

- Micah 6:6–8
- James 2:14–17
- Luke 4:16–21

For some years I have been intrigued by a single momentous word. The word? Justice. Two distinct visions of justice. There is the justice you know best, the justice intrinsic to our legal system, that stems in large measure from English common law. And there is the justice I know best, the justice intrinsic to Scripture, that stems from a covenant with God. The difference that distinguishes them I find strikingly challenging for a Catholic, indeed any Christian or Jew, as you struggle to link law with love, to shape a spirituality that unifies your life, does not turn you into a two-headed creature living two lives.

Three stages to my song and dance: (1) a swift word on the legal justice you profess; (2) an equally swift word on the biblical justice that is my preoccupation; (3) a critical question on their relationship: Can legal justice and biblical justice be harmonized in one and the same person?[1]

I

First, the legal justice you profess. It's central to your vocation. You see to it that just laws foster the common good, that human rights written into law are protected, that the scales of Lady Justice are not weighted in favor of the rich and powerful, that men and women remain innocent until proven guilty, that the punishment fits the proven crime. Your burden is precisely to insure that men and women receive what is their due, what they deserve. You are not to be swayed from justice by love or sentiment; your sway is the law on your books or the need to correct injustice. Your goddess is the Roman *Justitia*, the lady with scales and a sword, her eyes blindfolded or closed in token of impartiality. A proud profession indeed, for without you "America the Beautiful" would be a nation in anarchy, a country uncommonly unfree. "Equal before the law" is still an ideal, but largely because of you we are moving slowly but relentlessly toward it.

You are an incredibly powerful group. For this nation is founded on law, and so in large measure it is founded on you. True, our legal hands are not lily-white. We look back with shame on a Dred Scott decision that declared slaves to be property. We blush that in this "land of the free" women have been second-class citizens, that it is taking us longer to free women than to free the slaves. We weep because justice is so slow, weep when human beings rot in jail for months before they can be tried, weep when the men and women we imprison return to society more brutal than before. We get cynical when the powerful can delay or gerrymander justice. And surely most if not all of us here must at times grow black with helpless anger at a legal system that can sentence millions of the unborn to death because they are not persons, because they have no rights in law.

And still the law is a proud profession. Proud particularly for a paradoxical reason. Powerful you are, but powerful because you are...servants. And service has an honorable history. It goes back to ancient Athens, where the Greek word we translate as "liturgy" meant a burdensome public office or duty which the richer citizens discharged at their own expense for the people or the state. Service goes back to a Jesus who told us he took our flesh "not to be served but to serve"—in fact "to give his life" for others (Mt 20:28). Service goes back to lawyers like St. Thomas More, who went merrily to the scaffold declaring himself "the king's good servant but God's first."

And so for you. Bench, bar, schools of law, you are servants. And you serve not an abstract quality called justice; you serve your own flesh and blood. Strange at times, unsettling. For some of you serve by prosecuting the insider trader and the murdering mafioso, others by defending them. Sometimes you serve by shackling a sister or brother for years, sometimes by lifting their shackles. Some of you hassle us for the IRS, others keep corporations from being taxed to death. And every so often, while some of us shiver, you prove to 12 good folk and true that one of your own flesh should die by hanging or a lethal injection.

All this you do for one overriding purpose: the common good, the well-being of a wondrous rainbow of millions. Lift high your heads! Largely because of you we rarely eat one another alive.

II

Second, the biblical justice that preoccupies me. You see, when the prophet Micah announced to Israel, "What does the Lord require of you but to do justice?" (Mic 6:8), he was not imposing on God's people primarily an ethical or legal construct: Give each person what he or she deserves. Biblical justice embraces all that, but goes beyond it. Let me explain.

In contrast to a rugged individualism that pervades much of our culture, the Israelite lived in a world where "to live" was to be united with others by bonds of family or by covenant relationships.

> This web of relationships—king with people, judge with complainants, family with tribe and kinfolk, the community with the resident alien and [with the] suffering in their midst, and all with the covenant God—constitutes the world in which life is played out.[2]

Relationships. Biblical justice is fidelity to relationships that stem from a covenant. Within this context, in what sense is God just? Because God always acts as God should; God is unfailingly faithful to God's promises. When are people just? When they are in right relation in every aspect of their lives. Three levels: properly postured toward their God, toward their sisters and brothers, toward the whole of created reality.

Concretely, what did that mean for Israel? To be just, God's people had to love God above all else, with their whole heart and soul, with all their mind and strength. To be just, they had to love each human person as an image of God, as a brother or sister, like another self, whatever the color or smell, race or religion, no matter how hate-full or evil. To be just, they had to touch "things," nonhuman reality, earth and sea and sky, with respect, with reverence, as gifts of God not to be possessively clutched or rapaciously ravaged, only to be gratefully shared.

It was the Israelite tradition of justice that sparked the ministry of Jesus. He inaugurated a new covenant, where the most significant relationship is the monosyllable that says it all—love. And astonishingly, where loving others, already commanded in Leviticus (19:18), is said by Jesus to be "like" loving God (Mt 22:39). New Testament justice? Love God above all else; love one another as Jesus has loved us (Jn 15:12). Not a *quid pro quo,* but the kind of love that impelled God's unique Son to wear our flesh, to be born of a woman as we are born, to thirst and tire as we do; to respond with compassion to a hungry crowd, to the bereavement of a mother, to the sorrow of a sinful woman; to spend himself especially for the bedeviled and bewildered, the poverty-stricken and the marginalized; to die in exquisite agony so that others might live.

Through Christ, with Christ, in Christ we are called to bring closer to realization God's own vision of a single, all-embracing community: God, God's people, and God's earth.

III

Finally, the provocative issue: Is it possible to link in your lives secular justice and biblical justice? I mean, give to each what each deserves and give to all more than they deserve? Give to each what you have covenanted with the law to give, and give to all what you have covenanted with the Lord to give? A mission impossible? Let's see.

Legal justice is indeed an admirable way of life. The crucial question is: Should it be your *whole* life? From the perspective of a Catholic law center, the answer is no. Why? Because legal justice is not the whole of justice, only a single aspect thereof. For a still richer life, a totally just life, your vision of justice must expand. Not to change one law into another, legal justice into biblical, Blackstone into the Bible. Rather to enlarge your justice, so that justice covers your whole existence: forensic and domestic, legal and social, work and play.

This is not to denigrate legal justice. Yours is a service the Athenians of old and the prophets of Israel would applaud. More than that, it is a service that links you to the servant that was Jesus. For without you human rights would crumble beneath sheer power, human dignity collapse before the swift, the shrewd, and the savage, and "the land of the free" turn into the home of the slave.

And still it is not enough. Not for anyone convinced there is more to life than "law and order." Not for such as prize love above law, compassion over court convictions, family more than occupation.

Not for those who realize that the equality you dispense at the bar of justice is not enough to unite man and woman, black and white, Jew and Arab, the haves and the have-nots, the restless young and the rest-home aged, the crack pushers and the police who imprison them. Ironically, "equality before the law" tends not to unite but to divide.

Enter biblical justice. To Lady Justice's fairness it adds a word going swiftly out of fashion: fidelity. Fidelity to every relationship; *every* relationship. Not only the innocent you defend, but the pedophile you prosecute, the rapist you imprison for life, the bomber you doom to death. A mind-blowing, heart-rending dilemma. For biblical fidelity is synonymous with love. Not a mawkish, sickly sentimental feeling. Rather the tough love of a father punishing an unruly child. The tough love that calls for compassion—compassion for humans who are not particularly human; a compassion that continues to see in the serial murderer and the child abuser God's image, if ever so defaced. A compassion that tries ever so hard to imitate the Jesus who could love the sinner while despising the sin, who turned traditional morality on its head: "You have heard that it was said, 'You shall love your neighbor and hate your enemy.' But I say to you, Love your enemies" (Mt 5:43–44). This Jesus forces us to confront a sobering question: If our love, our compassion, goes out only to those who love us, only to those who live aright, only to our own kind, how Christlike is this, how do we differ from unbelievers?[3]

All of which raises a question for your heavy meditation. Can legal justice and biblical justice be harmonized in one and the same person at one and the same time? Or must the attorney, the jurist, the judge be for ever a two-headed creature, living two lives, one in court, the other at home; one on weekdays, in the grime and grit of lawlessness, of murder and the Mob, of cocaine and conspiracy, of spousal abuse and insider trading, the other on weekends, warmed by church or mosque or synagogue, transformed by a loving family and, perhaps, subpar golf?

I believe the harmony is possible. But not without a profound spirituality. I mean a personal relationship to Someone (capital S) who loves you far more than you love yourself. A relationship that can grace you if not always with specific answers, at least to live at times with ambiguity. If your answer is "Yes, it can be done," the consequences can be enormous. Not only a unique unity in your professional and personal life. Beyond that, a distinctive contribution of lay Christianity to a culture increasingly fragmented by a loss of love, by the ice-cold aphorism "Love those who love you, hate those who hate you."

Even if your answer at the moment is a regretful "No, it cannot be done," my high regard for you will not be diminished. I promise you the prayer St. Paul framed for the faithful of Philippi: "This is my prayer, that your love may overflow more and more with knowledge and full insight, to help you to determine what is best" (Phil 1:9–10).[4]

Gonzaga University
Spokane, Washington
September 23, 1997

43
CLOTHE YOURSELVES WITH
A COMPASSIONATE HEART
Homily for a Medical School Graduation

- Jeremiah 22:1–4
- Colossians 3:12–17
- Luke 10:25–37

Some years ago, I was privileged to speak at the annual Ohio Pastors Conference. What *I* said I have forgotten. What I have not forgotten was a sermon preached by an African American from Texas. He was preaching on the parable you have just heard, the Good Samaritan. He focused on the priest who came upon the fellow beaten half to death by robbers, the priest who "passed by on the other side" (Lk 10:31). That priest, the preacher claimed, could handle anything that had to do with the temple in Jerusalem: the Mosaic law, the Ark of the Covenant, the showbread in the sanctuary, the incense. What he could *not* handle was "the event on the Jericho road." That phrase rang out like a refrain throughout the sermon: "the event on the Jericho road."

This morning, women and men of medicine, I dare to lay before you the event on *your* Jericho road.[1] This morning's liturgy celebrates in ritual a rite of passage. You are passing from a hallowed temple, a center of medical learning, to a road that will lead to your ultimate medical goal. The next few years, I suggest, are like the movement from Jerusalem to Jericho, the event on *your* Jericho road.

Three stages to my presentation: (1) What is it you will be able to handle? (2) What is it you might "pass by on the other side"? (3) Where does the good Samaritan enter in?

I

First, what is it you will be able to handle? This you know in detail far better than I. Still, let me express it from the vantage point of someone who has watched you, admired you, been prodded by you, has even addressed your Surgical Rounds.

What can you handle? Obviously and increasingly, the instruments of your art and craft. If your residency placements are a fair sampling of our nation's placements, there is hardly an organ or nerve within our bodies that will escape your expert attention. I experienced one example last month, when under gifted hands ultrasound destroyed my cataracts and a lens implant focused anew rays of light—and I walked out within the hour.

The tools of your trade you handle, by necessity, with care. Beyond that, I trust that by choice you will touch them with reverence. Stethoscope and scalpel, X-ray and radioactive ray, drugs and microbes, CAT scan and MRI, all the modern miracles of technology that increasingly crowd your healthcare centers—none of these came forth from nothing. Human ingenuity, yes, but always at work on something originally from God's good earth, from something Catholic tradition calls a "trace" of God. In your hands these are no longer indifferent objects, like dust on a shelf. In your hands these are instruments of healing. To be touched by you to a broken body, to a shattered psyche. To heal God's human images, to help make the broken whole.

II

All that is a given; such tools of your trade you can handle; otherwise you would not be here. Of greater concern to me is what you might not be able to handle, might not want to handle, the event on your Jericho road you might "pass by on the other side." I mean the person inside the body. How? For time's sweet sake, I limit myself to one way of passing by: not listening.

I know, listening comes with the medical turf; it's as close to you as your stethoscope. But you can pass by without realizing that listening is an art surpassing the finest of instruments.

A pertinent story—it stems from the extensive experience of an esteemed colleague of yours, Dr. Robert Coles. He was working as a volunteer fifth-grade teacher in an impoverished Boston neighborhood. An African-American girl in the class, Cynthia, ten years old, had been with her mother to see a doctor at Children's Hospital. She was amazed at the number of "sick folks in one place." She didn't mind "all the people," only "some of them." A pause, then she specified: "The doctors, they be strutters. They need teaching." A classmate, Tom, asked her to explain. Her answer: "They're busy, they are—and they let you know it." Puzzled, Tom asked why working hard meant being a strutter. Cynthia's response: "They didn't give us credit for understanding anything. They're big on talking, on telling you this and that and something here and there, but they don't listen like they should. You go off on your own, and they'll cut you off."

Still unconvinced, Tom said, "Give them a break—they're in a rush, they've got to get their job done. You can't be polite all the time!" Cynthia: "For sure, it's a lot they have to do. But if you watch them, you'll see them being nice and relaxed with each other, and if it's one of them who comes and interrupts, they'll lend an ear, but if we try to tell them something, they hurry on." Dr. Coles "shuddered with embarrassment," suggested that the class get on with their spelling. But the ten-year-old was not through teaching, made sure her intended point had hit home: "If they'd listen, they'd learn more; that's how you learn—through your ears, not your mouth."[2] From the mouths of children....

It's not only children you can pass by without listening. It's all of us you are burdened and privileged to touch. I have suggested at Georgetown that the healthcare leaders of the 21st century—administrators and surgeons, internists and nurses, radiologists and anesthesiologists—will be the men and women who are concerned to discover where their patients come from and where they've been. Not only our medical history on a reception-room questionnaire, indispensable as this is. I mean my integral humanity, where I hurt deep inside, what I'm afraid of, what if anything I hope for, the love or lack of love that makes the world turn or stop for me.

Why all this time-consuming listening, with HMOs breathing down your backs? Not to turn doctors into daydreamers, residents into incurable romantics. But of this I am convinced: Intrinsic to your capacity to cure is your power to heal. In fact, even when to cure is not in the picture, to heal is still possible; for healing is broader than curing. I have seen it. I saw a doctor heal when a child afflicted with Down's syndrome left the hospital with infectious laughter. I saw a doctor heal when an African-American lady, blind and legless, looked up from her hospital bed and with a dazzling smile said, "How good it is to see you, Doctor!" I saw a doctor heal when just about the last words from a dying cardiac patient were, "Thank you, Doctor. You'll never know how much life your caring has given me." I saw a doctor heal when a cancerous young Jesuit dear to me returned from chemotherapy to our community at Georgetown strengthened to face a medically dismal prognosis (he has died since). You heal whenever you share, in some genuine fashion, the lot of the men, women, and children you serve—hurt a bit when we hurt a lot, weep a little when we weep profusely, feel diminished whenever a sister or brother dies.

Here you continue the healing mission of Jesus. Rarely, perhaps never, was his curing an end in itself. Leprosy or paralysis, blindness or madness, Jesus cured to remove obstacles—obstacles to an awareness of God's presence—or to elicit a fresh response to God's love.[3] I realize that this is rarely if ever your primary purpose as men and women of medicine. Perhaps it never entered your essay, "Why GUMed Should Accept Me." But isn't it worth recognizing that often such healing is in actuality the result of your curing? My flesh is part and parcel of a person. And that person, let me tell you, that unrepeatable "I," is a unique image of God; it is I trying to work out my own salvation, my own relationship with God, with my world. Like it or not, aware of it or not, you play a Christlike role in my agonizing efforts to love God above all else, to love others as Christ has loved me.

A twin miracle here: If you heal us, you may well heal yourselves, your own paralysis, your own blindness. More accurately, you let us heal you. Please listen to our stories.

III

Third, and perhaps most important, what does it take to get that way, to recognize the healer in your curing? How mimic the Samaritan who took such personal care of the half-dead Jew on the road to Jericho? What does it take? What the Samaritan had. Evangelist Luke had a remarkable Greek verb for it. We translate it "he was moved with pity" for the poor fellow. True enough, but it doesn't reproduce the flavor, the power, of the original. The Greek verb relates to a noun that means the "inward parts," the "entrails"; figuratively, the seat of our emotions, the seat and source of love, of sympathy, of mercy; it's what we call our heart. It's not an abstract "I love you"; it's deep feeling. And pity looks down on another from a superior perch. The Samaritan felt deep inside himself for the poor victim, did not see him as a hostile Jew, only someone as human, as vulnerable, as himself. Only one of God's children. Perhaps the closest

English word is "compassion," for to be compassionate is, literally, to "suffer with."

I do not say that your 18 hours of residency each day should be followed by a grand round of profound compassion; a few hours of sleep might be wiser. I do not say that my hiatal hernia should draw from you a deep groan of fellow feeling; a refill of my Pepcid will do very well, thank you. I do not say that the ER should resound with empathy; the stress there, "Chicago Hope"[4] tells me, is on haste and much shouting. I do say that a chronic compassion should pervade your professional life, be as much a part of you as your stethoscope or scalpel. I do say that it should well up at times—before a child with Down's syndrome, an unexpected heart failure in the OR, a leg you have amputated. I do say that compassion should at times press you to go the "extra mile," like the Samaritan who not only bandaged the Jew's wounds but "put him on his own animal, brought him to an inn" (Lk 10:34), paid for his care out of his own pocket—and this for an enemy.

Why? Because yours is not just another job; you are not higher-paid garbage collectors, white-jacketed plumbers. You are healers. And in the Catholic vision, I insist, you continue the healing mission of Jesus. But that takes compassion; and compassion is another word for love. Not a syrupy love; a tough love. The kind of love that led God's Son to a cross. The type of love that got four American missionary women raped and murdered in El Salvador. The love that brought a cancer-ridden Dr. Tom Dooley back to Laos.

How do you get compassionate? Some, I suspect, are born that way. And yet, Dr. Richard Selzer argues that

> A surgeon does not slip from his mother's womb with compassion smeared upon him like the drippings of his birth. It is much later that it comes. No easy shaft of grace this, but the cumulative murmuring of the numberless wounds he has dressed, the incisions he has made, all the sores and ulcers and cavities he has touched in order to heal....[5]

Genes and experience I do not deny. I do insist that the richest compassion of all, the compassion of which Jesus urged "Be compassionate just as [God] your Father is compassionate" (Lk 6:36), this is indeed a grace—none of us deserves it; but a grace I have no doubt God will be happy to give any of you who have the courage to ask for it. After all, you are doing God's work, you are continuing the healing mission of God's Son. So then, ask. Let this liturgy, this re-enacting of Jesus' supreme compassion on Calvary, be a plea for your own compassion, for the healing that will bring to others what your colleagues have brought to me: through health of body, new opportunities to love as Jesus loved.

In summary, let the plea you heard from St. Paul to the Christians of Colossae echo throughout your medical ministry. Scotch-tape it to your medical refrigerator: "As God's chosen ones, holy and beloved, clothe yourselves with a compassionate heart" (Col 3:12).[6] A compassionate heart.

Holy Trinity Church
Washington, D.C.
May 23, 1998

44
REMAKE AMERICA FOR OUR CHILDREN
Institute for Child Advocacy Ministry

- Matthew 19:13–15

Last evening Barbara Taylor spoke eloquently and persuasively about children.[1] More eloquently, more persuasively, than I can possibly do. Oh yes, I have preached passionately, have lectured limpidly, on children's issues. Some of it I have stolen unashamedly from Children's Defense Fund statistics: In the richest country on earth, one of every four children grows up below the poverty line. I have agonized over the children in my own Washington, D.C.: In one five-year period more than 250 of their playmates were killed by gunfire. And so some surviving little ones have been planning not their futures but their funerals—where to be waked, how to be dressed, how to look; for they do not expect to live very long. And so, like the mothers in and around Jesus' Bethlehem, I weep for our children, "refuse to be consoled, because they are no more" (Mt 2:18).

Still, I think it wise for me not to pursue the same path Barbara trod so experientially, with such expertise, such feminine insight. I shall rather focus on *adult* America as we march into a new millennium, shall ask how we grownups committed to a covenant might help to remake America for our children. Concretely, I shall confront you with three options, two examples, and one question.

I

First, permit me to invade your imaginations. How might you reimagine adulthood in Christianity's third millennium, so as to leave a living legacy for your children? In 1986, Harvard's 350th birthday, that prestigious university reported the three top goals declared by its entering freshmen: (1) money, (2) power, (3) reputation, fame.[2] Sounds today like (1) Trump, (2) Clinton, (3) Oprah. In reaction to that, I shall suggest three critical areas that confront adults in America's ongoing third century, three sets of options, choices, goals where you can make a difference, where unless you and your sisters and brothers do make a difference, our children will continue to be the most vulnerable humans in our society.

The first option: Will it be individualism or community? I am not downplaying individualism. Strong individuals were a powerful force in shaping an incomparable America. From Thomas Jefferson to F.D.R., from Eli Whitney to Thomas Edison, from Harriet Beecher Stowe to Susan B. Anthony, from Horace Greeley to William Randolph Hearst, from Sojourner Truth to Martin Luther King Jr., from Douglas MacArthur to Daniel Berrigan—there were always men and women who stood out from the crowd, paved new pathways. And not only the standouts. "Individualism," sociologist Robert Bellah and his coresearchers insist, "lies at the very core of American culture....Our highest and noblest aspirations, not only for ourselves, but for those we care about, are closely linked to our individualism."[3]

But that is not the individualism I have in mind. I am thinking of a critical change in American individualism. I mean what Bellah and company call a resurgence of late-19th-century *rugged* individualism, where the race is to the swift, the shrewd, the savage, and the devil take the hindmost; where in the last analysis the only one who really matters is the almighty I; to myself alone am I ultimately responsible. I am thinking of Lee Atwater, the architect of presidential politics who almost singlehandedly turned the Bush campaign around in 1988. Dying of a brain tumor at 40, this gifted man made this poignant confession:

> The '80s were about acquiring—acquiring wealth, power, prestige. I know. I acquired more wealth, power and prestige than most. But you can acquire all you want and still feel empty....It took a deadly illness to put me eye to eye with that truth, but it is a truth that the country, caught up in its ruthless ambitions and moral decay, can learn on my dime.[4]

And the greed that some defenders of the free market claim is necessary for capitalism to work, that greed has not spared any group—not Wall Street's Boeskys, not real estate's Keatings, not televangelism's Bakkers, not the private purveyors of deadly weapons to the underdeveloped world. Strangely, the rugged brand of individualism has invaded the postfeminist world.

The latest addition to the women's studies sections of book-
stores, *Bitch: In Praise of Difficult Women,* features on its cover a
topless picture of author Elizabeth Wurtzel. Beyond it lies a
seemingly unedited rant in which Wurtzel...demands for herself
and womankind the right to be rapacious, have fits and own
more than one Gucci bag. "I intend to scream, shout, throw
tantrums in Bloomingdale's if I feel like it and confess intimate
details of my life to complete strangers," she writes. "*I intend to
answer only to myself.*"[5]

Is there a counteragent? Yes indeed. It is a category that many
good Christians, including some devout Catholics, have forgotten:
the common good. The good an imaginative God had in mind on
the six days of creation; the good symbolized in the Garden of Eden,
in that original, all-embracing single community where, for a brief
shining moment, humanity was at peace with God, humans with one
another, humans with earth and sea and sky. It is the covenant God
cut with His chosen people when He freed them not only *from* slavery in Egypt but *for* a "contrast society" serving God and one
another without constraint. It is the covenant God cut with us in
Christ, the Son of God who, the Gospel of John declares, "was about
to die for the nation, and not for the nation only, but to gather into
one the dispersed children of God" (Jn 11:51–52). It is the continu-
ous Christian conviction that God created the material universe for
all humankind, that every man, woman, and child fashioned in the
likeness of God has a right to share in those riches of God's good
earth that are needed for human dignity. Not a denial of private
property; only a cry against its greedy misuse. It is the insight a
remarkably gifted Greek theologian named Origen preached early in
the third century:

> God...knows that what a man loves with all his heart and soul
> and might—this for him is God. Let each one of us now examine
> himself and silently in his own heart decide which is the flame
> of love that chiefly and above all else is afire within him, which
> is the passion that he finds he cherishes more keenly than all
> others....Whatever it is that weighs the heaviest in the balance of
> your affection, that for you is God. But I fear that with very
> many the love of gold will turn the scale, that down will come
> the weight of covetousness lying heavy in the balance.[6]

Very simply, what will drive America the rest of its third century? A despotism of rugged individualists or a democracy of individuals for others? Will the individualism we proudly cherish serve

the common good or greedy self-interest? And where will America's parents take their stand? Where will you take your stand?

The second option: Will it be ethical justice or biblical justice? Will it be human justice or God's kind of justice?

You see, when a fearless prophet named Micah declared to Israel, "What does the Lord require of you but to do justice?" (Mic 6:8), he was not imposing on God's people simply or primarily an ethical construct: Give to each man, woman, and child what is due to each, what each person has a strict right to demand, because he or she is a human being, has rights which can be proven from philosophy or have been written into law. What, then, was the justice God wanted to "roll down like waters" (Amos 5:24)? In a word, fidelity. Fidelity to what? To relationships, to responsibilities, that stemmed from their covenant with Yahweh. What relationships? To God, to people, to the earth. (1) Love God above all else, above every creaturely idol. (2) Love every human person like another self, another I, as if you were standing in his or her shoes, especially the paper-thin shoes of the downtrodden. (3) Touch the earth, things, all that is not God or the human person, with reverence, with respect, with awe, as a gift of God, a trace of divinity.

It is this Israelite tradition on justice that sparked the ministry of Jesus. He summed it up in the synagogue at Nazareth: "The Spirit of the Lord is upon me. For the Lord has anointed me, has sent me to preach good news to the poor, to proclaim release for prisoners and sight for the blind, to send the downtrodden away relieved" (Lk 4:18). That ministry he proclaimed pithily just before he was crucified for us: "Love one another as I have loved you" (Jn 15:12).

Ethical justice is indeed essential, but not enough. Essential because, unless we give others what they deserve, civilized existence is impossible, life becomes a jungle. And legislators will not listen to God-talk, at best only to the persuasions of human reason. Still, not enough for Jewish and Christian living, not enough to lift man and woman above sheer civility, above grudging giving to the impoverished, the less gifted, the less fortunate. "What they deserve" all too often results in a power struggle; all too often, as in our own dear country, the rich become richer and the poor get poorer.

Let me turn cruelly concrete. When one out of every four children lives below the poverty line in the richest country on earth; when countless Americans who claim to be people of compassion see in AIDS God's own plague on the promiscuous; when uncounted elderly sit unloved in nursing homes or grope in garbage cans for the food we waste unthinking; when women still cry out against the "feminization of poverty," against the powerlessness of women to shape the world in any but a masculine mold; when more than a third of the black people in the United States lack the basic necessities you and I take for granted; when our leaders still refuse to ban the production of land mines that each week kill or maim 500 men, women, and children across the world; when 75 percent of Americans clamor for a death penalty that Manhattan's District Attorney Robert Morgenthau claims "actually hinders the fight against crime"[7]; when Hispanics are still second-class citizens, Native Americans are homeless in their own homeland, and our Jewish sisters and brothers listen fearfully as more and more Americans claim the Holocaust which consumed six million of their dear ones is a gigantic hoax—here, I submit, a justice symbolized by a blindfolded lady with measuring scales and a sword is admirable but insufficient. Imperative is a fresh vision, the vision our Scriptures portray: Each man, woman, and child is a creation of God, shaped in God's own likeness, a sister or brother of mine, another I. In the Christian vision, every human person, however warped, is to be loved as Jesus loved and loves us. A tough theology, not easily translated into today's realities.

Again, very simply, what will drive America the rest of its third century? Only blindfolded Lady Justice or with her the justice demanded by a God who with eyes open gave His own Son to a crucifying death out of love for each human from the first Adam to the final Antichrist? And where will America's parents take their stand? Where will you take your stand?

The third option: Will it be information or appreciation? For years I have been captivated by an insight of revered Rabbi Abraham Joshua Heschel, an insight decades before Internet: Humankind "will not perish for want of information...only from lack of appreciation."[8]

Information is literally at our fingertips. Never in human history has information been so easily accessible—so much, so swift, so cheap. A manuscript from the Vatican Library or porn for the mentally impoverished; the latest statistics on assisted suicide in the Netherlands or belly-splitting malapropisms from church bulletins; old political cartoons and information on prescription drugs. Physicians can call up films on lung cancer, lawyers the latest on immigrant legislation in California. Preachers who rarely prepare a sermon can have the world's best at their bedside every Saturday night. And the young? They can be educated and entertained, play games and share a prayer, arrange their dates for the week and create a term paper without ever leaving their chairs—all this with feet up and a Bud Lite in their hands.

It's breathtaking, not to be piously despised in the light of eternity. But it raises a problem: not only refusing to discriminate between the "cool" and the "ugly," but perhaps more importantly, taking it all for granted. I mean the loss of wonder. With wonder we are born; look at children before the so-called age of reason. But as we grow older, most of us lose it. We get blasé and worldly-wise and sophisticated. We no longer run our fingers through water, shout at the stars, make faces at the moon. Water is H_2O, the stars have been classified, and the moon is not made of green cheese—Neil Armstrong walked on it. Rabbi Heschel saw this as our contemporary trap: "believing that everything can be explained, that reality is a simple affair which has only to be organized in order to be mastered. All enigmas can be solved, and all wonder is nothing but 'the effect of novelty upon ignorance.'"[9] Oh yes, the new can amaze us: a station in outer space, the latest computer game, the softest diaper in history. Till tomorrow; till the new becomes old; till yesterday's wonder is discarded, replaced, taken for granted. Little wonder Heschel concluded, "As civilization advances, the sense of wonder declines."[10]

When did I last marvel not at *what* I saw—Halley's Comet racing toward the sun, Michael Jordan soaring to the basket from the foul line—but *that* I see, that with a flicker of eyelids I can span a small world? Must I grow deaf with Beethoven before I touch my ears with reverence? Does it amaze me that I can shape an idea, tell you how I feel, touch my fingers to a loved one's face, to a flower? Must I envy Bill Gates, marvel at my Macintosh, gaze openmouthed at the computer that crushed chess champion Garry Kasparov, and never see myself, man or woman, as the most ingenious creation of them all, the image of God on earth? Is technology to make machines of our children or open them as never before to an ever-unfolding creation of which they are the stewards?

Again, very simply, what will drive America the rest of its third century? Only information piled upon information, or information selectively imbibed and salted with wonder? And where will America's parents take their stand? Where will you take your stand?

Happily, in all three options, all three choices, it's not an either/or; it's the traditionally Catholic, increasingly Christian both/and. I mean individualism for the building of community; ethical justice supplemented by biblical; information ingested with awe.

I conclude this section with a swift story and an intriguing insight. The story? A Sufi mystic was complaining to God about the woeful state of the world. Finally, in angry desperation, he cried out to God, "Why don't you do something about this?" God's reply? "I did. I made you."

In the context of that story, a thought-provoking insight from a powerful Presbyterian preacher and novelist, Frederick Buechner. The religious man or woman, he proclaimed, is "a queer mixture" of three persons: "the poet, the lunatic, the lover."[11] I pray that the poet may always find a place in you. For the poet is not primarily a versifier, fashioning delightful rhymes. A poet is a person of profound faith, seeing beneath the appearances of God's creation, seeing with new eyes, at times the eyes of Christ, believing the unbelievable, imagining the impossible. I pray that there may always be a fair measure of lunacy in you: the wild idea, the foolishness of Christ's cross, the mad exchange of all else for an ideal, perhaps for God ; for herein lies the Christian hope. And I pray that, however radical the risk, even on this world's crosses you will always mimic Christ the lover, arms flung wide, your body given to the coming century for America's soul, for a nation's new birth: a rebirth to individualism for the common good, to divine as well as human justice, to endless knowledge seasoned with ceaseless wonder.

II

Do those three options sound dreadfully abstract to you? Lest they abide in abstraction, let me exemplify the choices from life as real as you'll ever find it. Two stories; true stories. One story focuses on the power, divine Power, within an individual; the other centers on the power, divine Power, within community.

First, Sister Thea Bowman. I never met Thea, but this African-American nun taught me how to live and still tries to teach me how to die. She was born in 1937, grew up in Canton, Mississippi. A convert to Catholicism at ten, she joined the Franciscan Sisters of Perpetual Adoration at nineteen. For ten years she taught high school, at 35 earned a doctorate in English from the Catholic University of America. She became consultant for intercultural awareness in the Catholic Diocese of Jackson and professor of black theology at Xavier University in New Orleans. She spoke and sang at youth rallies, workshops, and services throughout the States, in Canada and Africa. At 43 she was diagnosed with breast cancer that had spread to the lymph nodes and bones. Six years later, March 30, 1990, she was dead. But these cold facts say little if anything about a woman who transformed whatever and whomever she touched.[12]

This lady was a word that challenged. Already advanced in her cancer, she told the assembled United States bishops in heart-rending, heart-lifting syllables what it means to be black and Catholic and American, then closed with a unique request:

> Now, bishops, I'm going to ask you-all to do something. Cross your right hand over your left hand. You've got to move together to do that. All right now, walk with me. See, in the old days, you had to tighten up so that when the bullets would come, so that when the tear gas would come, so that when the dogs would come, so that when the horses would come, so that when the tanks would come, brothers and sisters would not be separated from one another.[13]

"We shall live in love," she sang. And all the bishops swayed and sang. The U.S. bishops swayed and sang!

This lady was a word that sang. For Thea, music was the sound of black spirituality. Between songs on a recording made with a 50-voice choir she had shaped, she urged all who heard it:

> Listen! Hear us! While the world is full of hate, strife, vengeance, we sing songs of love, laughter, worship, wisdom, justice, and peace because we are free. Though our forefathers bent to bear the heat of the sun, the strike of the lash, the chain of slavery, we are free. No man can enslave us. We are too strong, too unafraid. America needs our strength, our voices to drown out her sorrows, the clatter of war....Listen! Hear us! We are the voice of negro America.[14]

This lady was a word that healed. As her wheel chair drove her cancerous flesh across the country, Thea's mission in life was never more evident: healing, making whole. On a September day in 1989, six months before her death, at St. Stephen's Church in Minneapolis, she celebrated healing ministry in a concert for all races AIDS-afflicted. Several sentences from her words that day are etched in my flesh—words we must by our lives etch into the hearts of our children:

> I have come tonight seeking a blessing. I have come tonight seeking a healing. I don't usually talk about myself, but tonight I want to tell you a little about me. I have cancer. More importantly, I have something in common with my brothers and sisters who have AIDS—weight loss, hair loss, loss of voice, weakness, fatigue, exhaustion.
>
> I'm here tonight to say, God IS. God made me. God loves me.

God gave me life, and I want to live as fully as I can live until I die. I want to live my best; I want to love my best; I want to do my best; I want to give my best.[15]

Thea's memory still inspires communities across our country. Such, good friends, is what one individual can do—one person who serves community; one person who loves God and people and all creation with a crucifying passion; one person whose wheel chair trembled with a woman of wonder, living fully to her last breath.

A second example. Last night I was uncommonly restless. I felt that God was trying to tell me something, to remind me of something. For the life of me, I could not recall it, and it murdered sleep. Ten o'clock passed, eleven, twelve, one—and at 1:19 by the bedside clock I remembered. What did I remember? Jericho...Joshua. Listen to the biblical account.

> The Lord said to Joshua: "See, I have handed Jericho over to you, along with its king and soldiers. You shall march around the city, all the warriors circling the city once. Thus you shall do for six days, with seven priests bearing seven trumpets of rams' horns before the ark. On the seventh day you shall march around the city seven times, the priests blowing the trumpets. When they make a long blast with the ram's horn, as soon as you hear the sound of the trumpet, then all the people shall shout with a great shout; and the wall of the city will fall down flat, and all the people shall charge straight ahead.
>
> (Jos 6:2–5)

And so it happened—but not only to Joshua, not only to Jericho's wall. I remembered the 1960s, the struggle of America's blacks for civil rights. I remembered Andy Young marching his warriors around the Capitol seven times. Why? Because he was convinced that if his people marched around the Capitol seven times, if his people were to utter a mighty cry, the walls of our Capitol would collapse. And so it happened. Against all the odds, the Civil Rights Act of 1964 passed our Congress.

It was the strongest civil rights bill in U.S. history. It ordered restaurants, hotels, and other businesses that serve the general public to serve all persons, no matter their race, color, religion, national origin. It barred discrimination by employers and unions, established the Equal Opportunity Commission. It cut off federal funds from any program or activity that allowed racial discrimination.[16]

III

But it is not only Joshua, not only Andy Young, who can make walls to fall. You too can topple the walls of Congress. Not so much with your marching feet; much more with your voices and your votes, with your songs and your outraged cry, "Save our children!"

On one condition. Only if all of us, with more colors than the rainbow, can, for this momentous moment, lay aside our ancient angers, our historic hates, and become a single community of love. Only if we can rise in our daily living from human justice to divine justice, from fairness to fidelity. Only if we love our God with all our heart and soul, all our mind and strength, reject whatever idols of earth hold us imprisoned. Only if, like the crucified Christ, we love every human image of God, however flawed, like another self—the poverty-stricken *and* the well-heeled, the battered *and* the beautiful, the ugly *and* the cool, the captive *and* the free. Only if we touch all of God's creation, everything God saw on the sixth day "was very good" (Gen 1:31), earth and sea and sky and all that is in them—touch it with reverence, reject the consumerism, the lust for more and more, that is savaging our society.

Then it is, good friends, that our cries have a splendid chance of toppling the walls of injustice. Then we may save the children who have no lobby comparable to tobacco and the gun, have no lobby save the love of God and His Christ that infects us, that drives us mercilessly and merrily to live and, yes, like Dr. King, to challenge death itself for the little ones who reveal what the kingdom of God is like.

Do you believe that? Do you really believe that a mass of committed Christians can topple the walls of injustice? Not by our naked humanity. Only with Christ, "the power of God and the wisdom of God. For God's foolishness is wiser than human wisdom, and God's weakness is stronger than human strength" (1 Cor 1:24–25).

Do you believe that? Twelve ordinary men once believed it, and our world has never been quite the same since. Women in every age have believed it, from Mary Magdalene whom tradition calls "apostle to the apostles," through Catherine of Siena challenging a pope to fidelity, to Marian here with her vision and Shannon here with her two-month-old Micah, and our world is immeasurably richer for their faith, their love, their courage.

Do you still believe you can do it? Do you still believe that in the power of Christ you can not only "save our children" but shape an America where individuals serve the common good, where all God's children receive what God has in mind when fashioning them? Then be just as God is just. Love as Christ loved—even unto crucifixion.

Do you believe it?

Institute for Child Advocacy Ministry
Clinton, Tennessee
July 22, 1998

NOTES

Preface

1. For the following five paragraphs, I am borrowing extensively (with some changes) from the first section of my 1997 address to the Catholic Coalition on Preaching, published in *Origins* 27, no. 18 (Oct. 16, 1997) 311–16.

2. From *The Poems of Gerard Manley Hopkins,* ed. W. H. Gardner and N. H. Mackenzie (4th ed.; New York: Oxford University Press, 1970) 90.

Homily 1

1. So Elisabeth Schüssler Fiorenza, quoted in my *Preaching: The Art and the Craft* (New York/Mahwah: Paulist, 1987) 77.

2. See Joseph A. Fitzmyer, S.J., *The Gospel according to Luke (I–IX)* (Garden City, N.Y.: Doubleday, 1981) 350 (on v. 35).

3. For important information on the title "Son of God," see Fitzmyer, ibid. 205–8.

4. Augustine, *Sermon 215,* no. 4 (Patrologia latina 38, 1074).

5. Patrick J. Bearsley, S.M., "Mary the Perfect Disciple: A Paradigm for Mariology," *Theological Studies* 41 (1980) 461–504, at 479–80.

6. For the text see my collection *Tell the Next Generation: Homilies and Near Homilies* (New York/Ramsey: Paulist, 1980) 39–43, at 43.

7. Jesus was quoting Ps 31:6. "In the later rabbinical tradition Ps 31:6 was used as part of the evening prayer that a disciple should utter before going to sleep" (Joseph A. Fitzmyer, S.J., *The Gospel according to Luke (X–XXIV)* (Garden City, N.Y.: Doubleday, 1985) 1519 (on v. 46).

Homily 2

1. I have this story from the sermon of a Protestant preacher, who heard it from a woman doctor from Mafraq, over coffee in the Beirut Intercontinental Hotel. I have shortened the story somewhat, without omitting essentials. I have used the story before, in my homily on the first of Jesus' last words from his cross, "Father, Forgive Them," in my collection *Love Is a Flame of the Lord* (New York/Mahwah, N.J.: Paulist, 1995) 17–21, at 20–21.

2. See Louis F. Hartman, C.SS.R., and Alexander A. Di Lella, O.F.M., "Daniel," *The New Jerome Biblical Commentary,* ed. Raymond E. Brown, S.S., Joseph A. Fitzmyer, S.J., and Roland E. Murphy, O.Carm. (Englewood Cliffs, N.J.: Prentice-Hall, 1990) 25:30, p. 417.

3. See ibid.

4. Based on Dan 9:4–10.

5. This homily was preached at the Theological College across from the Catholic University of America, Washington, D.C.

6. On the Lucan form of the Our Father, see Joseph A. Fitzmyer, S.J., *The Gospel according to Luke (X–XXIV)* (Garden City, N.Y.: Doubleday, 1985) 896–907.

7. A currently popular coffee.

8. I am aware that the so-called "first words of Jesus from the cross" do not appear in very early important manuscripts of Luke and in some ancient translations (see Fitzmyer [n. 6 above] 1503). No matter; the cross itself is a mute cry for forgiveness; apart from forgiveness Calvary makes no sense.

Homily 3

1. At the Franciscan Renewal Center in Scottsdale, Arizona, the liturgical readings from Cycle A replaced the readings from Cycle B for the third Sunday of Lent. This included the Gospel of the Samaritan woman at the well. I was asked to link that Gospel story with a concern for immigration which had brought a group of men and women to the Center. On the Friday before this Sunday, I had addressed them on "Immigrant: Biblical and American."

2. John L. McKenzie, "Samaritans," in his *Dictionary of the Bible* (New York: Macmillan, 1965) 765–66, at 766.

3. See the article by historian David M. Kennedy, "Can We Still Afford to Be a Nation of Immigrants?" *Atlantic Monthly* 278, no. 5 (November 1996) 52–54, 56, 58, 61, 64, 66–68; also the article by economist George J. Borjas, "The New Economics of Immigration," ibid. 72–80.

4. I am presuming that Jesus' request for water was granted. Obviously, "living water" for well water was not a *quid pro quo.*

5. See Raymond E. Brown, S.S., *The Gospel according to John (i–xii)*

(Garden City, N.Y.: Doubleday, 1966) 178: "Within the scope of Johannine theology, there are really two possibilities: living water means the revelation which Jesus gives to men, or it means the Spirit which Jesus gives to men."

Homily 4

1. More exactly, Isa 61:1a,b,d; 58:6d; 61:2a.
2. See Joseph A. Fitzmyer, S.J., *The Gospel according to Luke (I–IX)* (Garden City, N.Y.: Doubleday, 1981) 528.
3. I am indebted here to an enlightening essay on Jeremiah by Carroll Stuhlmueller, C.P., in his *Thirsting for the Lord: Essays in Biblical Spirituality* (Garden City, N.Y.: Image Books, 1979) 62–70.
4. Abraham J. Heschel, *The Prophets* (New York: Harper & Row, 1962) 19.
5. E. J. Tinsley, *The Gospel according to Luke* (London/New York: Cambridge University, 1965) 53.
6. Heschel, *The Prophets* 24.
7. See the account in the *Washington Star,* May 26, 1979, D-1 and D-2.

Homily 5

1. In the Latin, "Accende lumen sensibus."
2. Here I am indebted to a remarkably insightful article by a professor of English at Boston College, J. A. Appleyard, S.J., "What Do the Oscars Tell Us?" *America* 178, no. 9 (March 21, 1998) 16–19, 22.
3. Ibid. 18.
4. Ibid. 16.
5. Ibid. 17.
6. I should note here that on this Fourth Sunday of Lent I took advantage of the option allowing the readings from Cycle A.

Homily 6

1. New York: Harper & Row, 1985.
2. Ibid. 181.
3. Ibid. xii.
4. This homily was preached to priests of the Archdiocese of Cincinnati, Ohio, during a Preaching the Just Word retreat/workshop codirected by Walter J. Burghardt, S.J., and Raymond B. Kemp.
5. See important information, in brief form, in Robert L. Kinast, "Healing," *The New Dictionary of Catholic Spirituality,* ed. Michael Downey (Collegeville, Minn.: Liturgical, 1993) 466–68.
6. Lawrence Boadt, C.S.P.

Homily 7

1. See Ps 35:23: "Wake up! Bestir yourself for my defense,/ for my cause, my God and my Lord!" For the complex background, see Joseph A. Fitzmyer, S.J., "The Semitic Background of the New Testament *Kyrios*-Title," in his *A Wandering Aramean* (Missoula, Mont.: Scholars, 1979) 115–42; also his "New Testament *Kyrios* and *Maranatha* and Their Aramaic Background," in *To Advance the Gospel: New Testament Studies* (New York: Crossroad, 1981) 218–35. For a swift scholarly synopsis, useful for homilists, see Fitzmyer's *The Gospel according to Luke (I–IX)* (Garden City, N.Y.: Doubleday, 1981) 200–204.

2. I am aware of Raymond Brown's suggestion, based on Lindars, that "the Thomas story (which has no Synoptic parallels) has been created by the evangelist who has taken and dramatized a theme of doubt that originally appeared in the narrative of the appearance to the disciples....Thomas has become here the personification of an attitude" common to all the disciples. See Raymond E. Brown, S.S., *The Gospel according to John (xiii–xxi)* (Garden City, N.Y.: Doubleday, 1970) 1031. He proposes that the statement "He showed them his hands and side" (Jn 20:20) "was originally preceded by an expression of doubt, as in Luke xxiv 37–39, but that the evangelist has transferred this doubt to a separate episode and personified it in Thomas" (ibid. 1032). This scholarly suggestion, for all its merits, fits the classroom better than the pulpit; but it is worth mentioning here for more profound meditation on the part of believers.

3. Brown, ibid. 1048.

4. See the homily "Let Christ Easter in Us" in my collection *Dare To Be Christ: Homilies for the Nineties* (New York/Mahwah: Paulist, 1990) 51–56, at 52.

Homily 8

1. See Margaret Carlson, "Does He or Doesn't He?" *Time* 151, no. 16 (April 27, 1998) 22.

Homily 9

1. Actually, the singular is used, but the NT follows the Aramaic and Hebrew preference for a distributive singular; see Raymond E. Brown, *The Gospel according to John (xiii–xxi)* (Garden City, N.Y.: Doubleday, 1970) 618.

2. Because the liturgical readings from John's Gospel during Easter weekdays are so cut up, without regard for context, I have presumed to add verse 27 to the Gospel for this day.

3. This homily was preached to priests of the Archdiocese of New York on the first full day of the retreat/workshop Preaching the Just Word.

4. Here I am indebted in part to sections of an informative, wise, and forward-looking book by William J. Bausch, *The Parish of the Next Millennium* (Mystic, Conn.: Twenty-third, 1997).

5. Ibid. 40–41, quoting from the (London) *Tablet,* March 16, 1996.

6. Ibid. 71.

7. See ibid. 74.

8. Léon-Joseph Cardinal Suenens, *Coresponsibility in the Church* (New York: Herder and Herder, 1968) 31.

9. I borrow the phrase from liturgist Aidan Kavanagh, quoted by Bausch, *The Parish* (n. 4 above) 194–95.

Homily 10

1. This homily was preached at the annual meeting of the Catholic Health Association of Canada, held in Saint John, New Brunswick, Canada, May 3–6, 1997.

2. Kaela Volkmer, in *Accompaniment* (A Newsletter for the Family and Friends of Jesuit Volunteers: International) 12, no. 2 (spring 1997).

3. I am not suggesting that love is the *only* way in which humans imitate their God.

4. I have this from Bernie S. Siegel, M.D., *Love, Medicine & Miracles* (New York: Harper & Row, 1988) 2.

5. Quoted by Alain K. Laing, "Hippocrates," *World Book Encyclopedia* 9 (1975) 227.

6. Volkmer, in *Accompaniment* (n. 2 above).

7. Siegel (n. 4 above) xii; emphasis mine.

8. Ibid. 181.

Homily 11

1. This homily was preached to the members of the Jesuit community of Gonzaga College High School, Washington, D.C., at its weekly gathering for Eucharistic liturgy. The community consists of Jesuits who work at the school, others who staff the parish of St. Aloysius Gonzaga and the Horace McKenna Center for the poor, and others who have individual ministries, e.g. my project Preaching the Just Word.

2. Karl Rahner, S.J., *Ignatius of Loyola* (London/New York: Collins, 1979) 11–13.

3. Herbert Vorgrimler, *Understanding Karl Rahner: An Introduction to His Life and Thought* (New York: Crossroad, 1986) 11.

4. See Raymond E. Brown, S.S., *The Gospel according to John (xiii–xxi)* (Garden City., N.Y.: Doubleday, 1970) 700.

5. St. Augustine, *On John* 93.1 (Patrologia latina 35, 1864).

Homily 12

1. See Myles M. Bourke, "The Epistle to the Hebrews," *The New Jerome Biblical Commentary*, ed. Raymond E. Brown, S.S., Joseph A. Fitzmyer, S.J., and Roland E. Murphy, O.Carm. (Englewood Cliffs, N.J.: Prentice-Hall, 1990) 60:8, p. 923.
2. Hilary of Poitiers, *Commentary on Matthew* 2.5 (Patrologia latina 9, 927).
3. So Emile Mersch, *The Whole Christ: The Historical Development of the Doctrine of the Mystical Body in Scripture and Tradition* (London, 1949) 273.
4. Augustine of Hippo, *Confessions* 8.7; tr. F. J. Sheed, *The Confessions of St. Augustine* (New York: Sheed & Ward, 1943) 170.
5. *Dead Man Walking* is the title of a powerful film, the true story of a nun's effect on a convict condemned to die.
6. To understand the emphasis here, it is pertinent to note that this homily was preached during my project Preaching the Just Word, this time to priests of the Diocese of Honolulu, the same day on which a biblical scholar, Jesuit John R. Donahue, opened to them the significance and richness of biblical justice.

Homily 13

1. See Anthony F. Campbell, S.J., "1 Samuel," in *The New Jerome Biblical Commentary*, ed. Raymond E. Brown, S.S., Joseph A. Fitzmyer, S.J., and Roland E. Murphy, O. Carm. (Englewood Cliffs, N.J.: Prentice-Hall, 1990) 9:1–39, pp. 145–54
2. Ibid. 9:7, p. 147.
3. Here I am mightily indebted to Abraham J. Heschel's *The Prophets* (New York: Harper & Row, 1962), especially the opening chapter, "What Manner of Man Is the Prophet?" (3–26). Also, I am including and extending ideas first presented in a chapter of my book *Preaching: The Art and the Craft* (New York/Mahwah: Paulist, 1987) 29–38.
4. Heschel has seven; I omit two: the prophet as conceding little to human weakness and exaggerating mightily, and the prophet as God's counselor.
5. Heschel, *The Prophets* 4.
6. Ibid. 231.
7. Dogmatic Constitution on the Church 12.
8. Encyclical *On Social Concern*, Dec. 30, 1987, no. 31.
9. Ibid.
10. Ibid. 28.
11. Heschel, *The Prophets* 224.
12. This homily was preached at the presbyteral convocation, Jan. 12–15, 1998, of the Diocese of Owensboro, Kentucky.

Homily 14

1. To grasp the thrust of this homily, one must realize that it was preached to the St. Aloysius Gonzaga Jesuit Community on the day (January 19 in 1998) on which our country celebrated the life and death of Martin Luther King Jr.
2. C. F. D. Moule, *The Gospel according to Mark* (London/New York: Cambridge University, 1965) 27.
3. See C. S. Mann, *Mark* (Anchor Bible 27; New York: Doubleday, 1986) 235–36.
4. See John W. O'Malley, S.J., "Reform, Historical Consciousness, and Vatican II's Aggiornamento," *Theological Studies* 32 (1971) 573–601.
5. Ibid. 600; emphasis in the text.
6. From Taylor Branch, *Parting the Waters: America in the King Years 1954–63* (New York: Simon and Schuster, 1988) 882–83.
7. *Sister Thea Bowman, Shooting Star: Selected Writings and Speeches*, ed. Celestine Cepress, FSPA (Winona, Minn.: Saint Mary's Press, 1993) 37.
8. Ibid. 44.

Homily 15

1. Oxford and New York: Oxford University, 1997.

Homily 16

1. This is one possible explanation of the name. See Daniel J. Harrington, S.J., "The Gospel according to Mark," *The New Jerome Biblical Commentary* 41:23, p. 604.
2. This homily was preached during a Preaching the Just Word retreat/workshop for priests of the Diocese of Austin, Texas.
3. I am aware that Mark may be putting together incidents that happened at different times. Even so, it is legitimate, for homiletic purposes, to deal with them as a unity.
4. A Yiddish word, "mad, crazy, insane," frequently used by my very early Jewish friends to suggest that someone is "not all there."
5. Mt 12:24 identifies the opponents as Pharisees.
6. Vatican II, Decree on the Ministry and Life of Priests, no. 4.
7. Ibid. (tr. *The Documents of Vatican II*, ed. Walter M. Abbott, S.J. [New York: Herder and Herder, 1966] 540).
8. Ibid., no. 5 (tr. *Documents* 541).

Homily 17

1. Taken from *USA Today,* Dec. 20–22, 1996, 13A–14A, 17A–18A.
2. See John P. Meier, *A Marginal Jew: Rethinking the Historical Jesus* 2: *Mentor, Message, and Miracles* (New York: Doubleday, 1994): "...rambling, sometimes incoherent, yet concrete and bizarre narrative" (650); "it is difficult to say how much of the story may be pressed for historical facts" (652); "too many layers of literary activity and theological imagination have been superimposed" (653).
3. See the same expression in Mk 3:14: Jesus "appointed twelve whom he also named apostles, *to be with him,* and to be sent out to proclaim the message."
4. C. D. F. Moule, *The Gospel according to Mark* (New York: Cambridge University, 1965, repr. 1978) 42–43.
5. This homily was preached to priests of the Diocese of Tulsa, Oklahoma, as part of a Preaching the Just Word retreat/workshop.
6. Robert Hutchinson, "Does Your Justice Liturgy Do Justice to Liturgy?" *Salt,* November/December 1993, 28–32, at 32.

Homily 18

1. I am aware of the difficulties associated with the question of historicity in the New Testament traditions about Peter; aware too that there are differences among the evangelists in their treatments of Peter. For a splendid ecumenical discussion of such issues, see *Peter in the New Testament: A Collaborative Assessment by Protestant and Roman Catholic Scholars,* ed. Raymond E. Brown, Karl P. Donfried, and John Reumann (Minneapolis: Augsburg/New York: Paulist, 1973).
2. See Raymond E. Brown, S.S., *The Gospel according to John (xiii–xxi)* (Garden City, N.Y.: Doubleday, 1970) 1104–5.
3. On the difficulties in this text, the preacher would do well to consult Brown, ibid. 1106–8.
4. Léon-Joseph Suenens, *Coresponsibility in the Church* (New York: Herder and Herder, 1968) 31.
5. William J. O'Malley, "The Goldilocks Method," *America* 165, no. 14 (Nov. 9, 1991) 334–39, at 336.

Homily 19

1. This homily was preached at a Mass for Peace and Justice on the first day of a Preaching the Just Word retreat/workshop for priests and lay associates of the Diocese of Honolulu.
2. Joseph A. Fitzmyer, S.J., *The Gospel according to Luke (I–IX)* (Garden City, N.Y.: Doubleday, 1981) 225.
3. Ibid.

4. See Raymond E. Brown, S.S., *The Gospel according to John (xiii–xxi)* (Garden City, N.Y.: Doubleday, 1970) 653–54.
5. See ibid. 737–38.
6. See Constitution on the Church in the Modern World, no. 78.
7. Ibid.
8. From King's famous address "I Have a Dream" to 300,000 between the Capitol and the Washington Monument.

Homily 20

1. See Irene Nowell, O.S.B., "Tobit," *The New Jerome Biblical Commentary,* ed. Raymond E. Brown, S.S., Joseph A. Fitzmyer, S.J., and Roland E. Murphy, O.Carm. (Englewood Cliffs, N.J.: Prentice-Hall, 1990) 38:1–24, pp. 568–71.
2. See ibid. 38:4 and 6, pp. 568–69.
3. This homily was preached to priests of the Diocese of Springfield-Cape Girardeau, Missouri, in the course of my project Preaching the Just Word.
4. George M. Anderson, S.J., "Talking about Religion: An Interview with George H. Gallup, Jr.," *America* 175, no. 12 (Oct. 26, 1996) 19–22, at 21; emphasis mine.
5. Ibid. 20.

Homily 21

1. See Daniel J. Harrington, S.J., *The Gospel of Matthew* (Sacra pagina 1; Collegeville, Minn.: Liturgical, 1991) 309–11.
2. This homily was delivered to priests and permanent deacons of the Diocese of Davenport, Iowa, at a Preaching the Just Word institute.
3. *Washington Post,* May 19, 1998, A20.

Homily 22

1. This homily was preached during a Preaching the Just Word institute for priests, permanent deacons, and transitional deacons of the Diocese of Raleigh, North Carolina.
2. I have borrowed these two paragraphs from a homily of mine, "Salt of the Earth, Light of the World," in my collection (now out of print) *Grace on Crutches: Homilies for Fellow Travelers* (New York/Mahwah: Paulist, 1986) 155–59, at 156.
3. *Communities of Salt and Light: Parish Resource Manual,* ed. Department of Social Development and World Peace, United States Catholic Conference (Washington, D.C.: USCC, 1994).
4. Ibid., Appendix, p. 1.
5. Ibid.

6. Paul VI, *Evangelization in the Modern World,* nos. 27, 29, 34, 36 (tr. *The Pope Speaks* 21, no. 1 [spring 1976] 16, 17, 19, 20).
7. *Communities* (n. 3 above), Appendix, p. 3.

Homily 23

1. This homily was delivered to priests of the Archdiocese of Los Angeles, California, on the first full day of a Preaching the Just Word retreat/workshop.
2. Here and later, I am borrowing heavily from my "Crisis, Cross, Confidence: A Priest for *This* Season," *Emmanuel* 97 (1991) 64–73, 110–11.
3. Quoted words from Roger Balducelli, O.S.F.S., "The Decision for Celibacy," *Theological Studies* 36 (1975) 219–42, at 242.

Homily 24

1. See Robert L. Kinast, "Healing," *The New Dictionary of Catholic Spirituality,* ed. Michael Downey (Collegeville, Minn.: Liturgical, 1993) 466–68, at 467.
2. See *Sister Thea Bowman, Shooting Star: Selected Writings and Speeches,* ed. Celestine Cepress, FSPA (Winona, Minn.: Saint Mary's Press, 1993) 37.
3. Ibid. 117.
4. Quoted in the *New York Times,* Sept. 6, 1997, 19.

Homily 25

1. Joseph A. Fitzmyer, S.J., *The Gospel according to Luke (I–IX)* (Garden City, N.Y.: Doubleday, 1981) 757.
2. Ibid. 758.
3. This homily was preached at a liturgy during a Preaching the Just Word retreat/workshop for priests and pastoral administrators of the Diocese of Great Falls-Billings, Montana.
4. Mark 6:16 has Herod believing that "John, whom I beheaded, has been raised"; not so Luke.
5. See the council's Declaration on the Relationship of the Church to Non-Christian Religions, nos. 2–3.
6. *Nestorii sermo* (ACO 1, 5, 1, 30); *Liber Heraclidis* 2, 1 (tr. Nau 176); *Nestorii tractatus* (ACO 1, 5, 1, 38).
7. John Courtney Murray, S.J., *The Problem of God: Yesterday and Today* (New Haven: Yale University, 1954) 45.
8. Ibid. 44.

9. Here I am indebted to a soul-searing essay by Monika Hellwig, "Re-Emergence of the Human, Critical, Public Jesus," *Theological Studies* 50 (1989) 466–80, esp. 467.
10. Ibid.
11. New York/Ramsey: Paulist, 1982.

Homily 26

1. Literally, "the good part." But see Joseph A. Fitzmyer, S.J., *The Gospel according to Luke (X–XXIV)* (Garden City, N.Y.: Doubleday, 1985) 894: "The positive degree of the adj. is often used in Hellenistic Greek for either the superlative or comparative, both of which were on the wane."
2. This homily was preached during a convocation of the priests of the Diocese of Belleville, Illinois, the focus of which was my project Preaching the Just Word.
3. Some manuscripts omit "into her home."
4. See Fitzmyer (n. 1 above) 891–95.
5. Ibid. 892.
6. Barbara Reid, O.P., professor of Scripture at the Chicago Theological Union, with remarkable insights into biblical justice.
7. See, e.g., Karl Rahner, S.J., *Ignatius of Loyola,* with an Historical Introduction by Paul Imhof, S.J. (London/New York: Collins, 1979) 11–13.
8. Herbert Vorgrimler, *Understanding Karl Rahner: An Introduction to His Life and Thought* (New York: Crossroad, 1986) 11.
9. New York: New American Library, 1961.
10. *U.S. Catholic* 63, no. 10 (Oct. 10, 1998) 50.
11. Ibid.

Homily 27

1. The occasion was Georgetown University's Third Century Campaign Kickoff Weekend.
2. See Joseph A. Fitzmyer, S.J., *The Gospel according to Luke (I–IX)* (Garden City, N.Y.: Doubleday, 1981) 573–74.
3. See Leviticus 13:49.
4. Father Leo J. O'Donovan, S.J., president of Georgetown University.
5. Head coach of the Georgetown University basketball team.

Homily 28

1. This homily was preached on the first full day of a Preaching the Just Word retreat/workshop for priests, permanent deacons, and lay ministers of the Diocese of Phoenix, Arizona.

2. Marian Wright Edelman, Introduction to Arloc Sherman, *Wasting America's Future: The Children's Defense Fund Report on the Costs of Child Poverty* (Boston: Beacon Press, 1994) xx.
3. Ibid. xvi–xvii; emphasis in text..
4. Louis S. Richman, "Struggling To Save Our Kids," in a Special Report in *Fortune* 126, no. 3 (Aug. 10, 1992) 34–40, at 34.
5. In a message (September 1990) to the World Summit for Children, quoted in an editorial by Anthony J. Schulte, O.F.M., "Make Room in the Inn for the World's Children," *St. Anthony Messenger* 98, no. 7 (December 1990) 26.
6. Quoted ibid.
7. The Greek of this sentence—a protasis expressing reality ("if you have") and an apodosis contrary to fact ("you would say")—"implies that the faith of the apostles is not even the size of a mustard seed" (Joseph A. Fitzmyer, S.J., *The Gospel according to Luke (X–XXIV)* [New York: Doubleday, 1985] 1142).
8. On Lucan faith see Fitzmyer, ibid. 1142–43, but especially his *The Gospel according to Luke (I–IX)* (New York: Doubleday, 1981) 235–37, 712–14.
9. The arithmetic is less than accurate, since at least several million Catholic children must be numbered among the 16 million children at risk.

Homily 29

1. This homily was preached before the annual Memorial Day Concert held on the Capitol Lawn, for relatives and friends of the concert's producer, Jerry Colbert, at the Washington Court Hotel.
2. Figures from pertinent articles in the *World Book Encyclopedia,* 1975 edition.

Homily 30

1. This homily was preached to priests of the Diocese of Fall River, Massachusetts, on the first full day of the retreat/workshop Preaching the Just Word.
2. Origen, *Homily 17 on Luke* (Griechische christliche Schriftsteller 49, 105).
3. Epiphanius, *Panarion* 78.11 (GCS 37, 462).
4. Here I am indebted to Joseph A. Fitzmyer, S.J., *The Gospel according to Luke (I–IX)* (Garden City, N.Y.: Doubleday, 1981) 418, 429–30.
5. Ibid. 430.
6. See Patrick J. Bearsley, S.M., "Mary the Perfect Disciple: A Paradigm for Mariology," *Theological Studies* 41 (1980) 461–504.
7. Augustine, *Sermon 233* 3.4 (Patrologia latina 38, 1114).

Homily 31

1. See J. Gilchrist, "Lateran," *New Catholic Encyclopedia* 8 (1967) 403–6.
2. See J. E. Steinmueller, "Temples (in the Bible)," ibid. 13 (1967) 998–1000.
3. See Joseph A. Fitzmyer, S.J., *Paul and His Theology: A Brief Sketch* (2nd ed.; Englewood Cliffs, N.J.: Prentice-Hall, 1989) 68–69.
4. Jerome Murphy-O'Connor, O.P., "The First Letter to the Corinthians," *The New Jerome Biblical Commentary,* ed. Raymond E. Brown, S.S., Joseph A. Fitzmyer, S.J., and Roland E. Murphy, O.Carm. (Englewood Cliffs, N.J.: Prentice-Hall, 1990) 49:23, p. 802.
5. This homily was preached to priests of the Archdiocese of Los Angeles, California, on the first full day of a Preaching the Just Word retreat/workshop. On that morning a Scripture scholar had presented the biblical idea of justice, which I proceeded to utilize in my homily.
6. Origen, *Homily on the Book of Judges* 2.3.
7. See Lynn White Jr., "The Historical Roots of Our Ecological Crisis," *Science* 155 (1967) 1205.
8. See Dennis Olson, "God the Creator: Bible, Creation, Vocation," *Dialog: A Journal of Theology* 36, no. 3 (summer 1997) 169–74, at 173.
9. Ibid. 173–74.

Homily 32

1. This Preaching the Just Word retreat/workshop was held for bishops of Region 12, in the northwest section of the United States, comprising Alaska, Oregon, Idaho, Montana, the State of Washington, and Yukon in Canada.
2. *The Autobiography of St. John Neumann, C.SS.R., Fourth Bishop of Philadelphia,* translation and commentary by Alfred C. Rush, C.SS.R. (Boston: St. Paul Editions, 1977). For further information see Michael J. Curley, C.SS.R., *Venerable John Neumann, C.SS.R., Fourth Bishop of Philadelphia* (New York: Crusader Press, 1952); also his *The Provincial Story: A History of the Baltimore Province of the Congregation of the Most Holy Redeemer* (New York: The Redemptorist Fathers, Baltimore Province, 1963) chapter 5, "Heroic John Neumann," 94–104; and Leo Knowles, *Saints Who Spoke English* (St. Paul, Minn.: Carillon Books, 1979) 163–76.
3. *Autobiography,* Introduction 13.
4. Ibid. 22.
5. Curley, *Venerable John Neumann* 6 ("bookworm" in *Autobiography* 23).
6. Ibid.
7. Ibid. 27.
8. Ibid.

9. Ibid. 28. Josephinism was an Austrian state-church system of the Enlightenment period that subjected the Church and its ministers to the sovereign power of the State. For details see F. Maass, "Josephinism," *New Catholic Encyclopedia* 7 (1967) 1118–19.

10. For these details see Curley, *Venerable John Neumann* 361.

11. Curley, ibid. 199.

12. Ibid. 207–8.

13. See the letter of Neumann's coadjutor, James Frederick Wood, in Curley, ibid. 327.

14. For Neumann's early trials, see Curley, ibid. 197–232.

15. Curley, ibid. 218.

16. See ibid. 263.

17. English text ibid. 284.

18. Curley, ibid. 337–60, lists four "four principal duties of a bishop of a diocese" that come down to us from Scripture, the councils, and the great bishops in all ages: preaching, conferring of sacraments, spiritual administration, and temporal administration, and applies them to the Bishop of Philadelphia.

19. Council of Trent, Session 5, Decree 2, no. 9 (*Conciliorum oecumenicorum decreta,* ed. J. Alberigo [Freiburg: Herder, 1962] 645).

20. *The Complete Works of Saint Alphonsus Liguori* (Centenary Edition 22.324).

Homily 33

1. R. W. Chambers, *Thomas More* (Westminster, Md.: Newman, 1949). For a scathing appraisal of Chambers, see Richard Marius, *Thomas More: A Biography* (New York: Knopf, 1984) xx: "cloying, unrelenting, often unthinking defense of More in every particular."

2. Marius, *Thomas More* 514.

3. Robert Bolt, *A Man for All Seasons: A Play in Two Acts* (New York: Vintage Books, 1960).

4. This homily was preached to priests of the Diocese of Wheeling-Charleston, West Virginia, during the liturgy on the first full day of the project Preaching the Just Word. The title of the homily reproduces words reportedly spoken by More just before his execution.

5. R. S. Sylvester, "More, Sir Thomas, St.," *New Catholic Encyclopedia* 9 (1967) 1136–40, at 1137.

6. Its authorship has been questioned; see the Introduction to Richard S. Sylvester's edition of *The History of King Richard III,* Vol. 2 in *The Complete Works of St. Thomas More* (New Haven: Yale University, 1963) xvii–lxv.

7. Marius, *Thomas More* 12.

8. Ibid. 518.

9. Ibid. 519.

10.   Sylvester, "More" (n. 5 above) 1136–37.

11.   So Marius, *Thomas More* 518.

12.   So Sylvester, "More" 1138–39.

13.   Marius, *Thomas More* xxiv.

14.   Ignatius of Antioch, *Letter to the Romans* 4.1–2 (tr. James A. Kleist, S.J., *Ancient Christian Writers* 1 [Westminster, Md.: Newman, 1946] 81–82).

15.   Bolt, *A Man for All Seasons* (n. 3 above) xiii.

16.   Marius, *Thomas More* 515.

17.   Ibid. 483.

18.   Quoted ibid. 485.

19.   Quoted ibid. 488–89.

Homily 34

1.   I owe this reminder to a pamphlet by Thomas J. Coffey, S.J., *Kateri Tekakwitha* (Auriesville, N.Y.: Tekakwitha League, 1982) 3–4.

2.   This homily was preached during the Eleventh Annual Summer Institute for Priests, a significant segment of Seton Hall University's National Institute for Clergy Formation.

3.   Here I am indebted to the fine article by Marie Therese Archambault, "Tekakwitha, Kateri," *Encyclopedia of North American Indians,* ed. Frederick E. Hoxie (New York: Houghton Mifflin, 1996) 623–25. I should note that on the details of Kateri's life the articles and books are not always consistent.

4.   Ibid. 623.

5.   See J. D. L. Leonard, "Tetakwitha, Kateri," *New Catholic Encyclopedia* 13 (1967) 978–79, at 979.

6.   Archambault (n. 3 above) 624.

7.   See Margaret R. Bunson, *Kateri Tekakwitha, Mystic of the Wilderness* (Huntington, Ind.: Our Sunday Visitor, 1992) 37.

8.   John Courtney Murray, S.J., "The Danger of the Vows," *Woodstock Letters* 96 (1967) 420–27, at 427. This famous conference was reconstructed after Father Murray's death from two of his personal copies, one with his own handwritten emendations, together with a number of slightly varying mimeographed copies. He was reluctant to publish the conference without updating it in the spirit of Vatican II; he never found the opportunity.

9.   Roger Balducelli, O.S.F.S, "The Decision for Celibacy," *Theological Studies* 36 (1975) 219–42, at 242.

10.   See Paul Yu-Pin, "Christian Influence in Post-War China," *America* 71 (1944) 34.

11.   G. Voss, "Missionary Accommodation and Ancestral Rites in the Far East," *Theological Studies* 4 (1943) 556.

Homily 35

1. This homily was preached to priests of the Archdiocese of New York during a Preaching the Just Word retreat/workshop.
2. Selected from the letter as reproduced by John J. Wynne, S.J., *The Jesuit Martyrs of North America* (New York: Universal Knowledge Foundation, 1925) 154-74.
3. Quoted by Wynne, ibid. 182-83.
4. See ibid. 215-21; Francis Parkman, *The Jesuits in North America in the Seventeenth Century: France and England in North America, Part 2* (Boston: Little, Brown, 1940) 195, 511-13; L. Pouliot, "North American Martyrs," *New Catholic Encyclopedia* 10 (1967) 506-7. Wynne and Parkman, though somewhat dated, are especially useful for the quotations, sometimes quite lengthy, from the historically indispensable *Jesuit Relations and Allied Documents*.
5. For details see Edward E. Malone, O.S.B., *The Monk and the Martyr* (Studies in Christian Antiquity 12; Washington, D.C.: Catholic University of America, 1950).
6. J. N. D. Kelly, *Jerome: His Life, Writings, and Controversies* (New York: Harper & Row, 1975) 138.
7. Steven Payne, O.C.D., "Edith Stein: A Fragmented Life," *America* 179, no. 10 (Oct. 10, 1998) 11-14, at 13.
8. Ibid. 11-12.
9. From an essay "Love of the Cross," quoted by Payne, ibid. 13.

Homily 36

1. For a justification of this translation, see Roland E. Murphy, O.Carm., "Canticle of Canticles," *The New Jerome Biblical Commentary*, ed. Raymond E. Brown, S.S., Joseph A. Fitzmyer, S.J., and Roland E. Murphy, O.Carm. (Englewood Cliffs, N.J.: Prentice-Hall, 1990) 29:24, p. 465.
2. See Evelyn Whitehead and James D. Whitehead, "Christian Marriage," *U.S. Catholic* 47, no. 6 (June 1982) 9.

Homily 37

1. See Raymond E. Brown, S.S., *The Gospel according to John (i-xii)* (Garden City, N.Y.: Doubleday, 1966) 103-10.

Homily 38

1. I am not implying that this understanding was that of the Hebrew writer(s); it stems from further reflection down the ages.

2. See Evelyn Whitehead and James D. Whitehead, "Christian Marriage," *U.S. Catholic* 47, no. 6 (June 1982) 9. I am aware that this quotation recurs in many of my wedding homilies; but it says so much so briefly that I see no need to apologize.

3. See *Washington Times*, Aug. 5, 1997, A1.

Homily 39

1. Second Vatican Council, Constitution on the Sacred Liturgy, no. 7.

2. Columbia, Missouri, is Susie's city of birth; New York, the most recent city of her employment. Mexico City is where Gerry's mother and sisters live; Louisville, where Susie and Gerry will live and work.

3. Robert M. Morgenthau, "What Prosecutors Won't Tell You," Op-Ed, *New York Times*, Feb. 7, 1995.

4. Bernie S. Siegel, M.D., *Love, Medicine & Miracles* (New York: Harper & Row, 1988) 181.

5. See ibid. xii.

Homily 40

1. See Roland E. Murphy, O.Carm., "Canticle of Canticles," in *The New Jerome Biblical Commentary,* ed. Raymond E. Brown, S.S., Joseph A. Fitzmyer, S.J., and Roland E. Murphy, O.Carm. (Englewood Cliffs, N.J.: Prentice-Hall, 1990) 29:24, p. 465.

2. Bernie S. Siegel, M.D., *Love, Medicine & Miracles* (New York: Harper & Row, 1985; Perennial Library edition, 1988) 181.

3. Ibid. xii.

4. A well-known TV character presiding quite autocratically over civil suits.

5. One of two Communion hymns during the ceremony.

Homily 41

1. Joseph A. Fitzmyer, S.J., *Paul and His Theology: A Brief Sketch* (2nd ed.; Englewood Cliffs, N.J.: Prentice-Hall, 1989) 78 and 83.

2. I say "disciples" instead of "apostles" because it is not clear from Acts 2:1 whether "they" who "were all together in one place" were only the Twelve or included the "about 120" believers mentioned in Acts 1:15.

3. So suggests Roland E. Murphy, O.Carm., "Canticle of Canticles," *The New Jerome Biblical Commentary,* ed. Raymond E. Brown, S.S., Joseph A. Fitzmyer, S.J., and Roland E. Murphy, O.Carm. (Englewood Cliffs, N.J.: Prentice-Hall, 1990) 29:24, p. 465.

4. Leo I, *Sermon 7 on the Nativity of the Lord* 2.6 (Patrologia latina 54, 217–18, 220–21.

5. See Kevin Godfrey, O.F.M.Conv., "Hospitality," *The New Dictionary of Catholic Spirituality,* ed. Michael Downey (Collegeville, Minn.: Liturgical, 1993) 515–16.

6. Ibid. 515.

7. Ibid. 516.

Homily 42

1. This Red Mass was sponsored by the Gonzaga University Law School, Spokane, Washington.

2. John R. Donahue, S.J., "Biblical Perspectives on Justice," in *The Faith That Does Justice: Examining the Christian Sources for Social Change,* ed. John C. Haughey, S.J. (Woodstock Studies 2; New York: Paulist, 1977) 68–112, at 69.

3. See the strong text in Mt 5:43–48.

4. To put this homily in context, it may help to know that the Red Mass is celebrated in many Catholic dioceses at the opening of the judicial year, often as a votive Mass in honor of the Holy Spirit. It has a venerable history that traces back to 13th-century France, England, and Italy. On the origin of the name, scholars are not at peace. In one theory, the priest-celebrant was vested in red, and so the judges of the High Court in Edward I's reign (1272–1307), all of them doctors of the law, conformed to ecclesiastical tradition and also wore red robes. Others hold for an origin with more profound content: The liturgical red signifies a willingness to defend the truth inspired by the Holy Spirit, even if it demands one's own blood.

Homily 43

1. The occasion for this homily was the graduation Mass for the 1998 class of the Georgetown University Medical Center, Washington, D.C.

2. Robert Coles, "Secular Days, Sacred Moments," *America* 176, no. 1 (Jan. 4–11, 1997) 8.

3. See Robert L. Kinast, "Healing," *The New Dictionary of Catholic Spirituality,* ed. Michael Downey (Collegeville, Minn.: Liturgical, 1993) 466–68, at 467.

4. A popular TV program on the trials and tribulations of a Chicago hospital.

5. Richard Selzer, *Mortal Lessons: Notes on the Art of Surgery* (New York: Simon and Schuster, 1976) 46, 48.

6. "A compassionate heart"—perhaps the best translation of two difficult Greek words, *splagchna oiktirmou,* literally "the bowels of compassion, of mercy." Here Paul uses a noun, *splagchna,* that corresponds to the verb Luke uses, *esplagchnisthe,* when Jesus says that the Samaritan "was moved with compassion" (10:30).

Homily 44

1. This sermon, like Barbara Taylor's, was delivered in the Great Preachers Series during the 1998 Samuel DeWitt Proctor Institute for Child Advocacy Ministry sponsored by the Children's Defense Fund at the former Alex Haley Farm, Clinton, Tennessee, July 20–24. It is twice as long (about 36 minutes) as my usual homily, but this congregation, especially the large contingent of African Americans, would have felt cheated by less.

2. See *Time* 128, no. 10 (Sept. 8, 1986) 57.

3. Robert N. Bellah et al., *Habits of the Heart: Individualism and Commitment in American Life* (Berkeley: University of California, 1985) 141.

4. Quoted from Thomas B. Edsall, "GOP Battler Atwater Dies at 40," *Washington Post,* March 30, 1991, 1 and 7, at 1.

5. Quoted from Ginia Bellafante, "It's All about ME!" *Time* 151, no. 25 (June 29, 1998) 54–60, at 59; italics at end mine.

6. Origen, *Homily on the Book of Judges* 2.3.

7. Robert M. Morgenthau, Op-Ed, "What Prosecutors Won't Tell You," *New York Times,* Feb. 7, 1995.

8. Quoted from *Between God and Man: An Interpretation of Judaism from the Writings of Abraham J. Heschel* (New York: Harper, 1959) 40.

9. Ibid. 40.

10. Ibid. 41.

11. Frederick Buechner, *The Magnificent Defeat* (New York: Seabury, 1966) 23.

12. See *Sister Thea Bowman, Shooting Star: Selected Writings and Speeches,* ed. Celestine Cepress, FSPA (Winona, Minn.: Saint Mary's Press, 1993).

13. Ibid. 37.

14. Ibid. 44.

15. Ibid. 117.

16. See William C. Havard, "Civil Rights," *World Book Encyclopedia* 4 (1975 ed.) 468b.

Comprehensive Index for Homily Books by Walter J. Burghardt, S.J.

compiled by
Fr. Brian Cavanaugh, T.O.R.

Reference Key: **TNG** (*Tell the Next Generation,* 1980)
LSJ (*Sir, We Would Like to See Jesus,* 1982)
PYW (*Still Proclaiming Your Wonders,* 1984)
GOC (*Grace on Crutches,* 1986)
ENH (*Lovely in Eyes Not His,* 1988)
TCL (*To Christ I Look,* 1989)
DBC (*Dare to Be Christ,* 1991)
CMC (*When Christ Meets Christ,* 1993)
SWB (*Speak the Word with Boldness,* 1994)
LFL (*Love Is a Flame of the Lord,* 1995)
JRD (*Let Justice Roll Down Like Waters,* 1998)
TTP (*Christ in Ten Thousand Places,* 1999)

LITURGICAL SEASONS:

29th Mon. (Yr. 2)	JRD, p. 104
30th Sun. (A)	GOC, p. 140
30th Sun. (B)	LSJ, p. 132
30th Sun. (C)	PYW, p. 139
30th Mon. (Yr. 1)	LFL, p. 98
31st Sun. (A)	JRD, p. 108
31st Sun. (B)	ENH, p. 128; TCL, p. 102
31st Mon. (Yr. 2)	JRD, p. 113
32nd Sun. (B)	PYW, p. 144
32nd Sun. (C)	DBC, p. 93
32nd Mon. (Yr. 1)	LFL, p. 102; TTP, p. 138
32nd Mon. (Yr. 2)	JRD, p. 117
33rd Sun. (A)	LSJ, p. 137; GOC, p. 146; TCL, p. 107
33rd Sun. (B)	LSJ, p. 143; PYW, p. 149; TCL, p. 113
33rd Sun. (C)	PYW, p. 155; ENH, p. 134; SWB, p. 123
34th Mon. (Yr. 1)	JRD, p. 121
Christ the King:	TNG, p. 63; PYW, p. 174

FEASTS:

Baptism of the Lord	JRD, p. 127
Body and Blood of Christ (B)	LSJ, p. 157; JRD, p. 136
Body and Blood of Christ (C)	PYW, p. 168; TCL, p. 121
Epiphany	CMC, p. 27
Epiphany, Mon.	LFL, p. 10
Trinity Sunday (A)	LSJ, p. 151
Trinity Sunday (B)	TTP, p. 145
Trinity Sunday (C)	DBC, p. 77; SWB, p. 82
Trinity Mon. (C)	SWB, p. 88
Trinity Tues. (C)	SWB, p. 92
Trinity Wed. (C)	SWB, p. 96
Triumph of the Cross	LSJ, p. 168
Arrupe, Pedro, SJ	CMC, p. 179
John Paul I	TNG, p. 216
Murray, John Courtney	TNG, p. 211
Sadat, Mohammed el	LSJ, p. 196
Birth of John the Baptist	CMC, p. 57; LFL, p. 131
Conversion of St. Paul	PYW, p. 163; SWB, p. 174
North Amer. Martyrs	TTP, p. 175
Our Lady of Sorrows	TTP, p. 149

THEMES:

Wedding	TNG, p. 83; LSJ, p. 186, 189; GOC, p. 155, 160, 165, 170, 175; PYW, pp. 201, 206; ENH, pp. 163, 168, 173, 177, 182; TCL, pp. 174, 180, 186, 191, 196, 201; DBC, pp. 101, 106, 112, 117, 123, 129, 135, 141, 146, 152, 157; CMC, pp. 81, 87, 93, 98, 103, 109, 115, 121, 127; SWB, pp. 131, 141, 146, 151, 157; LFL, pp. 109, 114, 120, 125; JRD, pp. 175, 180, 186, 191, 196; TTP, pp. 183, 188, 193, 198, 204
Wedding: 50th Anniv.	CMC, p. 153

SCRIPTURE READINGS:

Genesis 1:26–2:3	PYW, p. 206; TCL, p. 186; DBC, p. 152; CMC, p. 98; SWB, pp. 131, 151; LFL, pp. 120, 125; JRD, pp. 141, 180
Genesis 2:4–9, 15	TCL, p. 161
Genesis 2:18–24	PYW, p. 201; GOC, p. 160; ENH, pp. 173, 177; TCL, p. 196; DBC, pp. 101, 106; CMC, pp. 81, 93; SWB, p. 141; JRD, pp. 175, 191; TTP, p. 193
Genesis 12:1–4a	LSJ, p. 41; DBC, p. 16; SWB, p. 19; JRD, p. 15
Genesis 12:1–9	JRD, p. 74
Genesis 14:18–20	DBC, p. 179; LSJ, p. 157; JRD, p. 136
Genesis 18:16–33	JRD, p. 79
Genesis 22:1–19	LFL, p. 57
Exodus 12:1–8, 11–14	TNG, p. 58; PYW, p. 61, 67; JRD, p. 132
Exodus 14:5–18	JRD, p. 83
Exodus 17:3–7	GOC, p. 31; ENH, p. 26; TTP, p. 17
Exodus 17:8–13	ENH, p. 122; JRD, p. 94
Exodus 23:20–24	JRD, p. 89
Leviticus 19:1–2, 11–18	JRD, p. 10
Numbers 6:22–26	CMC, p. 153
Numbers 21:4–9	LSJ, p. 168
Dt 4:32–34, 39–40	CMC, p. 208; TTP, p. 145
Dt 6:4–7	JRD, p. 219
Dt 10:12–22	SWB, p. 136
Dt 26:4–10	DBC, p. 173